Dr. Anderson's Interpretive Guide to Acts and the Pauline Epistles (Acts–Philemon)

By

STEVEN D. ANDERSON

Ph.D., Dallas Theological Seminary

Dr. Anderson's Interpretive Guide to the Bible
Volume 7

December 2014 edition

Copyright © 2014 by Steven David Anderson. All rights reserved. Not to be reproduced without the explicit written consent of the author.

Cover photograph (taken by the author): stairway to the temple of Artemis (Diana) in Jerash (Gerasa)

Printed by CreateSpace, An Amazon.com Company

Self-published by the author

Author's webpage: http://Bible.TruthOnly.com
Author's blog: http://TruthOnlyBible.wordpress.com

ISBN-10: 1500745995
ISBN-13: 978-1500745998

Citation for *The Chicago Manual of Style* (Turabian) and *The SBL Handbook of Style*:
Anderson, Steven D. *Dr. Anderson's Interpretive Guide to Acts and the Pauline Epistles (Acts–Philemon)*.
    December 2014 ed. Dr. Anderson's Interpretive Guide to the Bible 7. Grand Rapids: Steven D.
    Anderson, 2014.

Table of Contents

TABLE OF CONTENTS III

PREFACE VIII

STYLE NOTES IX

    Quotations of the Bible ix
    A Note on the Divine Name ix
    Common Abbreviations ix
    Abbreviations of the Books of the Bible x

INTERPRETIVE GUIDE TO ACTS 1

    AUTHOR 2
    WRITING STYLE 3
    RECIPIENTS 7
    DATE AND OCCASION OF WRITING 8
    PURPOSE AND MESSAGE 9
    TEXTUAL BASE 9
    PAUL'S MISSIONARY JOURNEYS 11
    OUTLINE OF ACTS 12
        Summary Outline 12
        Expanded Outline 12
    ARGUMENT OF ACTS 15
        The Development of the Church in Jerusalem, 1:1–8:1a 16
        The Extension of the Church to Palestine and Syria, 8:1b–12:25 20
        The Extension of the Church to the Uttermost Part of the World, 13:1–28:31 23
    BIBLIOGRAPHY OF ACTS 31

INTERPRETIVE GUIDE TO ROMANS 34

    HISTORICAL BACKGROUND 34
    AUTHOR 35
    DATE AND OCCASION OF WRITING 35
    PURPOSE AND MESSAGE 36
    WRITING STYLE 37
    TEXTUAL BASE 37
    OUTLINE OF ROMANS 38
        Summary Outline 38
        Expanded Outline 38
    ARGUMENT OF ROMANS 40
        Salutation, 1:1-7 40
        Introduction, 1:8-17 41
        Universality of Condemnation in Sin Apart from Christ, 1:18–3:20 41
        Justification by Faith in Christ as the Solution to Sin, 3:21–4:25 43
        The Eternal Security of the Justified Believer, 5:1–8:39 43
        Israel's Status in the Church Age Explained, 9:1–11:36 47
        Service in View of Salvation, 12:1–15:13 51
        Directions regarding Paul's Coming, 15:14-33 52
        Conclusion, 16:1-27 52
    BIBLIOGRAPHY FOR ROMANS 54

INTERPRETIVE GUIDE TO 1 CORINTHIANS 57

    HISTORICAL BACKGROUND 57

AUTHOR	58
DATE AND OCCASION OF WRITING	59
PURPOSE AND MESSAGE	59
OUTLINE OF 1 CORINTHIANS	60
Summary Outline	*60*
Expanded Outline	*60*
ARGUMENT OF 1 CORINTHIANS	61
Introduction, 1:1-9	*61*
Redress of Divisions in the Church, 1:10–4:21	*62*
Redress of Scandals in the Church, 5:1–6:20	*64*
Responses to Questions Sent by the Church, 7:1–11:1	*65*
Exhortation to Hold Fast to Apostolic Traditions, 11:2-34	*66*
Corrective on Spiritual Gifts, 12:1–14:40	*67*
Corrective on the Resurrection, 15:1-58	*69*
Closing Remarks, 16:1-24	*70*
BIBLIOGRAPHY FOR 1 CORINTHIANS	71
INTERPRETIVE GUIDE TO 2 CORINTHIANS	**73**
AUTHOR	73
DATE AND OCCASION OF WRITING	73
PURPOSE AND MESSAGE	75
OUTLINE OF 2 CORINTHIANS	75
Summary Outline	*75*
Expanded Outline	*75*
ARGUMENT OF 2 CORINTHIANS	76
The Basis of Paul's Relationship with the Corinthians, 1:1–7:16	*76*
Preparation for Paul's Upcoming Visit to Corinth, 8:1–13:14	*79*
BIBLIOGRAPHY FOR 2 CORINTHIANS	82
INTERPRETIVE GUIDE TO GALATIANS	**84**
AUTHOR	84
ADDRESSEES	85
HISTORICAL BACKGROUND, DATE, AND OCCASION OF WRITING	85
PURPOSE AND MESSAGE	86
CHRONOLOGY OF THE MINISTRY OF PAUL	86
THE RELATIONSHIP OF THE LAW TO THE CHURCH	87
OUTLINE OF GALATIANS	88
ARGUMENT OF GALATIANS	89
Greeting, 1:1-5	*89*
The Divine Origin of Paul's Gospel, 1:6–2:21	*89*
Defense of Justification by Faith, Apart from the Works of the Law, 3:1–5:12	*89*
The Nature of Life in the Spirit, Free from the Law, 5:13–6:10	*91*
Closing Remarks, 6:11-18	*91*
BIBLIOGRAPHY FOR GALATIANS	93
INTERPRETIVE GUIDE TO EPHESIANS	**95**
TITLE AND DESTINATION	95
Evaluation of the Title, "To the Ephesians"	*96*
HISTORICAL BACKGROUND	99
AUTHOR	100
DATE AND OCCASION OF WRITING	100
PURPOSE AND MESSAGE	101
OUTLINE OF EPHESIANS	101

  Argument of Ephesians 102
   Salutation, 1:1-2 .... *102*
   The Calling of the Church, 1:3–3:21 .... *102*
   The Conduct of the Church, 4:1–6:20 .... *103*
   Closing Remarks, 6:21-24 .... *104*
  Bibliography for Ephesians 105

INTERPRETIVE GUIDE TO PHILIPPIANS 107

  Historical Background 107
  Author 107
  Date and Occasion of Writing 107
  Purpose and Message 108
  Outline of Philippians 108
  Argument of Philippians 108
   Introductory Matters, 1:1-30 .... *109*
   Exhortation to Have a Sacrificial Mind, 2:1-30 .... *110*
   Exhortation to Have a Spiritual Mind, 3:1-21 .... *111*
   Behavior Which Should Result from Having the Christian Mind, 4:1-9 .... *112*
   Closing Remarks, 4:10-23 .... *112*
  Bibliography for Philippians 114

INTERPRETIVE GUIDE TO COLOSSIANS 117

  Historical Background 117
  The Colossian Heresy 117
  Author 118
  Date and Occasion of Writing 119
  Purpose and Message 119
  Outline of Colossians 119
  Argument of Colossians 120
   Salutation, 1:1-2 .... *120*
   Doctrinal: Instruction regarding the Person of Christ, 1:3–2:7 .... *120*
   Polemical: Defense of the Sufficiency of Christ, 2:8-23 .... *120*
   Applicational: Exhortation to Life in Christ, 3:1–4:6 .... *121*
   Closing Remarks, 4:7-18 .... *121*
  Bibliography for Colossians 122

INTERPRETIVE GUIDE TO 1 THESSALONIANS 124

  Historical Background 124
  Author 124
  Date and Occasion of Writing 125
  Purpose and Message 125
  Outline of 1 Thessalonians 125
  Argument of 1 Thessalonians 126
   Salutation, 1:1 .... *126*
   Personal: Paul's Desire for the Thessalonians' Growth, 1:2–3:13 .... *126*
   Hortatory: Paul's Directions for the Thessalonians' Growth, 4:1–5:24 .... *126*
   Closing Remarks, 5:25-28 .... *127*
  Bibliography for the Thessalonian Epistles 128

INTERPRETIVE GUIDE TO 2 THESSALONIANS 131

  Author 131
  Date and Occasion of Writing 131
  Purpose and Message 132

    Outline of 2 Thessalonians 132
    Argument of 2 Thessalonians 132
        Salutation, 1:1-2 132
        Encouragement in the Midst of Persecution, 1:3-12 132
        Response to False Teaching concerning the Day of the Lord, 2:1-17 133
        Exhortation to Obedience, 3:1-16 133
        Closing Remarks, 3:17-18 133
    Bibliography 133

INTERPRETIVE GUIDE TO 1 TIMOTHY **134**

    Historical Background to the Pastoral Epistles 134
    Addressee 137
    Authorship of the Pastoral Epistles 139
    Date and Occasion of Writing 140
    Purpose and Message 140
    Outline of 1 Timothy 140
    Argument of 1 Timothy 141
        Salutation, 1:1-2 141
        Exhortation to Faithfulness to the Word, 1:3-20 141
        Directions for Maintaining Proper Roles in the Church, 2:1–3:13 141
        Directions for Guarding the Purity of the Church, 3:14–4:16 142
        Directions for Proper Treatment of Groups in the Church, 5:1–6:2 142
        Conclusion, 6:3-21 142
    Bibliography for the Pastoral Epistles 143

INTERPRETIVE GUIDE TO 2 TIMOTHY **146**

    Author 146
    Date and Occasion of Writing 146
    Purpose and Message 147
    Outline of 2 Timothy 147
    Argument of 2 Timothy 147
        Salutation, 1:1-2 147
        Introduction: The Imperative for Faithfulness in Ministry, 1:3-18 147
        Charge to Timothy, 2:1–4:8 148
        Closing Remarks, 4:9-22 148
    Bibliography 148

INTERPRETIVE GUIDE TO TITUS **149**

    Author 149
    Addressee 149
    Date and Occasion of Writing 151
    Purpose and Message 151
    Writing Style 151
    Textual Base 152
    Outline of Titus 152
    Argument of Titus 152
        Salutation, 1:1-4 152
        Directives regarding the Oversight of the Church, 1:5–3:11 153
        Closing Remarks, 3:12-15 153
    Bibliography 154

INTERPRETIVE GUIDE TO PHILEMON **155**

    Historical Background 155

AUTHOR	156
DATE AND OCCASION OF WRITING	156
PURPOSE AND MESSAGE	156
OUTLINE OF PHILEMON	157
ARGUMENT OF PHILEMON	157
BIBLIOGRAPHY FOR PHILEMON	158

Preface

The book you are reading is the seventh volume of an eight-volume series of interpretive guides for every book of the Bible. These interpretive guides originated in a massive, multi-year project that was part of my Ph.D. program in Biblical Studies at Dallas Theological Seminary, but they incorporate insights gained throughout a lifetime of Bible training and academic study.

All of the interpretive guides follow the same basic format and order: an introduction to the book; a discussion of introductory issues (such as author, date, writing style, and addressees); a paragraph-level subject outline of the book; an "argument" which traces the flow of thought throughout the book but also deals with macrostructure, theology, and interpretive issues; and an annotated bibliography. My bibliographies are not exhaustive, though some are more complete than others. My aim has been only to cite some important works. One does not need to read everything to arrive at the correct interpretation, and in fact cannot read everything if he tries.

These interpretive guides are similar enough to a Bible commentary so that some people would classify them as commentaries. However, they do not deal much with issues of translation or textual criticism, and do not deal extensively with interpretive details. This series is intended partly as an aid to reading, and partly as a starting point for more detailed exegesis. It is, essentially, a general guide to biblical interpretation, from which more specific interpretations may be developed. I believe that these guides fill a gap in the literature by providing a synthetic overview of every book of the Bible in a way that commentaries and introductions do not. Additionally, and more importantly, they are the product of my own careful study of the Scriptures, and are not simply a slightly revised repetition of what you can read in other resources.

My approach to the biblical text is also fairly unique for contemporary literature, which generally seeks to read the Bible through the grid of preformed theological ideas or background studies. My method of biblical interpretation emphasizes the primacy of the biblical text, and seeks to find its literal meaning. Although I use and often recommend recent commentaries and other scholarly literature, I am writing from a traditional point of view that you will not read in other contemporary literature.

My theological outlook is conservative and Baptistic. I believe in the inspiration and inerrancy of the Bible. I am opposed to destructive higher criticism, but not to scholarship. I am neither Calvinist nor Arminian. I hold to a premillennial, pretribulational eschatology; to a literal six-day creation; and to a literal and traditional interpretation of the Bible. There are few Bible scholars who agree on every detail of biblical interpretation and theology, but I think that most conservative evangelical students of the Bible will find these interpretive guides interesting and useful.

A word of warning on the bibliographies: there are many commentaries listed in my bibliographies for completeness or academic purposes which actually are bad, or even dangerous, works. It should not be assumed that a commentary is worth consulting simply because I have listed it in a bibliography. But scholars need to have a broad awareness of what other scholars are publishing.

Studying the Bible is a lifelong enterprise, and thus I plan to continually revise and update these interpretive guides as I continue to study God's Word. I welcome comments and specific corrections of typographical or grammatical errors, though I may not be able to respond to all feedback. See my author page at http://Bible.TruthOnly.com for contact information and information on electronic editions. Or, read my blog at http://TruthOnlyBible.wordpress.com.

This book was originally published in August 2014. The December 2014 edition incorporates minor corrections supplied by readers, and expanded material on the Pastoral Epistles (1 Timothy, 2 Timothy, Titus).

Dr. Steven D. Anderson
Grand Rapids, Michigan

Style Notes

Quotations of the Bible

Most extended biblical quotations in these interpretive guides are from the 1901 American Standard Version (ASV; not to be confused with the New American Standard Bible). Often the translation that I give is my own, or is my own modification of the ASV. Unlike more contemporary translations, the ASV is public domain, and can be quoted and modified freely without a publisher's permission or a royalty fee. I regard the ASV as the most accurate English Bible version, though I prefer to use the original Hebrew, Aramaic, or Greek text of the Bible.

A Note on the Divine Name

I usually use the divine name "Yahweh" (= "Jehovah") where it appears in the Hebrew text of the Old Testament, rather than substituting "the Lord." The fact that God the Father has a name has not historically been appreciated by the church, and still is not appreciated today, since the church has generally followed a Jewish superstition which developed during the intertestamental period by substituting "the Lord" for the personal name "Yahweh." While rendering יהוה as "the Lord" is theologically acceptable, it makes the Old Testament come alive when the reader realizes that Old Testament saints worshipped a God whose Person and name they knew, and did not merely know abstractly as "the Lord"—comparable in some ways to the use of "Jesus" as the personal name of God's Son in the New Testament. On the Jewish superstition which treats any utterance of the divine name as a sacrilege, see the following verses against it: Exod 3:15; 23:13; Josh 23:7; 1 Kgs 18:24-27, 36-37; Pss 20:7; 45:17; 69:36; Isa 56:6; Jer 44:26; Hos 2:17; Zech 13:2.

Common Abbreviations

For standard abbreviations used in the field of biblical studies, one can consult *The SBL Handbook of Style* (Peabody, MA: Hendrickson, 1999). Some common abbreviations used in these interpretive guides include:

ASV	1901 American Standard Version
ch.	chapter
KJV	King James Version
LXX	Septuagint (an ancient Greek translation of the Old Testament)
MT	Masoretic Text (the best preserved form of the Hebrew/Aramaic Old Testament)
NASB	New American Standard Bible
NIV	New International Version
NKJV	New King James Version
NRSV	New Revised Standard Version
NT	New Testament
OT	Old Testament
RSV	Revised Standard Version
v.	verse
v. l.	variant reading (*varia lectio*)

Abbreviations of the Books of the Bible

Gen	Genesis	Nah	Nahum
Exod	Exodus	Hab	Habakkuk
Lev	Leviticus	Zeph	Zephaniah
Num	Numbers	Hag	Haggai
Deut	Deuteronomy	Zech	Zechariah
Josh	Joshua	Mal	Malachi
Judg	Judges	Matt	Matthew
Ruth	Ruth	Mark	Mark
1 Sam	1 Samuel	Luke	Luke
2 Sam	2 Samuel	John	John
1 Kgs	1 Kings	Acts	Acts
2 Kgs	2 Kings	Rom	Romans
1 Chr	1 Chronicles	1 Cor	1 Corinthians
2 Chr	2 Chronicles	2 Cor	2 Corinthians
Ezra	Ezra	Gal	Galatians
Neh	Nehemiah	Eph	Ephesians
Esth	Esther	Phil	Philippians
Job	Job	Col	Colossians
Ps	Psalm	1 Thess	1 Thessalonians
Pss	Psalms	2 Thess	2 Thessalonians
Prov	Proverbs	1 Tim	1 Timothy
Eccl	Ecclesiastes	2 Tim	2 Timothy
Song	Song of Songs (Song of Solomon)	Tit	Titus
Isa	Isaiah	Phlm	Philemon
Jer	Jeremiah	Heb	Hebrews
Lam	Lamentations	James (or Jas)	James
Ezek	Ezekiel	1 Pet	1 Peter
Dan	Daniel	2 Pet	2 Peter
Hos	Hosea	1 John	1 John
Joel	Joel	2 John	2 John
Amos	Amos	3 John	3 John
Obad	Obadiah	Jude	Jude
Jonah (or Jon)	Jonah	Rev	Revelation
Mic	Micah		

Interpretive Guide to Acts

The book commonly known as "Acts" (short for "The Acts of the Apostles")[1] tells the story of how the church began. God chose to display His power to the world by building His church through men who were poor, mainly uneducated (Paul is the notable exception), and of low status in society. To the secular mind, it would take a group of people of noble birth, political power, and great cunning to get a new religion up and running. It could not be done by commoners from Galilee. Christianity lacked everything that the world said was necessary for success, yet no religion has ever been more successful. The apostles were never able to raise large sums of money to fund their work; they completely failed to win the support of powerful people and government officials; and their religion could only hold out the promise of hardship, rejection, and suffering in this life. There was no political or social agenda, and no hope of temporal riches, fame, or pleasure. Somehow, the new religion spread like wildfire in the very face of Satan's fiercest attacks, and has now withstood the vicissitudes of time for nearly two thousand years. The world has no explanation for it. The apostles' own explanation was that Christianity was a work of God, not a work of man, and therefore it could not be stopped by men, nor could it be spread or established by human strength.

Acts is a book of firsts, especially in chs. 1–15. It describes the beginning of the church, the first new converts in the church, the first baptisms, the first congregation, the first persecution, the first appointment of deacons, the first martyr, the first Samaritan converts, the first Gentile converts, the first use of the name "Christian," the first apostolic martyr, the first major missionary journey, and the first church council.

Acts is also a book of transition which lays out the bridge between the old dispensation and the new one. It begins with Jesus teaching the apostles about the kingdom outside Jerusalem, and ends, about thirty years later, with Paul teaching Gentile Christians about the kingdom in Rome. The entire book shows an increasing expansion of the church from its starting point in Jerusalem, and a shift from an exclusively Jewish and provincial religion to a predominantly Gentile and universal church. Acts encompasses a simultaneous movement of increasing blessing upon the church and increasing judgment upon Israel. Acts also marks a transition in the NT canon, connecting the Gospels to the Epistles. Acts is both the sequel to the Gospels and the background to the Epistles. The Epistles would not make sense on their own, without the historical background given in Acts. Likewise, it would be difficult to understand the connection between the ministry of Jesus in the Gospels and the Christian church as we know it without the link provided by Acts, which records the continuation of Jesus' work through the apostles to found the church.

Some Bible teachers say that it is dangerous to base doctrines on Acts because it is a transitional book. But 2 Tim 3:16 affirms that all Scripture is profitable for doctrine. We *can* and *should* base Christian doctrines on Acts, though, just like any other book of the Bible, we need to understand what is happening in the larger historical and theological context, lest an isolated verse or passage be misread out of its context.[2] In fact, Acts is a crucial book for many areas of theology, such as missiology, ecclesiology, pneumatology, eschatology, soteriology, and Israelology. It also sets forth examples that,

---

[1] Although the title which the church has given to this book seems to imply that it describes the history of all the apostles, it really focuses on the ministries of Peter and Paul, because these were the two apostles whose work was of greatest significance for the founding of the church. It might have been more accurately titled, "The Origin of the Church."
Alphabetically "Acts" is the first book in the Bible.

[2] By way of comparison, virtually no one would say that we should not base doctrines on 1 Corinthians, even though 1 Cor 14 lays out rules for speaking in tongues that do not apply directly in a modern situation, in which the gift of tongues is no longer operative.

when understood in their historical context, teach important lessons about how to do evangelism, how to respond to persecution, and how to do ministry. The fact that some have claimed verses in Acts as a basis for false doctrines should not lead us to reject the legitimacy of Acts as a doctrinal textbook any more than the abuse of Romans or of any other part of Scripture.

Author

It is clear from the headings of the Gospel of Luke and the book of Acts that they form a two-part series composed by the same author. This author's name, according to the universal testimony of the early church, is Luke. Some of the earliest references in the church Fathers include Irenaeus (ca. 140–ca. 202) in *Haer.* 3.14.1, Clement of Alexandria (ca. 160–ca. 220) in *Strom.* 5.12 and the fragmentary *Adumbr. in 1 Pet*, and the *Anti-Marcionite Prologue to Luke* (probably ca. A.D. 190). To these can be added the abundant references in the Fathers to Lucan authorship of the third Gospel, along with the title ΚΑΤΑ ΛΟΥΚΑ in early manuscripts. Significantly, no one in the early church questioned Lucan authorship of Acts or showed knowledge of any alternative tradition. This tradition is powerful, because if the early church were simply inventing a name to give authority to the books of Luke and Acts, Luke would not be the first choice, since he is not one of the more prominent companions of Paul and is never named in the books attributed to him.

The testimony of the Fathers is strongly corroborated by internal evidence within the book of Acts itself. Although the writer does not name himself, there are three sections of the book in which events are narrated in the first person plural, "we": 16:10-17, 20:5–21:18, and 27:1–28:16.[3] The "we" sections fall in the narratives of Paul's second missionary journey, third missionary journey, and journey to Rome, and clearly indicate that the writer was a companion and ministry partner of the apostle Paul. Since, however, the writer does not refer to himself in the third person, all of Paul's companions who are named in the narrative may be eliminated as potential authors: Timothy (16:1), Silas/Silvanus (15:22), Barnabas (4:36), Apollos (18:24), Mark (12:25), Aquila (18:2), Tychicus (20:4), Trophimus (20:4), Sopater (20:4), Secundus (20:4), Aristarchus (27:2), Gaius of Macedonia (19:29), Gaius of Derbe (20:4), Jason (17:7), and Erastus (19:22). Titus may be excluded as well, since Paul states in Gal 2:1-3 that Titus accompanied him to Jerusalem in Acts 15, which is not one of the "we" sections. Luke is virtually the only frequent companion of Paul's who could have written the book. Further, the references to Luke in both Col 4:14 and Phlm 24 show that Luke was a companion of Paul's in his first Roman imprisonment, as was the author of Acts. Second Timothy 4:11 states that Luke was Paul's only companion in his second Roman imprisonment—meaning that Luke was Paul's amanuensis for 2 Timothy, which is widely recognized to exhibit a Greek style much closer to that of Acts than most of Paul's epistles. Conversely, there is no mention of Luke in any of the letters which Paul wrote during periods in the narrative of Acts not covered by the "we" sections. Everything fits with Lucan authorship, and there is nothing to suggest otherwise.

Relatively little is known about the personal life of Luke, as he is only mentioned by name three times in the NT (Col 4:14; 2 Tim 4:11; Phlm 24). The reference in Col 4:14 identifies him as "the beloved physician." Surely as he traveled with Paul, he must have attended to the physical problems Paul developed as a result of all his beatings and deprivations and travels in disease-ridden areas. Luke also was apparently a pastor of the church at Philippi between Acts 16 and 20:6, where he may have used his secular profession to provide himself an income. Obviously he was highly educated, a native speaker of Greek, and trained in Greek schools. Yet his writings show an intimate familiarity with the OT and Judaism, which implies that Luke was a Jewish proselyte prior to his conversion to Christianity. Colossians 4:14 may be taken as an indication that Luke was a Gentile, since Paul puts the salutations from Jews in a separate section (Col 4:10-11). If he was a Gentile, he would be possibly the only Gentile author of Scripture (the writer of Job is another possibility). Luke may have been a freedman, as

---

[3] It seems that the writer was with Paul for the entire narrative from 20:5 until the end of the book.

physicians were often slaves; but of this we have no certain knowledge. For evidence that Luke may have been from Syrian Antioch, as stated by Eusebius (*H.E.* 3.4.6) and Jerome (*Vir. ill.* 7; *Praef. in Comm. in Mt.*), see Bruce, *Acts of the Apostles*, 8-9. "In that case he may well have been one of the earliest Christian converts whom St Paul admitted to the full rights of Christian brotherhood, and with whom St Peter was afterwards, for one weak moment, ashamed to eat."[4] Beyond this, we know of Luke simply as "the faithful companion of St Paul, both in his first Roman imprisonment, when he still had friends about him, and in his second Roman imprisonment, when friend after friend deserted him and was 'ashamed of his chain.' . . . To [Luke]—to his allegiance, his ability, and his accurate preservation of facts—we are alone indebted for the greater part of what we know of the Apostle to the Gentiles."[5]

To the extent that Luke's writings betray his personality, we may form a picture of him as a man who was keenly observant, both of details and of the big picture, who demanded perfection in all his endeavors, and who spared no effort to achieve it. His writing shows a greater attentiveness to the literary canons of classical Greek than any other NT books, and yet this attentiveness is overridden by an even greater concern for the precise preservation of history.

Luke was an eyewitness to at least a third of the events in Acts, including the ones recorded from 20:5 to the end of the book. He was also an eyewitness to 16:9-40. Since Luke was a companion of Paul's for several years, Paul could have personally told Luke about events in his ministry to which Luke was not an eyewitness. Luke probably already knew much of this information from other sources within the network of Paul's ministry team. It is simply not known whether or to what extent Luke was present for the events recorded in chs. 1–12, regarding the founding of the church in Jerusalem and Judea; if he were present, there would be no reason for him to narrate events in the first person. However, while Luke was with Paul in Rome during his first imprisonment, he likely had ready access to Barnabas, Mark, and Peter, each of whom was present for most of the events recorded in chs. 1–12 (see below under "Date"). Luke could also have spoken with James and other eyewitnesses during Paul's imprisonment in Caesarea. For the report of secret proceedings of the Sanhedrin (4:15-17; 5:34-39), Luke could have gotten this information from someone in the council who converted to Christianity, most likely Paul (see also 6:7; 15:5; Luke 23:50-51). Thus, Luke would appear to be in an ideal position to draw up an account of the founding of the church, which was of course finally made inerrant, perfect, alive, and powerful by the work of the Spirit of God inspiring the words Luke wrote. "Luke contributes more to the NT than any other writer: in bulk his contribution exceeds that of Paul. His Gospel is the longest of the NT documents, and Acts is the second longest. Both works represent the limits of a single roll of papyrus."[6]

Writing Style

The writing style of Acts is universally acknowledged as the best in the New Testament as measured by the literary standards of classical Greek, rivaling that of the best extrabiblical Greek authors of the day. Even in English, one can tell that Luke has a superior ability for literary artistry. Although there are clear stylistic correspondences between the Gospel of Luke and Acts, the style of Acts is closer to classical Greek because the Gospel of Luke is based on apostolic teaching and eyewitness reports which Luke does not feel at liberty to alter substantially. In Acts, however, Luke is the narrator and is a personal eyewitness to many of the events, which he records in idiomatic Greek style. Thus, although Acts and Luke are of

---

[4] F. W. Farrar, *The Gospel according to St. Luke* (Cambridge Bibles for Schools and Colleges; Cambridge: Cambridge, 1880), 19.

[5] Farrar, *Luke*, 18, 20.

[6] F. F. Bruce, *The Acts of the Apostles: The Greek Text with Introduction and Commentary* (3rd ed.; Grand Rapids: Eerdmans, 1990), 33.

similar length—and all agree that they were written by the same author—the classical enclitic particle τέ occurs 151 times in the NA^{27} text of Acts, but only nine times in Luke.[7] Likewise, eight out of the thirteen partial fourth class conditions in the New Testament, as listed by Wallace, are found in Acts, whereas Luke only contains one. Again, Acts contains four of the five archaic future infinitives in the NT, and Luke has none. Thus, although in one sense, Acts, Luke, and Hebrews are on the same literary level, their style differs. Acts is the pinnacle of Greek literary style in the NT. Simcox's comments speak for most:

> The Acts is, of all the books included in the N. T., the nearest to contemporary if not to classical literary usage—the only one, except perhaps the Epistle to the Hebrews, where conformity to a standard of classical correctness is consciously aimed at.
>
> The fact is, that St. Luke is the most versatile of the N. T. writers; his mind, if not the greatest among them, was the most many-sided. . . . he writes in a Hebraistic or Hellenic style, according as he is describing events that took place in a Hebrew or in a Hellenic society. . . . if we give any weight to the tradition that he was a native of Antioch, he may have been a bilingual Syrian, as much at home among "Hebrews" as among Hellenists or Hellenes.[8]

Metzger's evaluation is similar:

> The Third Gospel and Acts reveal the hand of the most versatile of all the New Testament authors. The elaborately constructed preface to his Gospel (1:1-4) is a period of the purest Greek, one which may be compared, without too much disadvantage to Luke, with the prefaces to the histories of Herodotus and Thucydides. His breadth of culture is shown by his employing a good number of words and literary constructions unused or very rare in the rest of the New Testament. Thus his two books contain about 750 words not occurring elsewhere in the New Testament—more than 250 are in the Gospel and about 500 in Acts. He is familiar with nautical terms, which are correct without being strictly technical (Acts 27). . . .
>
> In characteristic details Luke commends himself as a capable littérateur. He uses the optative mood, which is totally lacking in Matthew, John, James, and Revelation, twenty-eight times. He makes frequent and generally idiomatic use of participles. Among Hellenistic authors who show certain affinities with Luke, so far as his vocabulary is concerned, are Polybius, Dioscorides, and Josephus.[9]

Mussies could also be quoted:

> Like the latest books of the LXX canon, the whole NT was written in the period of beginning Atticism. Apart from such incidental cases as *-tt-* in *elatton* and *kreittonos* in Heb 7:7, both of which may have been permanent exceptions, it is only Acts which shows some Atticistic tendencies. It is here only that the old-fashioned word *naun* is used (27:41) by the side of *ploion* (27:37, 39, 44), that optatives are found in dependent clauses (17:27; 27:12, 39), and that the obsolete future participles (8:27; 22:5; 24:11, 17) and future infinitives (11:28; 24:15; 27:10) are mainly present in the NT.
>
> Only the author of Acts varies his style in accordance with the Greek stylistic ideal, which manifests itself in his use of alternating synonyms in one and the same context. In the story of Ananias and Sapphira (5:1-11) and its introduction (4:32-37), he uses three different words for "to

---

[7] The 151 occurrences in Acts comprise seventy percent of the 215 total NT occurrences of τέ.

[8] William Henry Simcox, *The Writers of the New Testament: Their Style and Characteristics*, vol. 2 of *The Language of the New Testament* (The Theological Educator; London: Hodder and Stoughton, 1890), 16-19.

[9] Bruce M. Metzger, "The Language of the New Testament" (*IB*, vol. 7; New York: Abingdon Press, 1951), 47. Note that the optative mood verb εἴη occurs in a *v. l.* in John 13:24 which is printed in the text of NA^{27}, and would, if accepted, contradict Metzger's assertion that the optative is "totally lacking" in John.

sell": *pōleō* (4:34, 37), *pipraskō* (4:34; 5:4), and *apodidomai* (5:8); in the pericope of the apostles' imprisonment there are three words for "prison": *tērēsis dēmosia* (5:18), *phylakē* (5:19, 22), and *desmōterion* (5:21, 23). Compare in the story of the jailkeeper in Philippi the words *phylakē* (16:23, 24, 27) and *desmoterion* (16:26); the use of *naus* besides *ploion* may also be a case in point. He has two words for "many": *polloi* and *hikanoi*, two for "one another": *heautous* (28:29) and *allēlous* and the expression *allos pros allon* (2:12), two words for "other": *allos* and *heteros*, three for "to be": *eimi, ginomai,* and *hyparchō,* and there are some six for "the next day": *hē aurion, hē epaurion, hē hetera, hē epiousa, hē echomenē hēmēra,* and *deuteraioi*. It is even thinkable that such a variant as *ēlthamen* (28:14) between *ēlthomen* (28:13) and *eisēlthomen* (28:16) goes back to the original and was deliberately chosen; compare also the shift from 1st declension sg. *Lystran* (14:6 and 16:1) to 2d declension pl. *Lystrois* (14:7 and 16:2). The variation between *Ierosalēm* and *Hierosolyma* has an extra dimension: the former is mainly used in contexts where in reality the conversation should be assumed to have been carried on in Aramaic (with some exceptions).

This stylistic tendency then may shed some light on the literary taste of both the author and Theophilus, his first addressee. Nevertheless, there are also Semiticisms in Acts, such as the frequency of the periphrastic conjugation (1:10, 13, 14; 2:5, and elsewhere; on these, see Fitzmyer *Luke I–IX* AB).[10]

Metzger notes the change in style between chs. 1–12 and chs. 13–28:

> In the first part, containing testimony from Palestinian witnesses, Luke retains proportionately more Semitic coloring than in the remaining chapters. In the latter, where Paul's missionary journeys into Gentile lands are described, the author appropriately clothes his account in more elegant Greek, which would have been quite out of character in the first part.[11]

Simcox also notes this change: "As we go on after ch. xiii. in the Acts, the Hellenic element in the language becomes more and more predominant."[12]

Luke is very careful in his use of language. His speeches tend to use different style than his narratives. He also seeks to preserve the exact vocabulary that was used in each place and period. For example, Paul is called by his Hebrew name "Saul" until he begins his first missionary journey, after which point he is always referred to by the Roman name "Paul" (13:9). Luke refers to "Barnabas and Saul" before the first missionary journey (11:30; 12:25; 13:2, 7), then switches to "Paul and Barnabas" as Paul gains in prominence (13:43, 46, 50; 15:2, 22, 35; cf. 13:13, "Paul and his company"). However, he carefully reverses the order when the two apostles traveled to Jerusalem, where Barnabas had greater stature (15:12, 25), and also in 14:14, when the crowds were calling Barnabas "Zeus" and Paul "Hermas," making Barnabas more prominent. In Acts 15:14, Luke carefully records the Aramaic form of Peter's name that James used in his speech, Συμεών, in contrast to the angel's message to Cornelius, in which the Greek form Σίμων is used (Acts 10:5, 18, 32; 11:13).[13]

Luke always uses the correct term for each Roman official in each province. Different provinces used different terms for the same officials, depending on the kind of province it was.

---

[10] Gerard Mussies, "Languages (Greek)," in *The Anchor Bible Dictionary*, vol. 4 (New York: Doubleday, 1992), 202-3.

[11] Metzger, "The Language of the New Testament," 48.

[12] Simcox, *Writers of the New Testament*, 16-19.

[13] Other examples: 4:27, 30—"thy holy Child/Servant Jesus"; 5:20—"the words of this Life"; 5:41—"the Name"; 6:7—"the word of God increased"; 9:2—"the Way."

Luke, unlike the other evangelists, sets the gospel story in a context of world history—referring, e.g., to the Emperors Augustus and Tiberius by name (Lk. 2:1; 3:1). He does this to an appreciably greater degree in his second volume, especially when the gospel leaves the confines of its Palestinian homeland and moves through the wide open spaces of the Roman Empire. Even in its Palestinian homeland we meet Roman governors of Judaea and members of the colorful family of the Herods; beyond its frontiers we meet governors of other Roman provinces and a variety of civic officials. Luke's accuracy, as has long been recognized, is especially evident in his use of the manifold designations for such public persons.[14]

Both Sergius Paulus (13:7) and Gallio (18:12) were correctly titled as *anthupatoi* (deputies or proconsuls), officials in charge of senatorial provinces. The magistrates at Philippi were *strategoi* (16:20, 22, 35, 36, 38). The "rulers of the city" of Thessalonica were properly called *politarchoi* (17:6, 8). He knew that the town clerk or scribe (*grammateus*; 19:35) at Ephesus had political authority over the people and responsibility toward Rome. He was aware that Felix the governor (*hegemon*; 23:24) held the same position in Judea that Pilate once had (Matt. 27:11), the ruler of an imperial province. "The chief man of the island" (28:7) of Malta was literally "the first man" (*ho protos*), a technical term for the ruling official. For these reasons, Luke must be known as a first-class ancient historian.[15]

To these examples may be added Luke's proper designation of Herod Antipas as a tetrach (τετραάρχης, Acts 13:1; cf. Luke 3:1, 19; 9:7), in contrast to Herod Agrippa I and II, who are both properly called "king" (βασιλεὺς, Acts 12:1; 25:13); the designation of the attendants of the chief magistrates of the Roman colony of Philippi as ῥαβδοῦχοι in 16:35; and the mention in Ephesus of "Asiarchs," high officials of the province of Asia (19:31). Luke's use of πολιτάρχας (from πολιτάρχης, "politarch") in Acts 17:6, 8 for Thessalonian officials is noteworthy because this term is only used in these two verses in all of Greek literature—the usual literary term was πολίαρχος, with the dialectical variant πολίταρχος used only once in literature and otherwise occurring, along with πολιτάρχας, only in non-literary papyri and inscriptions. The majority of the inscriptional uses (eighteen of thirty-two) are from Thessalonica, which was ruled by a council of five or six politarchs,[16] and the term is found on an inscription on the Varder Gate on the west side of the city which dates to the time of Paul.[17] It is hardly coincidental that Luke uses this extremely rare technical term in just the right place in the narrative—he is obviously a historian of rare ability and accuracy.

When it is remembered that the status of provinces, with the designations of their governors, varied from time to time, Luke's precision is the more noteworthy: there were no works available to him for ready reference on such matters as there are to the modern historian. Luke probably reproduces such data from an accurate memory, as one who was around and observant at that time and in those places.[18]

A unique terminological distinction of Acts is its designation of believers. In Acts, believers are usually called disciples, whereas in the epistles, they are usually called saints. The term μαθητής (*disciples*) occurs twenty-eight times in Acts, whereas it does not occur once in the epistles. Likewise, the

---

[14] Bruce, *The Acts of the Apostles*, 31.

[15] Robert G. Gromacki, *New Testament Survey* (Grand Rapids: Baker, 1974), 158.

[16] Bruce, *The Acts of the Apostles*, 370.

[17] J. W. Simpson Jr., "Thessalonians, Letters to the" (in *Dictionary of New Testament Backgrounds*; Downers Grove: IVP, 1993), 933-34.

[18] Bruce, *The Acts of the Apostles*, 32.

term "saints" occurs in the ASV forty-one times in the epistles, and only four times in Acts (9:13, 32, 41; 26:10)—once in a speech by Paul, once in an event reported to Luke by Paul, and twice in events reported to Luke by Peter. It is also significant that Luke uses ξύλον for the cross in Peter's addresses in Acts 5:30 and 10:39, since Peter does not use σταυρός in his epistles, only ξύλον (1 Pet 2:24).[19]

Recipients

Luke formally addresses both his Gospel and the book of Acts to a man named Theophilus (Luke 1:3; Acts 1:1). This name does not occur elsewhere in the NT, though "Theophilus was a perfectly ordinary personal name, attested from the third century B.C. onward."[20] However, "Theophilus" is likely a nickname, as it means "lover of God"; by way of comparison, the Apostolic Father Ignatius (writing ca. 105–110) refers to himself in each of his letters by the name Theophorus, meaning "owned by God." In Luke 1:3, Theophilus is addressed by the appellation κράτιστε (*most excellent*), which was used to address people of high rank in the socio-political order; this term is used elsewhere in the NT only in address to the governors Felix (Acts 23:26; 24:3) and Festus (Acts 26:25). The only man of such rank whom we know was a Christian at the time Luke wrote was Sergius Paulus, the proconsul of Cyprus whose conversion is described as the first major event in Paul's first missionary journey (Acts 13:4-12). It would be natural that when Luke told the story of how the church began, he would include the story of his addressee's conversion. As there is no evidence of the conversion to Christianity at this early period of anyone else to be addressed as κράτιστε, it can be assumed with reasonable confidence that Theophilus is a Christian nickname for Sergius Paulus.

The man Sergius Paulus (Latin, "Paullus") is amply attested by extrabiblical historical sources. Reasoner notes that "This proconsul is not attested in [extant] pagan literature, but we do find his name on ancient coins of Cyprus (*Cat. Greek Coins*, "Cyprus," 119-21). The Sergii Pauli were a senatorial family of the first century; the name therefore fits one of consular status."[21] Nobbs surveys proposed archeological attestations of Sergius Paulus, and concludes that he is probably named as "Lucius Sergius Paullus" in an inscription along the Tiber River in Rome dating to the early years of Claudius' reign.[22] In addition, it is likely that a monument erected in Pisidian Antioch by L. Sergius Paullus and dedicated to his parents is identifiable with the son of the Sergius Paulus of Acts 13.[23] There are indications from inscriptions that Sergius Paulus' family were Christians.[24]

Sergius Paulus was an ideal convert. He was highly intelligent, called "a man of understanding" by Luke (Acts 13:7). He actually initiated contact with Paul and Barnabas, summoning them to his courtroom or residence, and requesting to hear the gospel from them. Formerly he had been under the influence of a Jewish magician named bar Jesus/Elymas, who opposed Paul's message. Paul demonstrated that he had greater power than Elymas by smiting him with temporary blindness, and

---

[19] Luke also uses ξύλον in Paul's sermon at Pisidian Antioch (Acts 13:29). Although Paul prefers σταυρός, he does use ξύλον in Gal 3:13.

[20] F. F. Bruce, *The Book of the Acts* (rev. ed.; NICNT; Grand Rapids: Eerdmans, 1988), 29.

[21] Mark Reasoner, "Political Systems" (*Dictionary of Paul and His Letters*; Downers Grove: IVP, 1993), 721.

[22] Alanna Nobbs, "Cyprus" (in *The Book of Acts in Its Graeco-Roman Setting*, vol. 2 of *The Book of Acts in its First Century Setting*, Grand Rapids: Eerdmans, 1994), 284-87.

[23] Ibid., 287.

[24] Ibid. For a criticism of this identification, see B. van Elderen, "Some Archaeological Observations on Paul's First Missionary Journey," *Apostolic History and the Gospel* (Exeter: Paternoster, 1970, 151-61.

Sergius Paulus converted immediately. Yet Luke notes that he was astonished by the teaching of the Lord more than by the miracle (13:12). The story of Sergius Paulus and Elymas, as the initial event in Paul's first missionary journey, sets a pattern which will be repeated time and again throughout Paul's missionary endeavors, which is Jewish hostility to the gospel contrasted with Gentile openness. Of this pattern, Sergius Paulus was the first prototype, and so it was that Luke's addressee himself has a prominent role in the story of how the church began.

It seems that Theophilus/Sergius Paulus was Luke's patron, i.e., that Theophilus paid Luke to write a thoroughly researched story of the origins of Christianity, and to send him the result. Regarding Luke's dedication of both volumes to Theophilus, Bruce notes that

> Such dedications were common form in contemporary literary circles. For example, Josephus dedicated his *Jewish Antiquities*, his *Autobiography*, and his two volumes *Against Apion* to a patron named Epaphroditus. At the beginning of the first volume *Against Apion*, he addresses him as "Epaphroditus, most excellent of men"; and he introduces the second volume of the same work with the words: "By means of the former volume, my most honored Epaphroditus, I have demonstrated our antiquity."[25]

Ferguson notes that

> the formal dedications to Theophilus in Luke and Acts mark these works for the book trade and are one indication of the author's familiarity with the literary conventions of the Hellenistic world; they are the only books in the New Testament with this feature, which shows that they were intended for a wider audience than that of the Christian communities and reflect a higher level of culture.[26]

The standard use of a dedication to mark a book for public circulation shows that Luke did not intend for these works to be read by Theophilus alone, but rather to be widely disseminated. Luke's primary audience was the church, though his Gospel has an evangelistic appeal, and Acts presents an apologetic for the legitimate and supernatural origins of Christianity.

Date and Occasion of Writing

Acts ends with Paul's release after a two-year imprisonment in Rome, implying that the book was composed shortly thereafter. Paul arrived in Rome in the spring following Festus' succession of Felix as procurator of Judea, which most likely occurred in the summer of A.D. 59.[27] Thus, his imprisonment of "two full years" (28:30) would have ended in the spring of 62, and Luke must have published Acts later in 62. The occasion of writing was the maturation and universal extension of the church, coupled with the request by Luke's patron for a record of how the church began.

Since the preface to Acts states that it was written after Luke's Gospel, and since Luke states that he was with Paul both on the journey to Jerusalem and on the journey to Rome, it would seem that during the two years in which Paul was imprisoned in Caesarea, Luke did research for his Gospel, interviewing sources, traveling, and organizing the material. His Gospel contains much information that could only

---

[25] Bruce, *The Book of the Acts*, 29-30. See also L. C. A. Alexander, "Luke's Preface in the Context of Greek Preface-Writing," *NovT* 28 (1986), 48-74.

[26] Everett Ferguson, *Backgrounds of Early Christianity* (3rd ed.; Grand Rapids: Eerdmans, 2003), 132.

[27] See the excellent discussion of this chronological problem in Joel B. Green, "Festus, Porcius," in *The Anchor Bible Dictionary*, vol. 2 (New York: Doubleday, 1992), 795.

have come from primary source interviews. It stands to reason, then, that Luke published his Gospel before Paul left for Rome, and that he then spent the two years in which Paul was at Rome doing the research to write Acts. Paul's prison epistles indicate that Luke was with Paul for at least part of his first Roman imprisonment (Col 4:14; Phlm 24), so he must have used this time to interview Paul and others who were in Rome at about the same time—notably Peter (1 Pet 5:13), Barnabas (Heb 13:24), Mark (1 Pet 5:13), Timothy (Phil 1:1; Col 1:1), and Silas (1 Pet 5:12), among others—in order to collect the material needed to write Acts. Since virtually all of the material in Acts was personally witnessed by either Peter, Barnabas, Mark, Paul, or Luke, and most by at least two of these, everything fits with a composition of the book in Rome in A.D. 60–62, and with publication of the book from Rome shortly after Paul's release.

The date of composition of the Gospel of Luke also has direct bearing on the question of the date of composition of Acts.[28] Since Acts is really vol. 2 of a two-part work, one would expect that there was not a delay of decades between the two writings, but that Luke began his research for Acts immediately after publishing his Gospel, and completed his research and writing in no more than a couple of years. The Gospel of Luke must, at a minimum, have been composed before the writing of 1 Timothy in A.D. 64 and had opportunity to circulate, since Paul quotes from Luke 10:7 in 1 Tim 5:18, prefaced by the words, "For the scripture saith," and in parallel with a quotation from Deuteronomy. When Luke's opportunity to do research and interview sources is considered, however, his Gospel must be viewed as having been composed in Palestine and Acts in Rome. Luke was in Rome in A.D. 60–62 and had the time and access to the sources which he needed to write Acts, so there is no reason why he would have waited to write or publish the book.

Purpose and Message

The purpose of both Luke and Acts is stated in Luke 1:1-4: to give Luke's patron Theophilus a reliable record of the origins of Christianity. Luke's story of the origins of Christianity actually begins in his Gospel with the births of John and Jesus (Luke 1–2). Acts is a continuation of Luke's Gospel. The purpose of the book of Acts is to tell the story of the beginning of the church of Jesus Christ from the Ascension to the expansion of the church to the ends of the earth. The message of Acts is that Christianity is the fulfillment and natural continuation of true Judaism, which began as a remnant of faithful Jewish disciples of Jesus in Jerusalem, and expanded into a worldwide church as a consequence of the Jews' rejection of the good news about Jesus the Messiah.

Textual Base

Some scholars consider the text of Acts to be the most problematic in the New Testament. Metzger's *Textual Commentary* gives 224 pages to Acts, compared with 205 pages for the Gospels and 246 pages for Romans–Revelation. In reality, however, this is a problem which Metzger himself has created by giving undue weight to the Western text simply because it is early and significantly different from the so-called Alexandrian text. The Western text is weakly attested (D and three fragmentary papyri are the significant witnesses), whereas the Alexandrian text is attested by all the early and strong witnesses to the Gospels and the Epistles, as well as by the well-preserved P^{74} and P^{45}. Canons of internal evidence also

---

[28] This is in response to writers such as Bruce, who suggests that Luke could have written Acts decades after the last events recorded in the book (*The Acts of the Apostles*, 9-18). Naturally, commentators who hold that Mark was the first Gospel written, and who date Luke after A.D. 70 as a result, simply have a precommitment to the view that Acts had to have been written later, no matter how contrary to logic this may seem.

point to the secondary and expansionistic nature of the Western text, which is one-tenth longer than the Alexandrian text.[29]

The major papyri in Acts are P^{74} and the third-century P^{45} (P^{91} is also third-century). Since P^{74} is seventh-century, it is not as significant as most papyri. The primary witnesses to the Alexandrian text in Acts are P^{45} ℵ B sa. Secondary Alexandrian witnesses are P^{50} A (C) Ψ 33 (11:26–28:31) 81 104 326. Western witnesses are P^{29} P^{38} P^{48} D E 383 614 1739 syr^{hmg} syr^{palms} cop^{G67} early Latin Fathers, Ephraem.

---

[29] See Bruce M. Metzger, *A Textual Commentary on the Greek New Testament* (2nd ed.; Stuttgart: Deutsche Bibelgesellschaft, 1994), 223.

Paul's Missionary Journeys

	First Missionary Journey	Second Missionary Journey	Third Missionary Journey
Texts	Acts 13:1–14:28	Acts 15:36–18:22	Acts 18:23–21:16
Dates	early A.D. 47–end of A.D. 48	middle of A.D. 49–late A.D. 52	early A.D. 53–May 26, A.D. 57
Ministry Partners	Barnabas, John Mark (left early)	Silas (Silvanus), Timothy, Luke, Aquila and Priscilla (Prisca)	none primary; Timothy, Luke, Erastus, Gaius, Aristarchus, Tychicus, Trophimus, Sopater, Secundus
Focus of Ministry	Galatia	Corinth	Ephesus
Itinerary	Syrian Antioch → Seleucia → Cyprus (Salamis, Paphos) → Perga → Pisidian Antioch → Iconium → Lystra → Derbe → Lystra → Iconium → Pisidian Antioch → Perga → Attalia → Syrian Antioch	Syrian Antioch → Syria → Cilicia → Derbe → Lystra → Galatia → Phrygia → Troas → Samothrace → Neapolis → Philippi → Amphipolis → Apollonia → Thessalonica → Berœa → Athens → Corinth → Cenchreæ → Ephesus → Cæsarea → Jerusalem → Syrian Antioch	Syrian Antioch → Galatia → Phrygia → Ephesus → Macedonia → Greece → Philippi → Troas → Assos → Mitylene → Chios → Samos → Miletus → Cos → Rhodes → Patara → Tyre → Ptolemais → Cæsarea → Jerusalem
Associated Epistles	Galatians (between first and second journeys, early A.D. 49)	1 Thessalonians (from Corinth, spring A.D. 50), 2 Thessalonians (from Corinth, late A.D. 50)	1 Corinthians (from Ephesus, spring A.D. 56), 2 Corinthians (from Macedonia, late summer/early fall A.D. 56), Romans (from Corinth, late A.D. 56)
Major Events	conversion of Sergius Paulus; address at Pisidian Antioch; healing and stoning at Lystra	split with Barnabas; call of Timothy; Macedonian vision; beating at Philippi; conversion of the Philippian jailor; riot in Thessalonica; sermon at Mars' Hill; trial before Gallio	conversion of John's disciples at Ephesus; powerful ministry at Ephesus; riot at Ephesus; return to Macedonia and Greece; raising of Eutychus; farewell to the Ephesian elders; journey to Jerusalem

Other journeys: anti-missionary journey to Damascus (9:1-25), journey to Tarsus (9:26-30), ministry in Antioch (11:25-30; 13:1-3), journey to Rome (27:1–28:31), mainly undocumented travels between his first and second imprisonments (possibly to Spain).

Paul wrote one epistle after his first journey, two on his second, three on his third, four in his first Roman imprisonment, and three later.

Outline of Acts

Summary Outline

I. The Development of the Church in Jerusalem 1:1–8:1a
II. The Extension of the Church to Palestine and Syria 8:1b–12:25
III. The Extension of the Church to the Uttermost Part of the World 13:1–28:31

Expanded Outline

I. The Development of the Church in Jerusalem 1:1–8:1a
   A. From the resurrection to Pentecost 1:1-26
      1. Introduction and setting 1:1-5
      2. Final instructions and ascension 1:6-11
      3. The interim setting 1:12-14
      4. The replacement of Judas 1:15-26
   B. The beginning of the church 2:1-47
      1. The coming of the Spirit 2:1-4
      2. The reaction of the people 2:5-13
      3. Peter's sermon 2:14-36
      4. The response to the gospel 2:37-42
      5. The progress of the church 2:43-47
   C. The ministry of Peter and John 3:1–4:37
      1. The healing of the lame man 3:1-10
      2. Peter's sermon 3:11-26
      3. The opposition to Peter and John 4:1-31
         a. The arrest of Peter and John 4:1-4
         b. Peter's defense 4:5-12
         c. The verdict 4:13-22
         d. The response of the church 4:23-31
      4. The progress of the church 4:32-37
   D. The ministry of the apostles 5:1–6:7
      1. The demonstration of apostolic power 5:1-16
         a. Apostolic power demonstrated to the church 5:1-11
            i. The lie and death of Ananias 5:1-6
            ii. The lie and death of Sapphira 5:7-11
         b. Apostolic power demonstrated to Israel 5:12-16
      2. The opposition to the apostles 5:17-42
         a. The arrest, rearrest, and trial 5:17-32
         b. The verdict and result 5:33-42
      3. The appointment of apostolic coworkers 6:1-6
      4. The progress of the church 6:7
   E. The ministry of Stephen 6:8–8:1a
      1. Stephen's ministry and arrest 6:8-15
      2. The high priest's inquisition 7:1
      3. Stephen's defense 7:2-53
         a. Recitation of Israel's history 7:2-50
         b. Application to the Jews 7:51-53
      4. The martyrdom of Stephen 7:54–8:1a

II. The Extension of the Church to Palestine and Syria 8:1b–12:25
A. The impetus of the extension 8:1b-3
B. Extension of the church to Samaria 8:4-25
    1. Philip's ministry in Samaria 8:4-8
    2. The belief of Simon the sorcerer 8:9-13
    3. Peter and John in Samaria 8:14-24
    4. Conclusion of the Samaritan ministry 8:25
C. Extension of the church to Ethiopia 8:26-40
D. The conversion and growth of Saul 9:1-30
    1. The vision on the Damascus road 9:1-9
    2. The visit of Ananias 9:10-19a
    3. Saul's ministry in Damascus 9:19b-22
    4. Saul's escape from Damascus 9:23-25
    5. Saul's visit to Jerusalem 9:26-30
E. The progress of the church 9:31
F. The growth of the church in coastal Judea 9:32-43
    1. The healing of Aeneas 9:32-35
    2. The raising of Dorcus 9:36-43
G. Extension of the church to the Gentiles 10:1–11:18
    1. Cornelius' vision 10:1-8
    2. Peter's vision 10:9-16
    3. The arrival of Cornelius' messengers 10:17-23a
    4. The meeting with Cornelius 10:23b-33
    5. Peter's address 10:34-43
    6. The admission of Gentiles into the church 10:44-48
    7. The Jewish acceptance of Gentile believers 11:1-18
H. Extension of the church to Antioch 11:19-26
I. The shift in the center of the church 11:27–12:25
    1. The Judean church supported by Antioch 11:27-30
    2. James killed and Peter persecuted 12:1-19
    3. Judgment of Herod 12:20-23
    4. The progress of the church 12:24
    5. The ascendance of Barnabas and Saul 12:25

III. The Extension of the Church to the Uttermost Part of the World 13:1–28:31
A. Paul's first missionary journey 13:1–14:28
    1. The commissioning of Barnabas and Saul 13:1-3
    2. The ministry in Cyprus 13:4-12
    3. The ministry at Pisidian Antioch 13:13-52
        a. The coming to Antioch 13:13-15
        b. Paul's sermon 13:16-41
        c. The initial response 13:42-43
        d. Belief and rejection 13:44-52
    4. The ministry at Iconium 14:1-7
    5. The ministry at Lystra 14:8-18
    6. Rejection and return 14:19-28
B. The Jerusalem Council 15:1-35
    1. The dispute over the Law 15:1-5
    2. The council called 15:6
    3. Peter's opinion 15:7-11
    4. Paul and Barnabas' report 15:12
    5. James' judgment 15:13-21

  6. The letter sent 15:22-29
  7. The delegation to Antioch 15:30-35
 C. Paul's second missionary journey 15:36–18:22
  1. The split between Paul and Barnabas 15:36-41
  2. The church plants revisited 16:1-5
  3. Travels through Asia Minor 16:6-10
  4. Ministry at Philippi 16:11-40
   a. The initial converts 16:11-15
   b. The demon-possessed girl 16:16-18
   c. Paul's ministry through suffering 16:19-34
   d. Paul's release and departure 16:35-40
  5. Ministry at Thessalonica 17:1-9
  6. Ministry at Berea 17:10-15
  7. Paul at Athens 17:16-34
   a. The dispute with the philosophers 17:16-21
   b. Paul's sermon 17:22-31
   c. The response to the message 17:32-34
  8. Paul at Corinth 18:1-17
   a. Paul's initial ministry in Corinth 18:1-4
   b. Paul's continued ministry in Corinth 18:5-11
   c. Paul's trial in Corinth 18:12-17
  9. Paul's return trip 18:18-22
 D. Paul's third missionary journey 18:23–21:16
  1. The return visit to Galatia and Phrygia 18:23
  2. The ministry of Apollos 18:24-28
  3. Paul's ministry at Ephesus 19:1-41
   a. Conversion of John's Ephesian disciples 19:1-7
   b. Paul's ministry in Ephesus 19:8-20
   c. Paul's journey plans 19:21-22
   d. The riot in Ephesus 19:23-41
  4. Travels from and to Asia 20:1-6
  5. Discourse and miracle at Troas 20:7-12
  6. Travels through Asia 20:13-16
  7. Paul's address to the Ephesian elders 20:17-38
   a. The elders called 20:17
   b. Review of Paul's ministry in Ephesus 20:18-21
   c. Overview of Paul's present situation 20:22-27
   d. Paul's charge to the Ephesian elders 20:28-35
   e. The farewell 20:36-38
  8. The journey from Miletus to Tyre 21:1-6
  9. The meeting with the Caesarean church 21:7-14
  10. The journey from Caesarea to Jerusalem 21:15-16
 E. Paul's journey to Rome 21:17–28:31
  1. Paul in Jerusalem 21:27–23:24
   a. Paul's acceptance by the Jerusalem church 21:17-26
   b. Paul assaulted 21:27-36
   c. Paul's request 21:37-40
   d. Paul's defense 22:1-21
    i. The entreaty to hear 22:1
    ii. The Jews' attentiveness 22:2
    iii. Paul's conduct before his conversion 22:3-5

                iv. Paul's conversion 22:6-16
                v. Paul's commission to minister 22:17-21
            e. Opposition and deliverance 22:22-29
            f. Paul's trial before the Sanhedrin 22:30-23:10
                i. The trial called 22:30
                ii. The trial conducted 23:1-10
            g. Paul's vision and charge 23:11
            h. The plot against Paul 23:12-24
        2. Paul and Felix 23:25–24:27
            a. The letter to Felix 23:25-30
            b. The journey to Felix 23:31-35
            c. The trial before Felix 24:1-23
                i. The Jews' accusation 24:1-9
                ii. Paul's defense 24:10-21
                iii. Felix's verdict 24:22-23
            d. Felix's subsequent dealings with Paul 24:24-27
        3. The trial before Festus 25:1-12
            a. The request for the trial 25:1-5
            b. The trial conducted 25:6-12
        4. The hearing before Agrippa 25:13–26:32
            a. Agrippa informed about Paul 25:13-22
            b. The hearing convened 25:23-27
            c. Paul's defense 26:1-23
            d. Paul's apology to the court 26:24-29
            e. Agrippa's verdict 26:30-32
        5. From Caesarea to Rome 27:1–28:15
            a. From Caesarea to Crete 27:1-8
            b. The storm 27:9-26
            c. The shipwreck 27:27-44
            d. Arrival at Malta 28:1-6
            e. Events in Malta 28:7-10
            f. From Malta to Rome 28:11-15
        6. Paul in Rome 28:16-31
            a. Paul's lodging in Rome 28:16
            b. The meeting with the Jews called 28:17-22
            c. Paul's preaching to the Jews 28:23-28
            d. Paul's stay in Rome summarized 28:30-31

Argument of Acts

Acts begins with Jesus teaching the Eleven about the kingdom outside Jerusalem, and ends with Paul teaching Gentiles about the kingdom in Rome. In between is the story of how this movement took place. Some exegetes divide the book of Acts into two sections, with chs. 1–12 describing the development of the church with Jerusalem as the center and Peter as the central apostle, and chs. 13–28 describing the development of the church with Antioch as the center and Paul as the central apostle. The problem with this is that parts of chs. 1–12 are not about Peter, most notably 8:26–9:30, and Antioch loses its prominence by the end of the book. Thus, it seems better to trace the major sections of the book according to commission given to the apostles in 1:8, with chs. 1–7 describing the development of the church in Jerusalem, chs. 8–12 describing the development of the church in Judea and its environs, and chs. 13–28 describing the extension of the church throughout the known world. In any case, it is clear that the structure of the book is both chronological and geographical, paralleling the expansion of the church through time.[1]

The Development of the Church in Jerusalem, 1:1–8:1a

The first major section of Acts, from 1:1 to 8:1a, describes the initial founding and development of the church in Jerusalem. The apostles proclaimed the fulfillment of the ancient promises to Israel in the Person and work of Jesus of Nazareth, and while some accepted the message gladly, the majority in Jerusalem rejected it.[2]

From the resurrection to Pentecost, 1:1-26. The first chapter describes events between the ascension and Pentecost, and lays the groundwork for the origin of the church. The very first verse (1:1) presents this book as a continuation of Jesus' work and teaching as recorded in Luke's Gospel, though it will now be Jesus' work through the church. After a brief introduction in 1:1-5 which anticipates the outpouring of the Spirit, Jesus gives final instructions to the disciples in 1:6-11, then ascends.[3] The commission of the apostles to found the church is stated in 1:8, and parallels Luke's aim in this book of giving a history of the church's origin. The setting in which the disciples found themselves during the week-long interval between the ascension and Pentecost is described in 1:12-14. The twelve gathered daily for prayer with the women who followed Jesus, along with Jesus' mother and brothers, who had only just believed in Jesus following His resurrection (cf. John 7:5; 1 Cor 15:7). The replacement of Judas was the final event preparatory to Pentecost (1:15-26).[4]

---

[1] Toussaint proposes that the movement of the book of Acts is marked by a progress report at the end of each unit (Stanley D. Toussaint, "Acts," in *The Bible Knowledge Commentary: New Testament*, ed. John F. Walvoord and Roy B. Zuck [Wheaton, IL: SP Publications, 1983], 352-53). The list of progress reports he gives include 2:47, 6:7, 9:31, 12:24, 16:5, 19:20, and 28:30-31. The last progress report tells of the triumph and worldwide spread of the gospel. While his structure is interesting and worthy of consideration, it is possible to interpret these progress reports as other than structural indicators, and it is questionable whether, for example, 28:30-31 is a true progress report.

[2] The apostles initially sought to transform Judaism into a New Covenant community defined by faith in Jesus as the Messiah, instead of an Old Covenant community defined by Jewish identity markers. They were not starting a new religion, but instead were loyal adherents of the Jewish Scriptures, literally interpreted. As Judaism progressively disowns the Nazarenes in Acts, however, the church acquires an identity independent of Judaism. Biblical Judaism is assimilated into the church, which grows with the hand of God's blessing upon it, while Old Covenant Judaism quickly fades into insignificance.

[3] Two key theological points are contained in this opening section. First, after forty days of being taught by Jesus about the kingdom of God (1:3), the disciples still believed that the kingdom was literal, earthly, future, and for Israel (1:6). In His reply, Jesus does not correct their beliefs concerning the nature of the kingdom (1:7). Second, the return of Jesus is said to be in the same manner as His ascension (1:11). This means it is a literal, visible, personal, and bodily return in glory. It even means that Jesus will return to the same place as He ascended from, namely, the Mount of Olives (Zech 14:4). People will literally see Jesus descending from the sky in a cloud (Matt 24:30), just as the disciples could see Him ascending into the sky in a cloud.

[4] In Matt 19:28, Jesus promised that the twelve apostles would sit upon twelve thrones in the kingdom, judging the twelve tribes of Israel. Therefore a replacement was needed for Judas to fill out the number of the apostles, and also to have twelve witnesses to the resurrection. Paul could not have been the twelfth apostle, because he did not meet the criteria set forth by Peter in 1:21-22. The replacement for Judas had to have been with Jesus throughout His earthly ministry. It should also be noted that Paul sets himself apart from the other apostles as a different kind of apostle (1 Cor 15:5-8; Gal 2:8). Paul never claimed to be one of the twelve (compare 1 Cor 15:5 with 15:8). Luke

The beginning of the church, 2:1-47. Chapter 2 describes the beginning of the church, mostly its first day of existence (2:1-42), but also several days or weeks immediately following (2:43-47). The dramatic moment at which the church began (cf. 11:15) is recorded in 2:1-4, as the Holy Spirit came powerfully upon the 120 in the Upper Room, permanently indwelling them and baptizing them into the body of Christ. The people who were in Jerusalem for the Feast immediately knew something miraculous had happened, because every foreign Jew heard the new Christians speaking in his own native language (2:5-13). The questioning of the multitudes concerning this strange phenomenon prompted Peter's great sermon of 2:14-36. Peter's message is that Jesus is the Lord and Messiah who will bring the coming judgment upon the world. You need to call upon the name of the Lord before the judgment comes so you will be saved in that day. Peter begins by linking the phenomenon of tongues with the outpouring of the Spirit at the inauguration of the New Covenant, following the eschatological judgment (2:14-21).[5] He then links the miracles Joel spoke of with those performed by Jesus, which is his first proof of Jesus' messiahship (2:22). Peter offers two other proofs of Jesus' messiahship: His resurrection (2:23-32)[6] and His ascension (2:33-35). Verse 36 is a concluding summary statement, which shows that the point of Peter's sermon is to prove Jesus' messiahship (Pss 16, 132) and Lordship (Ps 110).

The response to Peter's sermon is recorded in 2:37-42—three thousand people were saved and baptized.[7] The new church formed a tightly knit and devout community, listening to the apostles' teaching, praying, sharing their goods (κοινωνία), and eating meals with other believers (2:42). The further progress and growth of this new group of Spirit-empowered believers is described in 2:43-47. The church was a united body which delighted in hearing the Word taught, ministering to the saints, praising God, and sharing the good news about Jesus.

---

indicates in Acts 1:26 that Matthias was still numbered with the Eleven at the time of writing, and he refers to "the twelve" in 6:2, before the conversion of Paul.

[5] The signs accompanying Christ's first advent are typological prefigurements of those accompanying His second advent.

[6] It is significant that Peter staked his argument in this sermon on the resurrection of Jesus (2:32). If the resurrection never happened, the Sanhedrin could have disproved it easily by taking Jesus' corpse out of the tomb and putting it on public display. Christianity would have been ruined. That the opponents of Christianity did not do this shows that the tomb was empty.

[7] Acts 2:38 has long been used by some to argue for baptismal regeneration, i.e., the view that baptism saves. A question may be raised as to how Peter's original hearers would have understood his call. The concept of baptism that the Jews on the day of Pentecost would have been most familiar with was that of John's baptism. According to Mark 1:4 and Luke 3:3, John preached a baptism based on repentance for the purpose of the remission of sins. John was not baptizing people in order that they would repent; rather, his ministry of baptism was for the purpose of repentance (cf. Matt 3:11). People came to be baptized by John to signify that they were repenting of their sins (Matt 3:6). Hence, Peter's hearers would have understood that baptism was an outward sign of repentance. Baptism is associated with repentance as the act which naturally follows repentance and outwardly signifies conversion. The purpose of this whole conversion process is to have one's sins forgiven, though the sins are actually forgiven after the first step in the process rather than the final step. From a logical point of view, it is obvious that baptism follows a decision to forsake one's former lifestyle and identify with the church; one does not make this decision as he is being baptized.

There is a great irony in the whole debate over baptismal regeneration in this verse, however: Peter himself, along with the 120 in the Upper Room, went out and began to speak in tongues immediately after they received the Spirit, and there was no body of Christ to be baptized into before that. Since John's baptism is distinguished from Christian baptism—John's disciples had to be rebaptized in Acts 19:1-5—the first 120 themselves apparently never underwent Christian water baptism. In such a situation, Peter obviously could not be telling the people that they could only be saved through water baptism.

The ministry of Peter and John, 3:1–4:37. Chapters 3–7 highlight the ministries of specific leaders in the Jerusalem church in chronological sequence, showing the centrality of their role in the founding and upbuilding of the church. As the church becomes established, the most prominent ministry roles pass from the leading apostle (ch. 2) to the two leading apostles (chs. 3–4) to the twelve as a group (5:1–6:7) to a leader appointed by the twelve (6:8–8:1a). The mission of Peter and the other apostles was to found the church, and therefore the apostolic role was not meant to continue throughout the age except through the preservation of the apostles' teaching in the NT Scriptures.

The focus on the ministry of Peter and John in chs. 3–4 begins with a dramatic miracle in the temple (3:1-10). A lame man who was over forty years old (cf. 4:22) was healed instantly when Peter commanded him to walk in the name of Jesus of Nazareth. As a crowd gathered around, Peter delivered a sermon (3:11-26), beginning by explaining that the miracle was not performed by his own power (3:12). It came about because Jesus, whom the Jews denied and killed, has been raised from the dead, and it is through faith in His name that the lame man was healed (3:13-16). Peter then explains that the crucifixion of the Messiah was part of God's plan, and therefore not an event which cancelled out the promises to Israel (3:17-18). He urges the people to repent, first, so that their sins would be forgiven, and, second, so that Jesus the Messiah would return to Israel from heaven and establish His kingdom on earth (3:19-21).[8] Peter's argument is that the nation is under judgment for crucifying the Messiah, and must repent for the kingdom to come. In 3:22-25, he then warns of what is coming should the nation fail to repent. The message of the kingdom went to Israel first because they are the sons of the prophets, who foretold the ministry of the Messiah, and the sons of the Abrahamic Covenant, which promised blessing through the Messiah. However, if Israel hardens itself to the message, it will be temporarily pushed aside while the blessings through the Jewish Messiah go out to the nations.

As if to fulfill Peter's warning, the Sadducees, who believed that bodily resurrection was impossible, came to arrest Peter and John—the first direct opposition to the nascent church (4:1-4). At the trial the next day, the Sanhedrin did not even bother to challenge the miracle, but simply looked for a way to accuse Peter and John. Peter said in the apostles' defense that, far from being criminals, they were on trial for performing a good deed (4:9). He then argues that, far from leading the people astray, the apostles' teaching of the crucifixion and resurrection of the Messiah is fully in accord with the OT Scriptures (4:10-12). After a closed-door consultation, the Sanhedrin failed to find a way either to deny the miracle or to justify punishment of the apostles (4:13-17). However, they gave the apostles an order to stop preaching in the name of Jesus so as to manufacture a legal basis for future charges (4:18). This first climactic confrontation between the apostles and the Sanhedrin ended with the apostles only growing emboldened in their witness and commitment (4:19-22). The church, too, was encouraged and emboldened by the apostles' stance (4:23-31). They quoted Ps 2:1-2 to say, "opposition to the Messiah was predicted by the God who is sovereign in history, and so we will go on serving Him in the face of opposition."[9]

---

[8] The "seasons of refreshing" (3:19) apparently refer to roughly the same thing as "the times of restoration of all things" (3:21). Both references are to the messianic kingdom. However, "refreshing" has more to do with enjoyment of benefits, while "restoration" has more to do with straightening things out—restoring the Davidic kingdom to Israel (cf. 1:6), restoring the spiritual condition of the people (Matt 17:11; Luke 1:17), restoring creation from the curse, and restoring rule over the earth to redeemed man.

There is no verse that says the offer of the kingdom to Israel, which was presented at Jesus' first advent, has been rescinded. Thus, the generation of Jews which accepts Jesus as the Messiah will see the second advent (cf. Matt 23:39; Rom 11:25).

[9] The church is not saying that Psalm 2 has been completely fulfilled, but that the scene at Armageddon is only the ultimate expression of the opposition to God and His Messiah that has characterized the nations of the world throughout history. "The nations" is interpreted in 4:27 as including more than just the Sanhedrin—it encompasses the total rejection of the Messiah by all groups of people. The prayer is therefore for boldness, not for a removal of the opposition which is a part of God's plan.

The section ends with another progress report (4:32-37). In spite of the opposition, the church was fully united and energized, and demonstrated their love for one another by sharing their goods freely with any brother who had need.

The ministry of the apostles, 5:1–6:7. The section highlighting the ministry of the apostles (5:1–6:7) begins in 5:1-11 with a dramatic demonstration of apostolic authority. When a couple in the church, Ananias and Sapphira, envied the recognition Barnabas received for the gift he gave to the church (4:36-37), they sold a parcel of land and brought part of the proceeds to the apostles. This was, of course, no sin, but they lied to the apostles and said they were giving the full sale price (5:2, 8). What made this lie so bad is that the apostles were God's representatives, so they were really lying to the Holy Spirit. Ananias and Sapphira were both killed immediately after they spoke the lie to the apostles. Ananias and Sapphira were given the judgment they truly deserved for their lie to teach the church a lesson about God's power and holiness. Right at the beginning point of a new program, God uses those who transgress His commands as an object lesson to demonstrate His holiness (cf. Lev 10; Num 15:32-36; Josh 7).

The demonstration of apostolic authority to the church in 5:1-11 is followed by the demonstration of apostolic power to the people of Israel as a whole in 5:12-16. The apostles performed numerous miracles of various kinds, which resulted in the growth of the church in numbers and in reputation. The religious leaders, however, were provoked to jealousy, and arrested the apostles (5:17-18). After an angel released the apostles during the night, the Sanhedrin showed themselves to be such hardened sinners that they ordered their rearrest. and brought them to trial (5:19-28). Peter defended the apostles' actions by repeating the gospel message and demonstrating that they were preaching at God's command (5:29-32). The Sanhedrin was enraged at Peter's statement that they had murdered the Son of God and did not have the Holy Spirit in them, and they intended to put the apostles to death on the spot.[10] Rabbi Gamaliel stood up and intervened, giving wise counsel (5:34-35). He pointed out that when previous messianic claimants had died, their followers immediately ceased to believe in them, and so did the people (5:36-37). If Jesus' work went forward after His death, the only explanation is that there was divine power behind it, and that Jesus was a living Messiah who had risen from the dead (5:38-39). Gamaliel's speech is reported not only to relate how the apostles were released, but also because Gamaliel unwittingly gives a direct statement of a major theme of the book of Acts, which is the expansion of the church in the face of opposition, thereby demonstrating that the church is a work of God, not of men. The Sanhedrin agreed not to kill the apostles, but still had them flogged (5:40). The apostles had joy in the midst of persecution (cf. Luke 6:22-23), and continued to faithfully teach and preach Jesus as the Messiah (5:41-42).

The first schism in the church, which led to the first appointment of non-apostolic church officers, is recorded in 6:1-6. The apostles were not able to administer the church's benevolence fund and commit themselves to the study and teaching of the Word at the same time. Thus, they appointed a group of seven men who appear to function as deacons.

The section regarding the ministry of the apostles ends in 6:7 with another progress report, describing how the church continued to grow in Jerusalem, both numerically and spiritually.

The ministry of Stephen, 6:8–8:1a. The ministry of Stephen, the first Christian martyr, is recorded in 6:8–8:1a. After being appointed to the deaconate, Stephen began performing miracles and preaching—things previously done only by the apostles. His Spirit-empowered ministry was so effective that Stephen was completely unstoppable in debates with his opponents (6:9-10). These opponents therefore arrested

---

[10] Humanly speaking, it looked as if the church came within a hairbreadth of being crippled here. It would have been a severe blow to the church to have all twelve apostles killed right at the beginning. But God was in control the whole time, protecting and building up His church. This really was not a close call. The apostles' attitude is noteworthy—"We will do the right thing no matter what the cost, and let God worry about what might happen to the church if we die." Too many church leaders throughout history have yielded to compromising pressures in order to preserve their existence and supposed influence.

Stephen, and brought him before the Sanhedrin on false charges (6:11-15).[11] The high priest, probably Caiaphas, demanded that Stephen reply to the charges (7:1). The aim of Stephen's response (7:2-53) is to defend the gospel and announce that the Jews were under judgment.

> The first section (vv. 2-16) deals with Israel's patriarchal period and refutes the charge of blaspheming God (6:11). The second major section (vv. 17-43) deals with Moses and the Law and responds to the charge of blaspheming Moses (6:11) and speaking against the Law (6:13). The third section (vv. 44-50) deals with the temple and responds to the charge of speaking against the temple (6:13), and Stephen's allegedly saying that Jesus would destroy the temple and alter Jewish customs (6:14). Stephen then climaxed his address with an indictment of his hard-hearted hearers (vv. 51-53).[12]

There are three major themes in Stephen's address:[13] (1) There is progress and change in God's program; therefore the Mosaic system—including the tabernacle/temple—is temporary, added to the Abrahamic promise. There are stages in the development of God's plan, and the Mosaic system is only one stage. Moses even predicted the coming of a prophet like himself (7:36), who would have the ability to make a New Covenant with Israel. (2) The blessings of God are not limited to the land of Israel and the temple area. Israel's patriarchs and leaders were blessed outside of the land (7:2-16); the Law was given outside the land (7:38); the tabernacle was built outside of the land (7:44) and was replaced (7:47); and God is not restricted to one building/temple (7:48-50). (3) Israel's history is one of opposition to God. Joseph was rejected by his brothers (7:9); Moses was rejected by his people (7:27); and the people to whom Moses delivered the Law disobeyed it (7:38-43).

The Sanhedrin listened quietly to Stephen's clever defense in 7:2-50, being in agreement with the things he said, without realizing where he was going in his argument. But when Stephen revealed the point of his defense in 7:51-53, everything made sense, and they were outraged. The defendant indicted his accusers, accusing them of following the same pattern of disobedience as their forebears. This charge hit a nerve, and Stephen was immediately dragged out and stoned (7:54–8:1a). Stephen's dying prayer was that God would not hold this sin against his murderers, for he saw that they were acting "ignorantly in unbelief" (1 Tim 1:13). This prayer was dramatically answered only two chapters later in the narrative of Acts, as the ringleader of the opposition to Stephen, a young Pharisee named Saul, was converted through a vision of the risen Christ and commissioned as the great apostle to the Gentiles to complete the work Stephen had begun.

The Extension of the Church to Palestine and Syria, 8:1b–12:25

The second major section of Acts, 8:1b–12:25, describes the extension of the church to Palestine and Syria.

The impetus of the extension, 8:1b-3. The impetus of the church's geographical expansion is given in 8:1b-3—it was the persecution of the church at Jerusalem, resulting in believers scattering from Jerusalem

---

[11] The charges laid against Stephen, though false in the way they are presented, nevertheless contain enough truth to be able to see where their basis lay. First, Stephen was preaching that the temple was temporary and would be destroyed in judgment for the Jews' rejection of Jesus (cf. Dan 9:26; Matt 24:1-2; Acts 7:47-50). Second, Stephen was preaching that the Law of Moses was a temporary arrangement which had been fulfilled in Christ, so that believers in the Church Age are under a New Covenant system.

[12] Thomas L. Constable, *Notes on Acts* (2014 ed.; Sonic Light, 2014), 111.

[13] These themes are restated from Toussaint, "Acts," 369-70, with some direct quotes.

to the surrounding regions. Throughout the book of Acts, persecution is often the instrument God uses to force the church to expand. The persecutions also created a greater distance between Judaism and the church, giving the church its own self-identity, and purifying the church from false believers.

Extension of the church to Samaria, 8:4-25. As the church was scattered, believers preached the Word everywhere they went. One of the seven men appointed by the apostles in Acts 6:5, named Philip (cf. Acts 21:8), took the lead in preaching the gospel in Samaria, while the Spirit authenticated his message by miracles (8:4-8). One notable convert was a magician named Simon (8:9-13).[14] There was a need to authenticate the new converts from this new group of people, however. They had to be identified by the apostles, both to ensure that they were not starting some new religion and going off on their own, and to ensure acceptance of Samaritan converts by Jewish believers. Thus, Peter and John traveled from Jerusalem to Samaria and prayed for the Samaritan believers to receive the Holy Spirit (8:14-17). Luke then relates the story of Simon's attempt to buy apostolic power (8:18-24). Luke seems to think it is important to relate the story of Simon. Perhaps this is because Simon expresses what has been the wish and claim of a great many mystics and false prophets ever since, represented in our time by the Charismatic movement. Peter's response reveals that the desire to possess supernatural power emanates from a heart that is gripped by iniquity, no matter appearances to the contrary.

Extension of the church to Ethiopia, 8:26-40. After describing the conclusion of the apostles' Samaritan ministry (8:25), the final paragraph in ch. 8 relates how the gospel was taken to the faraway land of Ethiopia (= Nubia, i.e., northern Sudan; 8:26-40). Philip was told by God to leave Samaria and journey down the main road towards Egypt, going as far as Gaza (8:26). The reason was to set up an important meeting with a potential convert of great significance: a high official in the royal court of Ethiopia who was returning home after worshipping at Jerusalem (8:27). This man was reading Isa 53, and was confused, because mainstream Judaism had no explanation for this chapter (8:28-34). Philip used it as a springboard to explain the good news about Jesus the Messiah (8:35). The eunuch accepted the message, and, understanding that baptism was the initiation rite of the church, asked Philip to immerse him in a roadside pool (8:36-38). As Philip completed the task, the Spirit took him away to another place, where he continued to proclaim the gospel (8:39-40).

The conversion and growth of Saul, 9:1-30. The dramatic story of the conversion and growth of Saul (= Paul), which is a prelude to the conversion of the Gentiles (cf. 9:15), is recorded in 9:1-30. Paul's conversion is so important to the message of Acts that it is recorded two more times, in 22:1-21 and 26:1-23. Paul's conversion explains how the gospel moved from the Jews to the Gentiles, and it also is proof of the gospel message, for only a vision of the risen Christ could have brought about such a dramatic change of character in the church's leading persecutor. As Saul was on his way to Damascus to arrest Christians, he was knocked to the ground and blinded by the overpowering glory of the Lord Jesus (9:1-9). After spending (parts of) three days in blindness, praying, a Christian brother came and laid his hands on him, healing his eyes, and baptizing him (9:1-19a). After his conversion, and probably after a gap of three years in which Paul was taught directly by the Holy Spirit in Arabia (Gal 1:16-18), Paul began to preach the Christian gospel in Damascus (9:19b-22). Immediately, the Jews in Damascus laid a plot to kill Paul,

---

[14] There is a real question as to whether Simon's conversion was genuine, and it is difficult to answer it with complete confidence. If Luke had stated directly whether Simon was one of the ones who received the Holy Spirit in 8:17, this would solve the problem. On the one hand, it is possible for a genuine believer to do and say the things Simon does in 8:18-24, and 8:13 states that Simon did believe the gospel message. On the other hand, the Gospel of John makes clear that there is such a thing as false belief, and the word ἀπώλεια in 8:20 is never used elsewhere in the NT of physical death alone, but rather of eternal damnation (when used of persons). Still, there is a question as to whether Peter is (in 8:20-22) threatening Simon with physical death or eternal damnation, and whether he is calling Simon to repent of this one sin in particular, or of his sins in general.

forcing him to flee for his life (9:23-25)—a pattern that would be repeated time and again in the apostle's ministry. Paul went to Jerusalem, only to have the Jews there attempt to kill him shortly after he was accepted by the church, forcing him to flee to his hometown of Tarsus (9:26-30; cf. Gal 1:18-19).

The progress of the church, 9:31. Luke gives another progress report in 9:31, showing how the church, which had now spread throughout Judea, Galilee, and Samaria, continued to grow.

The growth of the church in coastal Judea, 9:32-43. In 9:32-43, Peter's ministry expands, moving its focus from Jerusalem to coastal Judea. This section is a precursor to Peter's Gentile mission in 10:1–11:18. Peter's ministry in coastal Judea was authenticated by two major miracles: the healing of a bedridden man named Aeneas (9:32-35), and the resurrection of a woman named Dorcas (9:36-43).

Extension of the church to the Gentiles, 10:1–11:18. Chapter 10 of Acts records a monumental event in the history of the church: the salvation of uncircumcised Gentiles and their admission into the church for the first time. Although the issues raised in this section are not fully resolved until ch. 15, it is clear that one no longer has to become a Jew to be saved—he needs only to believe on the Lord Jesus Christ. The section begins with a vision seen by the God-fearing Roman centurion Cornelius, in which an angel appeared to him and told him to send for Peter in Joppa (10:1-8). As Cornelius' messengers were on their way, Peter himself saw a vision which was intended to teach the principle that the church is one new man in Christ, without distinction between Jew and Gentile (10:9-16). Markers of Jewish identity and ceremonial dietary laws no longer had any spiritual significance. The Spirit then told Peter to receive the three messengers from Cornelius, which he did (10:17-23a). The next day, Peter arrived at Cornelius' house, where the centurion had gathered together his friends and family to hear Peter's message (10:23b-33). Peter's address contained several simple, yet earth-shattering, truths: God is no respecter of persons (10:34-35); Jesus of Nazareth was the Messiah, and He preached and ministered as such (10:36-38); Peter and the apostles are witnesses to Jesus' ministry, His crucifixion, and His resurrection from the dead (10:39-41); Jesus commanded the apostles to preach His return to judge the world (10:42); and all the prophets testify that faith in Jesus is the only means of salvation (10:43). Cornelius and those who were gathered with him accepted the message, and their approval by God was manifested by the coming of the Holy Spirit upon them, which was demonstrated by speaking in tongues (10:44-46). Peter then commanded them to be baptized, officially inducting them into the church—without circumcision (10:47-48). Peter then stayed for several days to teach the new believers (10:40b).

When Peter returned to Jerusalem, however, news of Cornelius' conversion had traveled ahead of him, and conflict awaited. Peter was accused of eating with uncircumcised men—something prohibited by Pharisaical tradition, but not by the Law of Moses (11:1-3). Peter answered the accusation by describing how the conversion of the uncircumcised was directly ordained and approved by God at every step of the way (11:4-17). The Jewish believers accepted Peter's defense (11:18), though the issue would not finally be resolved until Paul's ministry forced the church to make a definitive statement in ch. 15.

Extension of the church to Antioch, 11:19-26. The next paragraph, 11:19-26, describes how the church subsequently expanded entirely out of Palestine and spread to one of the largest cities in the Roman world, Syrian Antioch. In Antioch, it built on Peter's expansion of the gospel to the Gentiles, so that Gentiles were actively proselytized (11:20). The expansion of the church to Antioch precipitated a further expansion to the uttermost parts of the earth, since Antioch became the base for the missionary activity of Barnabas and Paul.

The shift in the center of the church, 11:27–12:25. The section which runs from 11:27 to 12:25 describes a shift in the center of the church from Jerusalem to Antioch. First, the churches in Judea are supported by the church at Antioch (11:27-30). Then James is killed, and Peter is persecuted and has to lower his profile (12:1-19). The church moves forward triumphantly in spite of the persecution (12:20-

24). The section ends with Barnabas and Saul in a position of greater prominence, even taking a member of the Jerusalem church with them to assist with their ministry (12:25).

The Extension of the Church to the Uttermost Part of the World, 13:1–28:31

The final sixteen chapters of Acts are focused entirely on the ministry of one man, the apostle Paul. The reason is simple: it was Paul who was largely responsible for taking the gospel to the Gentile world, then for evangelizing the whole Roman Empire. Paul's work flung back the horizons of Christianity, fulfilling the Great Commission. At the time of Paul's conversion, Christianity was narrowly confined to Jews in Palestine and Syria. By Paul's death, Christianity had spread throughout the Roman world, with Gentile Christians far outnumbering Jewish Christians. Shortly after Paul's defense of his gospel at the Jerusalem Council in A.D. 49, the other apostles followed his lead and scattered from Palestine to bring the good news about Jesus Christ to the ends of the earth, some travelling as far as Ethiopia and India. Paul's life had such a great impact that many secular scholars today consider him to be the founder of Christianity; and while this is an exaggeration, it is difficult to imagine a Christianity without Paul. It was Paul who effectively moved Christianity away from being another sect of Judaism, and established it as an entirely separate religion. Peter was the first to bring the gospel to the Gentiles, but Paul forced the issue of the relation of law and grace. It was Paul, with his massive intellect and an education second to none, who greatly strengthened the church with deep teaching, clarifying how Jew and Gentile relate to one another in the body of Christ, how the Church Age fits with God's plan for Israel, how the local church is to function, and how believers are to live. Paul's epistles have always been the backbone of the New Testament. Paul gave Christianity an intellectual credibility and a basis in scholarship that is acknowledged to this day. Before his conversion, Paul was recognized as the most zealous and hardest-working promoter of Pharisaical Judaism, and when he became a Christian, he took the same principled zeal, work ethic, and scholarship that he had developed in Judaism, and applied it to his Christian mission. Paul observes in 1 Cor 15:8-10 that though he was a latecomer to the apostolic band, "I labored more abundantly than they all: yet not I, but the grace of God which was with me." By the time of Paul's death, a new generation of teachers and evangelists had been raised up to continue the apostle's work, and his heroic martyrdom after a life of faithfulness has inspired the church ever since.

Paul's first missionary journey, 13:1–14:28. From Acts 1:8 to 8:1a, there is no missionary aspect to the church, except in Jerusalem. As late as 11:19, the believers were still speaking only to Jews. Acts 13 is a major transitional chapter, as it begins with the Jewish church in Antioch, and ends with the apostles turning from the Jews to the Gentiles (13:46). Paul's first missionary journey (13:1–14:28), though limited in its scope, marked a major shift in the direction of the church.

The opening paragraph records the commissioning of Barnabas and Saul by the Antiochene church at the prompting of the Holy Spirit through a prophet (13:1-3). This pair, accompanied by John Mark, sailed from the port of Seleucia to the island of Cyprus (13:4), Barnabas' original home (4:36). After preaching and journeying through the whole island, they reached the seat of provincial government, Paphos (13:5-6). Here Paul was summoned by the proconsul, Sergius Paulus, who was interested in the gospel, but was hindered by the opposition of a Jewish false prophet named Elymas (13:6-8). The confrontation ended with the blinding of Elymas and the conversion of the Gentile proconsul (13:9-12). The story of Sergius Paulus and Elymas, as the initial event in Paul's first missionary journey, sets a pattern that will be repeated time and again throughout Paul's missionary endeavors, which is Jewish hostility to the gospel contrasted with Gentile openness. This is also the point at which Paul takes on a leadership role (compare 13:7, "Barnabas and Saul," with 13:13, "Paul and his company"). The temporary blinding of Elymas is also significant as a symbol of Israel's temporary blindness and hardening during the Church Age (cf. Rom 11:25; 2 Cor 3:14-16). The blinding of this one individual Jew was a picture in miniature of the judgment which fallen upon his entire nation.

Paul and Barnabas then sailed to Asia Minor and journeyed north to strategic Roman colony of Pisidian Antioch (13:13-14). Here Paul and Barnabas attended the Sabbath-day synagogue service, and were invited to speak (13:15). Paul's sermon, recorded in 13:16-41, is divided into three sections by three direct addresses: the historical anticipation of and preparation for the coming of the Messiah, who is Jesus (13:16-25); the rejection, crucifixion, resurrection, and ascension of Jesus (13:26-37); and the imperative to receive Jesus as Christ (13:38-41). Paul's message is that the promises made to Israel were fulfilled in Jesus, who was rejected by Israel but approved by God, and who therefore must be believed upon by the audience in order to be saved. Justification is only possible through Jesus, not through the Law, and the Jews must repent of their rejection of Jesus to avoid national judgment. Initially, Paul received a positive response from some (13:42-43). However, the Jews became jealous on the next sabbath, when vast multitudes turned out to hear Paul preach, and they decisively rejected the gospel (13:44-45). Paul announced that he and Barnabas would take the offer of eternal life to the Gentiles instead, and the Jews drove them out of town (13:46-52).

Paul and Barnabas traveled eastward to Iconium, where their ministry had such a great impact that another riot began, and once again they were forced to flee (14:1-7). They moved south to Lystra, where Paul's healing of a lame man provoked great amazement (14:8-18), which quickly reversed itself when Paul's Jewish opponents arrived and stirred up the multitudes to stone Paul (14:19). Paul was miraculously able to walk away from the stoning after Barnabas and the believers held a prayer meeting over him (14:20). The apostles moved on to Derbe, and after preaching there, retraced their route through Lystra, Iconium, and Pisidian Antioch in order to teach the new Christians and appoint pastors for them (14:21-23).[15] They then returned to Syrian Antioch to give their sending church a report on their activities (14:24-28).

The Jerusalem Council, 15:1-35. Act 15:1-35 records another turning point in the history of the early church, which is the church's official approval of Paul's gospel to the Gentiles and official declaration of itself as a new entity that is not defined by Jewish identity markers. This declaration was prompted when Judean Christians arrived at the Antiochene church and told the Gentile Christians there that they could not be saved without keeping the Law of Moses (15:1). When Paul and Barnabas strenuously opposed them, the church at Antioch decided to send certain of their members with Paul and Barnabas to Jerusalem for an official declaration on the matter (15:2). As they gave a report to the Jerusalem church regarding their missionary work among the Gentiles, Christian Pharisees stood up and argued that the new converts must be circumcised and commanded to keep the Law of Moses (15:3-5). The apostles and elders gathered to consider the question (15:6). The issue before the council is whether the church is a sect within Judaism, in which membership is defined by observance of the Law of Moses, or whether it is an entirely new and independent entity defined solely by faith in Jesus Christ. After a lengthy discussion, Peter pointed out how Gentile converts had been approved by God in his own ministry work, and argued that the Judaizers were testing God by not accepting the Holy Spirit's induction of uncircumcised Gentiles into the church (15:7-10). Further, he argued that Jews must be saved in the same way as Gentiles, by grace alone and faith alone (15:11). Paul and Barnabas then rehearsed how God had performed the same signs and wonders among the Gentiles as He had among the Jews (15:12). However, a final verdict was not reached until James, the senior pastor at Jerusalem, could appeal to Scripture and apply it to the situation (Acts 15:15-21). James quotes Amos 9:11-12, an eschatological prophecy which describes the salvation of Gentiles in the future Davidic kingdom without losing their Gentile identity. Peter has already explained the theological basis for this phenomenon: the provision of salvation by grace through faith in Jesus, apart from the works of the law. This provision is already in effect in the present age, in which the Christ's church is awaiting the arrival of His kingdom. Thus, Gentile converts should not have to accept Jewish identity markers; they need only to observe moral essentials, of which James

---

[15] The term πρεσβυτέρους (*elders*) in 14:23 is distributive, and does not necessarily imply a plurality of elders in individual churches. The idea of κατ' ἐκκλησίαν is "church by church."

isolates four which would have been particular problems for pagan converts (15:19-21). The apostles and elders then sent out a letter to the church at large, which warned against the doctrine that men must keep the Law to be saved, confirmed Paul and Barnabas, and stated the conclusion of the council (15:22-29). This was a definitive statement that salvation is obtained by faith in Jesus Christ, apart from the works of the Law. Paul and Barnabas, accompanied by two witnesses from Jerusalem, then delivered the letter to the Antiochene church and remained there to minister (15:30-35).

Paul's second missionary journey, 15:36–18:22. After spending some time at Antioch, Paul suggested to Barnabas that they revisit the churches they had planted to check up on them—perhaps as a follow-up to Paul's epistle to the Galatians (15:36). It seems that Paul originally intended for this journey to be nothing more than a revisit of the churches that had already been planted, with some additional ministry in nearby areas. As it progressed, however, it developed into much more than this; Paul traveled all the way to Greece, evangelizing Macedonia and Achaia, and planting numerous and significant new churches. Actually, from here on out, Paul's entire life becomes a missionary journey, without any established headquarters. However, as Paul and Barnabas prepared to set out, they determined that they were unable to work in tandem for the time being, since they could not reach an agreement as to whether to take John Mark along with them (15:37-38). Thus, the two apostles split the assignment, with Barnabas taking Mark and traveling to his home area of Cyprus, and Paul traveling to Asia Minor with Silas (15:39-40).[16]

Paul journeyed overland through Syria and Cilicia (15:41) before reaching the area of his first missionary journey in Derbe and Lystra (16:1). While revisiting the churches he had previously planted and delivering to them the decree of the apostles and elders at Jerusalem (16:1-5), Paul sought out a young Jewish-Gentile man named Timothy to mentor and make useful, perhaps recognizing a mistake in his refusal to work with Mark. Paul, Silas, and Timothy then traveled westward through Asia Minor, intent on preaching the gospel, but with a more limited vision of reaching the world than what the Holy Spirit intended (16:6-8). God then told Paul directly that he should go preach in Macedonia, rather than staying in Asia Minor (16:9-10). He immediately crossed over the Aegean Sea to Philippi, which was a Roman colony and a major city at the very heartland of the Greco-Roman world (16:11-12). Initially, Paul's ministry in Philippi was successful, as several former Jewish proselytes became Christians (16:13-15). Satan wasted no time in opposing Paul, however, sending a demon-possessed slave girl to follow them around announcing their identity as servants of the Most High God who proclaim the way of salvation—a true message, but one which was distorted by the association with its source (16:16-17). Paul put up with this for several days, but finally decided he had to cast out the demon in spite of knowing what would follow (16:18). The owners of the slave-girl, upset that she could no longer tell fortunes, immediately dragged Paul and Silas before the magistrates on false charges; the missionaries were savagely beaten and thrown into the stocks (16:19-24). Satan's attempt to derail Paul's ministry at Philippi was thwarted, however, when Paul and Silas spent the evening praying and singing hymns in the stocks, then were unchained by a great earthquake (16:25-26). This led immediately to the salvation of the jailer and his family (16:27-34), then to the protection of the newly founded church at Philippi through the threat of legal action against the magistrates if further harm were done to the church (16:35-40).

---

[16] People with gentler personalities tend to see Barnabas as right and Paul as wrong. People with less sensitive personalities tend to see Paul as right and Barnabas as wrong. Really, the right thing to do was for them to go their separate ways, as they did. Paul's personality would not allow him to work well with Mark at the time, whereas Barnabas' personality would not permit him to do anything but work with Mark. Mark's subsequent ministry in the church is evidence that Barnabas was right to reenergize Mark, and that he did so effectively. However, Paul may not have been able to do what Barnabas did for Mark, since Barnabas had a special talent for restoring struggling believers. Conversely, Silas, as a Roman citizen, was better suited for mission work in Greece than Barnabas was. Thus, the best solution was the one that was reached—for the two apostles to go their separate ways on friendly terms, doing what each did best with the best partner for his work.

Paul then ministered in Thessalonica, following the same pattern as always—evangelizing the Jews in the synagogue, seeing many Gentile conversions, then being driven out of town when the Jews started a riot (17:1-9). Paul traveled fifty miles southwest to Berea, where he enjoyed a good response to the gospel but was driven out of town by the Jews once again (17:10-15). Paul then went to Athens and stayed there by himself while he waited for his ministry team to catch up (17:15). This marked a turn in his ministry from Macedonia (northern Greece) to Achaia (southern Greece). Athens was the center of Greek culture, religion, and philosophy, and Paul's presentation of the gospel at Athens was a significant event. Paul's spirit was deeply stirred by the idols which filled the city, and he divided his time between debating Jews in the synagogue and debating philosophers in the marketplace (17:16-18). The Greeks were fascinated by his new religious ideas, and for perhaps the only time in his life, a mob dragged Paul into a public gathering place for the sole purpose of hearing him present the gospel (17:19-21). Paul's sermon has three parts: (1) The Athenians acknowledged that they were searching for a God whom they did not know (17:22-23). (2) This is the Almighty Creator God who is sovereign in history, who reveals Himself to those who seek Him, who has given men an innate sense of His existence, and whose existence is even recognized by some of the Greeks' own poets (17:24-28). (3) God's creatures are morally accountable to Him, and must repent in order to be saved in the day when God judges the world through the Man whom He has appointed as Judge, as confirmed by His resurrection from the dead (17:29-31). Paul's sermon was cut off at this point, just as in 26:24 (cf. 22:22). The Greeks saw salvation as escape from the physical realm, and therefore Paul's doctrine of bodily resurrection seemed like foolishness to them (17:32; cf. 1 Cor 15:12, 35). However, there were a handful who accepted the gospel and followed Paul (17:33-34).

Paul then traveled from Athens to Corinth, a city of political, commercial, and geographical importance which lay at the crossroads of Greece (18:1). Corinth would become the central focus of Paul's second missionary journey, as he spent over a year and a half ministering there (18:11, 18). His ministry enjoyed initial success (18:2-4), then blossomed and multiplied after Silas and Timothy joined Paul and the Lord promised to protect him there (18:5-11). Following the typical pattern, the Jews rejected Paul, then accused him before the proconsul (18:12-13). This time, however, the proconsul refused to accept the case, and instead castigated the Jews for bringing a frivolous lawsuit (18:14-17). Some time later, Paul left Corinth, briefly visited Ephesus, then visited the mother church in Jerusalem and returned to his old home church of Antioch (18:18-22). The return to Antioch marks the end of Paul's second missionary journey.

Paul's third missionary journey, 18:23–21:16. Unlike Paul's first two missionary journeys, his third journey is really almost a continuation of his second, marked only by a brief furlough in Antioch, which was followed by the resumption of itinerant ministry (18:23). First, Paul revisited the churches in southern Turkey, checking up on their condition and strengthening them with his teaching (18:23).

The section from 18:24 to 19:7 records the extension of the church to the final group who had not yet believed on Jesus, which was the disciples of John the Baptist. It begins in 18:24-28 with the only paragraph in chs. 13–28 which is about the ministry of a man other than Paul—an eloquent Jew named Apollos. This was still part of the transitional period in which people like Apollos were saved as OT saints and/or as disciples of John, before the gospel had penetrated throughout the known world. They were not Christians, however, since they did not yet know about Jesus. After his conversion to Christianity through the ministry of Priscilla and Aquila, Apollos became a major player in the development of the church in the Greek world, first confounding the Jews at Ephesus, then moving to the intellectual center of Corinth to help the believers there.

Paul then traveled through southern Turkey to Ephesus, a major city of the Roman world which would become the focus of his third missionary journey (19:1). When he arrived, he found disciples of John, and gave apostolic confirmation of the extension of the gospel to this final group by laying his hands on them to receive the Holy Spirit (19:1-7). Paul's long and successful ministry in Ephesus is described in 19:8-20. As usual, he began in the synagogue, then began to meet separately with the Christians after the Jews kicked them out (19:8-9). Paul remained in Ephesus for more than two years, and had such an effective ministry that everyone in the province of Asia heard the gospel (19:10). Because Ephesus was a center for magic and idolatry, the Holy Spirit authenticated Paul's message with extraordinary miracles which demonstrated the power of God over Satan (19:11-16), resulting in mass conversions (19:17-20). After the Ephesian church had been established, the Spirit led Paul to make plans to revisit Greece, then to testify concerning Jesus to Jerusalem, then to Rome (19:21-22; cf. 23:11). As Paul was preparing to leave, however, a riot forced him out of town (19:23-41). Paul's ministry had such a great impact on the city of Ephesus, particularly among its Gentile population, that the silversmiths were afraid they would go out of business, and started a riot to oppose Paul and revitalize worship of Artemis. Paul left town, traveling through Macedonia to Greece, where he spent three months, probably at Corinth (20:1-3). He then began to retrace his journey, traveling back through Macedonia to Troas (20:4-6). While teaching the saints at Troas all day and all night on Sunday, Paul also performed the extraordinary miracle of raising a boy from the dead (20:7-12). Paul then continued on his journey, bypassing Ephesus so as not to be detained by friends who wished to entertain him (20:13-16). Paul then summoned the pastors of the churches in Ephesus to Miletus, and challenged them with a farewell address (20:17-35).[17] Paul's address has three parts: a review of his ministry in Ephesus (20:18-21), an overview of his present situation (20:22-27), and a charge to the elders (20:28-35). Paul's message is that the elders are to emulate his example by having the attitude and conduct of selfless servants, by faithfully teaching and preaching the Word, and by guarding against false teaching. Paul's address was followed by an emotional farewell which shows the deep affection of Gentile believers towards Paul, in contrast to the hostility he would face in Jerusalem (20:36-38).

After meeting with the Ephesian elders, Paul sailed from Miletus (in SW Turkey) to Tyre (in Lebanon; 21:1-3). While in Tyre, the church there met with Paul and told him not to go to Jerusalem because of what the Spirit had said would befall him there (21:4-6).[18] Paul then sailed south to Caesarea, the most direct route to Jerusalem (21:7-8). Once again, the Spirit foretold Paul's sufferings at Jerusalem, and the Christians pled with Paul not to go until he persuaded them that it was the Lord's will (21:9-14).[19] Paul's journey from Caesarea to Jerusalem (21:15-16) marks the end of his third missionary journey.

Paul's journey to Rome, 21:17–28:31. The final and climactic section of the book of Acts describes Paul's journey from Jerusalem to Rome, which mirrors the movement of the entire church from the Jewish world to the Gentile world. It begins with Paul proving to the Jerusalem church that he does not tell Jewish Christians to give up their Jewish identity, as he participates in temple rituals in accordance with the Law (21:17-26).[20] This led to a problem, however, for when the Jews from Asia Minor

---

[17] The statements in 19:25 and 19:38 that they would see Paul's face no more means that Paul is not going to revisit Ephesus anytime soon. To behold someone's face is to see him on a regular basis, as the Ephesians had seen Paul regularly before. It does not literally mean that the Ephesians and Paul would never see each other again. A comparison of 1 Tim 1:3 with 3:14, along with 2 Tim 1:18, seems to indicate that Paul did intend to visit Ephesus later, and the Ephesian elders could have visited Paul in prison even if he did not return to Ephesus. It should be noted that Luke wrote Acts after Paul had been released from prison and was free to travel about as he wished. If Paul had made a mistake here, one would think that Luke would either not record these statements, or else would include an explanation.

[18] This does not mean that the Spirit was telling Paul not to go to Jerusalem, but that the people were advising Paul not to go on the basis of what the Spirit told them would happen to Paul when he went. They naturally did not want to see their beloved pastor badly beaten and imprisoned.

[19] When Agabus prophesied, he did not say, "This will happen *if* Paul goes to Jerusalem," but "This will happen *when* Paul goes to Jerusalem." It is implied that the Spirit intended for Paul to go to Jerusalem.

[20] When Paul offered these sacrifices, he did not interpret them as making atonement for sin. They were likely not even understood as such by the Jews, since they were associated with a vow. Paul states in 1 Cor 9:20 that he

recognized Paul in the temple, they immediately instigated a mass assault on Paul, adding a false accusation against him to further infuriate the people (21:27-29). They immediately dragged Paul out of the temple and began to beat him, intending to kill him (21:30-31). The garrison of Roman soldiers which was housed in a fortress adjoining the temple urgently dispatched a unit to contain the riot, lest a popular revolt break out (21:31-32). Paul was rescued by the soldiers and carried into the fortress (21:33-36). He then requested to speak to the people from the stairs of the fortress, and the chief captain gave him permission (22:37-39).[21] Paul beckoned with the hand, and the people fell silent—even more so, when they heard this alleged Hellenist speaking to them in the Jerusalem dialect of Aramaic (21:40–22:2). This was an epic moment in the history of the nation of Israel (cf. 23:11; 2 Tim 4:17). Israel had already rejected Jesus and crucified Him. They had heard the preaching of Peter and the other apostles soon after, and rejected them as well. Now, over twenty years later, after Christianity had matured and spread throughout the Gentile world, with time running out for the nation before judgment fell, God sent his greatest apostle to Jerusalem to give the Jews one more chance to hear the message and repent. This was Paul's great moment to testify to the truth of the gospel of Jesus Christ before his own countrymen in Jerusalem at one of the major national feasts (cf. 9:15). The whole city was gathered together in and around the temple to hear the apostle speak. Before this time, what they had heard about Paul was based on secondhand knowledge, and without even visual recognition of him. Now he could at last explain to them who he was, how and why he had become a Christian, what he preached, and why he ministered among the Gentiles. From here on out, the Jews are left fully without excuse, for they have heard Paul's testimony from his own mouth in their own language, and have seen him with their own eyes. Their decisive rejection of Paul and his message left God no choice but to bring judgment.

Paul's defense has three parts: his conduct before his conversion (22:3-5), his conversion (22:6-11), and his commission to minister (22:12-21). His defense answers three accusations: that he is against the Jews, that he is against the Law, and that he is against the temple. Paul argues that the change in his life was so radical, the only way you could account for it is by a divine work. Thus, his defense is his testimony, his life history. He was a Hebrew of the Hebrews, the most zealous of the Pharisees, and a hater of Christianity. He did not believe in Jesus or bring the gospel to the Gentiles of his own accord, but because the Lord dramatically appeared to him and commissioned him to preach the gospel. Paul waits as long as he can to speak of the ἔθνη (*nations/Gentiles*), but finally has to mention the word in 22:21 to explain how he ended up preaching the gospel to Gentiles. Once again, it was not of his own accord, or because he was anti-Jewish, but because the Lord sent him. However, as soon as the Jews heard Paul's claim that the Jews had rejected the way of salvation and the Gentiles had accepted it—implying that most Jews were unsaved and that more Gentiles were being saved than Jews; also that Gentiles did not need to become Jews to be saved—they were infuriated (22:22). They unequivocally and totally rejected Paul and his gospel, calling for the apostle's immediate execution (22:22-24). They might have obtained their wish, had Paul not appealed to the legal rights guaranteed to Roman citizens (22:25-29).

The chief captain believed that Paul must have committed some terrible crime to so incense the Jews, but had no idea what it was. Thus, he called the Sanhedrin to assembly the next day, and brought Paul before them for a hearing (22:30). Paul recognized the danger of the setting and his inability to gain an acquittal, and only managed to get out of the predicament alive by inflaming tensions between the Pharisees and Sadducees (23:1-10). The chief captain should, by his own admission (23:28-29), have released Paul at this point, but returned him to prison instead. The next event is important for understanding what is happening in the narrative and why Luke is focusing on it. The Lord appeared to

---

was willing to live as a Jew in front of the Jews and as under the Law in front of those who are under the Law in order to win them to Christ. He also circumcised Timothy to avoid giving offense (Acts 16:3). In no case did he regard these things as contributing to salvation.

[21] What impressed the chief captain in 21:37 was probably not that Paul could say something in Greek, but that he could speak Greek without any hint of a Judean accent, and using the idiomatic "if it is permitted for me to say."

Paul and charged him to bear testimony concerning Him at Rome, as he had done at Jerusalem (23:11). Paul's original apostolic commission was to bear witness concerning Jesus before "the Gentiles and kings, and the sons of Israel" (9:15). Up to this point in Acts, Paul has borne witness to Jews and Gentiles throughout the Hellenistic world, and in ch. 22 he finally bore witness to his own countrymen in Jerusalem. In the remainder of Acts, Paul will complete his commission by bearing witness successively to Felix, Festus, Agrippa II, and Caesar. He also finally brings the gospel to the capital of the Gentile world, namely, Rome.

The next paragraph, 23:12-24, describes how Paul traveled the first leg of the journey to Rome. A plot to murder Paul was discovered by Paul's nephew, who informed the chief captain, Claudius Lysias (23:12-22). The chief captain determined immediately that he had to get Paul out of Jerusalem, at night and under heavy guard (23:23-24). Claudius included a letter to Felix explaining Paul's situation (23:25-30). Felix then received Paul and promised to try him himself (rather than referring his case to the governor of Cilicia) when his accusers came (23:31-35). The accusers came almost as quickly as possible, arriving in Caesarea five days later (24:1). Felix understood immediately that Paul was a big fish because of who traveled to Caesarea to bring the charges—the high priest, elders of the Jews, and a professional orator named Tertullus. The accusation against Paul was threefold: that he was an insurrectionist, a cult leader, and had attempted to profane the temple (24:2-9). Paul replied to these charges in his defense (24:10-21). First, he had only come to Jerusalem twelve days previously, which was not long enough to become a pest, and he had not instigated any sort of insurrection (24:11-13). Second, his belief in Jesus as Messiah is the fulfillment of the Jewish Scriptures, and therefore not an illegal cult (24:14-16). Third, he conducted himself in the temple according to the Law, and was assaulted for other reasons by Jews from Asia who were not among the accusers (24:17-19). Fourth, Paul's affirmation of the resurrection is the real reason why the Sadducean priests were trying to get rid of him; the issue is theological, not legal (24:20-21). Felix understood the hatred that Judaism had for Christianity, and knew that he had no legal grounds to convict Paul, but also realized that releasing Paul would infuriate the Jewish leadership. Thus, he kept Paul in Caesarea under detention until, allegedly, further witnesses could be called (24:22-23). This detention became indefinite, as Felix hoped for a bribe and sought to please the Jews (24:24-27). Importantly to the fulfillment of Paul's apostolic commission, this detention period included a compelling presentation of the gospel to Felix, which he refused. When the new procurator arrived, Porcius Festus, the first order of business for the chief priests and Jewish leaders was to demand a new trial against Paul (25:1-5). In the trial, Festus caved to the political pressure placed on him by the Jewish leadership, forcing Paul to appeal to Caesar (25:6-11). Festus was legally obliged to honor the appeal, thus moving Paul along on his journey to Rome (25:12). Shortly thereafter, King Agrippa II came to Caesarea to greet the new governor, and Festus described Paul's case to him (25:13-21). Agrippa requested to hear Paul's defense (25:22), and a hearing was convened the next day for the purpose of determining the nature of the charges against Paul (25:23-27).

Paul's defense before Agrippa (26:1-29) is far different than his defenses before Felix and Festus. Paul argues that he was a Hebrew of the Hebrews and a great opponent of Christianity, whose life was dramatically changed by an appearance of the risen Christ (26:4-18). He ordered his life in obedience to the commission given him by the Lord, preaching the gospel to all men everywhere (26:19-20). Paul gives Agrippa the straight story on his arrest: the Jews wanted to get rid of him because he was trying to draw people away from their form of Judaism (26:21). But the Christian gospel is the fulfillment of the OT prophets, so Paul is in no way anti-Jewish or anti-Torah (26:22-23). Paul's oration was interrupted by an outburst from Festus when he mentioned Christ's resurrection from the dead, since bodily resurrection was ridiculous to the Greco-Roman mindset (26:23-24). However, Paul, knowing that Agrippa did not have this same hang-up, appealed to him to convert to Christianity based on his belief in the prophetic message concerning Christ (26:25-27). Agrippa replied that he was almost persuaded to become a Christian (26:28), yet he did not respond to Paul's appeal to be saved (26:29).[22] After the hearing, Agrippa gave his verdict to Festus: You should have acquitted Paul (26:30-32).

Acts 27–28 describes the completion of Paul's commission, as the apostle to the Gentiles finally brings the gospel all the way to Rome. God sovereignly protects and directs Paul through a long and dangerous journey. God shows He is greater than Rome by bringing Paul to Rome safely in spite of faulty decisions made by Rome along the way. When Paul preaches in Rome, he attempts to evangelize the large Jewish community there, but is rejected by them. This seems to seal his approach of turning to the Gentiles.[23] There is no indication that Paul ever seriously attempted to evangelize a Jewish community after Acts 28. It is implied that Paul was released after the end of his two-year imprisonment,[24] probably in 62 A.D., and that this book of Acts was written shortly thereafter. Acts 27:24 indicates that Paul's case did indeed go to court, and he apparently was acquitted. However, the whole process took two full years. Probably the legal documentation associated with the case was lost in the shipwreck, and so had to be replaced. Then there was the usual backlog of cases and the time it would take for the accusers and witnesses to arrive from Judea. In any case, Paul preached the gospel freely in Rome for two full years, and was released afterward to do more work for the Lord. Acts ends with the church triumphant in spite of hell's fiercest opposition (cf. Matt 16:18). Luke's aim of showing the origin and universal spread of Christianity has been accomplished by the record of Paul's journey to Rome and successful ministry there, along with the final shift of the gospel to the Gentiles.

---

[22] The presentation of the gospel to Festus and Agrippa once again is a fulfillment of Paul's apostolic commission to bear witness concerning Jesus before kings.

[23] Everywhere Paul went, he preached the gospel to the Jews first, then to the Gentiles. But 28:25-28 have a stronger sense of finality, and seem to indicate a shift to Gentiles first because (οὖν) of the Jews' rejection. Elsewhere, Paul says "*I* will go to the Gentiles," indicating a personal decision; but here salvation itself is sent to the Gentiles. Whenever Israel receives the gospel, they will regain priority (Rom 11:23-24). The rejection of the gospel by the Jews has turned out for the spiritual benefit of the Gentiles; but when the Jews do accept Jesus as their King, this will be even more beneficial for the Gentiles (Rom 11:12, 15).

[24] This is demonstrated by the use of the aorist Ἐνέμεινεν in 28:30 instead of the present or perfect.

Bibliography of Acts

As the bibliography below shows, there are far more commentaries on Acts than an expositor could possibly consult. No attempt will be made here to survey each commentary, except to say that many of the conservative ones are quite useful. Both of Bruce's commentaries are excellent. Toussaint's is brief but lucid, and should be consulted. His is one of the few commentaries that is classically dispensational. Most commentaries do not deal with dispensational issues in Acts, i.e., with the apostles laying hands on people to receive the Holy Spirit at some times but not at others, with new converts speaking in tongues in some places but not in others, and so forth. Longenecker's commentary is worth reading. Lumby, Cook/Jacobson, and Barnes are classics. Bock's is useful, but should be used with caution because it comes from a progressive dispensational point of view and uses critical interpretive methodologies. The five-volume series *The Book of Acts in Its First-Century Setting* contains many helpful articles on the historical background of Acts.

Alexander, Joseph Addison. *Commentary on the Acts of the Apostles*. 2 vols. New York: Charles Scribner, 1875.

Barclay, William. *The Acts of the Apostles*. Philadelphia: Westminster Press, 1953.

Barnes, Albert. *Acts*. Notes on the New Testament, ed. Robert Frew. Reprint: Grand Rapids: Baker, 1949.

Barrett, C. K. *Preliminary Introduction and Commentary on Acts I–XIV*. Volume 1 of *A Critical and Exegetical Commentary on the Acts of the Apostles*. International Critical Commentary. Edinburgh: T & T Clark, 1994.

———. *Introduction and Commentary on Acts XV–XXVIII*. Volume 2 of *A Critical and Exegetical Commentary on the Acts of the Apostles*. International Critical Commentary. London: T & T Clark, 1998.

Bock, Darrell L. *Acts*. Baker Exegetical Commentary on the New Testament. Grand Rapids: Baker, 2007.

Bruce, F. F. *The Acts of the Apostles: The Greek Text with Introduction and Commentary*. 3rd ed. Grand Rapids: Eerdmans, 1990.

———. *The Book of Acts*. Rev. ed. New International Commentary on the New Testament, ed. Gordon D. Fee. Grand Rapids: Eerdmans, 1988.

Chance, J. Bradley. *Acts*. Smyth & Helwys Bible Commentary. Macon, GA: Smyth & Helwys, 2007.

Constable, Thomas L. *Notes on Acts*. 2104 ed. Sonic Light, 2014.

Conzelmann, Hans. *A Commentary on the Acts of the Apostles*. Hermeneia. Philadelphia: Fortress Press, 1987.

Cook, F. C. "The Acts of the Apostles: Introduction." In *The Bible Commentary: New Testament*, ed. F. C. Cook, vol. 2, 309-50. New York: Charles Scribner's Sons, 1902.

Dunn, James D. G. *The Acts of the Apostles*. Epworth Commentaries. Peterborough: Epworth Press, 1996.

Dunnett, Walter M. *The Book of Acts*. Grand Rapids: Baker, 1981.

Fitzmyer, Joseph A. *The Acts of the Apostles: A New Translation with Introduction and Commentary.* Anchor Bible. New York: Doubleday, 1998.

Gloag, Paton J. *A Critical and Exegetical Commentary on the Acts of the Apostles.* 2 vols. Edinburgh: T. and T. Clark, 1870. Reprint: Minneapolis: Klock & Klock, 1979.

Haenchen, Ernst. *The Acts of the Apostles: A Commentary.* Philadelphia: Westminster Press, 1971.

Harrison, Everett F. *Acts: The Expanding Church.* Chicago: Moody Press, 1975.

Howson, J. S., and H. D. M. Spence. *The Acts of the Apostles.* International Revision Commentary on the New Testament, ed. Philip Schaff, vol. 5. New York: Charles Scribner's Sons, 1883.

Jacobson, William. "The Acts of the Apostles: Commentary and Critical Notes." In *The Bible Commentary: New Testament*, ed. F. C. Cook, vol. 2, 351-534. New York: Charles Scribner's Sons, 1902.

Jensen, Irving L. *Acts: An Inductive Study.* Chicago: Moody Press, 1968.

Johnson, Luke Timothy. *The Acts of the Apostles.* Sacra Pagina 5. Collegeville, MN: Liturgical Press, 1992.

Kelly, William. *An Exposition of the Acts of the Apostles: Newly Translated from an Amended Text.* 3rd ed. London: C. A. Hammond, 1952.

Kent, Homer A., Jr. *Jerusalem to Rome: Studies in the Book of Acts.* Grand Rapids: Baker, 1972.

Kistemaker, Simon J. *Exposition of the Acts of the Apostles.* New Testament Commentary. Grand Rapids: Baker, 1990.

Larkin, William J., Jr. *Acts.* IVP New Testament Commentary Series. Downers Grove, IL: InterVarsity Press, 1995.

Lenski, R. C. H. *The Interpretation of the Acts of the Apostles.* Columbus, OH: Lutheran Book Concern, 1934.

Longenecker, Richard N. "The Acts of the Apostles." In *The Expositor's Bible Commentary*, vol. 9, 205-573. Grand Rapids: Zondervan, 1981.

———. "Acts." In *The Expositor's Bible Commentary: Revised Edition*, vol. 10, 663-1102. Grand Rapids: Zondervan, 2007.

Lumby, J. Rawson. *The Acts of the Apostles: With Maps, Introduction and Notes.* Cambridge Bible for Schools and Colleges. Cambridge: Cambridge, 1882.

———. *The Acts of the Apostles: With Maps, Notes and Introduction.* Cambridge Greek Testament for Schools and Colleges. Cambridge: Cambridge, 1891.

Marshall, I. Howard. *The Acts of the Apostles: An Introduction and Commentary.* Tyndale New Testament Commentaries. Grand Rapids: Eerdmans, 1980.
   Note: Marshall is concise and to the point.

Morgan, G. Campbell. *The Acts of the Apostles*. New York: Fleming H. Revell, 1924.

Munck, Johannes. *The Acts of the Apostles*. Revised by William F. Albright and C. S. Mann. The Anchor Bible. Garden City, NY: Doubleday, 1967.

Neil, William. *Acts*. New Century Bible Commentary. Grand Rapids: Eerdmans, 1973.

Pervo, Richard I. *Acts*. Hermeneia. Minneapolis: Fortress Press, 2009.

Peterson, David G. *The Acts of the Apostles*. Pillar New Testament Commentary. Grand Rapids: Eerdmans, 2009.

Polhill, John B. *Acts*. New American Commentary, vol. 26. Nashville: Broadman, 1992.

Rackham, Richard Belward. *The Acts of the Apostles: An Exposition*. Westminster Commentaries. London: Methuen & Co., 1901.

Ryrie, Charles Caldwell. *The Acts of the Apostles*. Colportage Library. Chicago: Moody Press, 1961. **Note:** This commentary is extremely brief.

Smith, Robert H. *Acts*. Concordia Commentary. Saint Louis: Concordia, 1970.

Thomas, W. H. Griffith. *Outline Studies in the Acts of the Apostles*. Grand Rapids: Eerdmans, 1956.

Toussaint, Stanley D. "Acts." In *The Bible Knowledge Commentary: New Testament*, ed. John F. Walvoord and Roy B. Zuck, 349-432. Wheaton, IL: SP Publications, 1983.

Williams, C. S. C. *A Commentary on the Acts of the Apostles*. 2nd ed. Black's New Testament Commentaries. London: Adam & Charles Black, 1964.

Williams, David John. *Acts*. New International Biblical Commentary. Peabody, MA: Hendrickson, 1990.

Witherington, Ben, III. *The Acts of the Apostles: A Socio-Rhetorical Commentary*. Grand Rapids: Eerdmans, 1998.

Interpretive Guide to Romans

Romans has long been recognized as a book of fundamental doctrinal significance, for it is the apostle Paul's great exposition of the Christian gospel. Romans explains and defends the need for all men to be saved by faith through grace, apart from the works of the Law; the nature and effectiveness of the solution from sin provided by Christ; the eternal security of the justified believer; the relation of Israel and the church; and the relation of Jewish and Gentile believers within the church. These are fundamental doctrinal issues, the correct understanding of which is requisite to understanding how to be saved, and to understanding the Bible as a whole. A person who understands the book of Romans properly will have the right hamartiology, the right anthropology, the right soteriology, the right ecclesiology, and the right eschatology. None of the cults understands Romans, and neither does any denomination or sect in the church that has a fundamentally flawed doctrinal position. This includes many churches which have made Romans a focus of their study and appeal to it to prove their doctrines, for familiar passages are often superficially understood.

Romans is the longest of Paul's epistles, as measured by the number of words in the book.[1] For this reason, it is placed first in the canonical order of Paul's epistles. If the Pauline epistles were arranged in chronological order, there would be five books before Romans—Galatians, 1 & 2 Thessalonians, and 1 & 2 Corinthians.

Romans is not only long; it is also deep. Many pastors have taken years to preach through Romans, and commentaries on Romans are often incredibly voluminous. All of Scripture is inexhaustibly rich, but because Romans explains and ties together so many of the Bible's core doctrines, and does so using intricate argumentation, understanding Romans requires an exceptional expenditure of time and effort. Such a study is, however, necessary and deeply rewarding to the person who seeks to comprehend the Christian doctrine of salvation by grace through faith in Christ in the present age.

Historical Background

Paul states in 15:23 that the church at Rome had been in existence for many years before he wrote. There is no specific record of the founding of the church at Rome, though 15:20-21 indicates that no apostles had yet traveled to Rome by the time Paul wrote this epistle. However, Roman Christians are mentioned as early as Acts 18:2, when Emperor Claudius temporarily expelled most Jews from Rome in A.D. 49 because, as the historian Suetonius relates, of disturbances surrounding one "Chrestus," i.e., Christ. Apparently unbelieving Jews were inciting riots against the Christians, as they so often did in the Greek cities which Paul evangelized. The Jews returned to Rome beginning from A.D. 54, following the poisoning of Claudius.

Jews from Rome were present in Jerusalem on the day of Pentecost (Acts 2:10), and apparently some became Christians, traveled back to Rome, established a church, and began to evangelize. In addition, since people from all over the Roman Empire were continually traveling to and from Rome, some Christians who had been evangelized during the missionary journeys of Paul and others would have taken up residence in Rome and joined the Roman church.

The city of Rome was, of course, a Gentile place, but also contained a significant Jewish population. The epistle to the Romans indicates that the church at Rome reflected the general makeup of the city. Verses such as 1:13, 11:13, and 15:27 indicate that the majority of the Roman church was Gentile, and yet it is clear that there was also a strong Jewish contingent, since Paul deals extensively in the epistle with

---

[1] In the Greek text of NA^{27}, Romans has 7,111 words, 1 Corinthians has 6,830 words, and 2 Corinthians has 4,477.

the relationship between Israel and the church, and with the relationship between Jewish Christians and Gentile Christians.

Ancient Rome was in some ways very much like modern-day America, in some ways different. It was a cesspool of iniquity, with raging mobs, rough soldiers, tyrants, public baths, and murderous sports. The upper classes lived in extreme opulence, yet two-thirds of the population were slaves. There were some four hundred pagan temples in the city, and magnificent public works of all sorts. Residents of Rome included not just native Latin Romans, but also peoples from all over the Roman world. Both Greek and Latin were commonly spoken. This was a challenging environment for church ministry, but also one with a unique potential for spiritual impact.

Author

Paul names himself as the author in 1:1 and describes himself elsewhere in the book (e.g., 1:8-15; 11:1, 13; 15:15-16, etc.). Paul was really the only apostle who could have written Romans. Paul dictated Romans to a man named Tertius, who identifies himself as the amanuensis in 16:22. This letter was probably delivered by a woman named Phoebe (16:1-2). Outside of the last two chapters, the Pauline authorship of Romans has never been disputed, not even by liberals, who recognize that it expresses the central themes of Paul's teaching.

It is interesting that an epistle to the church at Rome was written in Greek, since Rome was the center of the Latin-speaking world. In fact, many of the Christians whom Paul salutes in ch. 16 hailed from other parts of the empire, and may not have spoken Latin well if at all. Conversely, probably most of the native Romans in the church understood Greek well. One of the two languages had to be used when writing the letter, and since Paul was fluent in Greek but not Latin the former language was the natural choice. There were many people in Rome who could easily translate a Greek epistle into Latin as it was read, if that was necessary.

Date and Occasion of Writing

At the end of his third missionary journey, Paul left Ephesus and revisited Macedonia (Acts 20:1-2), writing two letters to the church at Corinth the same year. Paul spent three months in Corinth during the winter of 56/57 (Acts 20:3; 1 Cor 16:6), intending to return to Jerusalem afterwards with a gift for the needy Jerusalem church from the Gentile churches in order to help ensure acceptance of Gentile Christians by Jewish Christians (compare Rom 15:25 with Acts 19:21; 24:17; 1 Cor 16:1-8; 2 Cor 8–9). It was during Paul's stay in Corinth in the winter of 56/57 that he wrote the epistle to the Romans (so 15:26; 16:1-2, 23). Paul's three months in Corinth apparently allowed him time for settled reflection on what to write to the Romans and how to write it. The length of his stay also allowed for time for the letter to be delivered and an offering to be collected, then for the offering to be sent to Paul to take to Jerusalem. Probably Romans was written near the beginning of Paul's stay in Corinth, at the end of A.D. 56.

At the time when Romans was written, the world was ripe for a full explanation of the Christian gospel. Judaism, pagan religions, and Greek philosophy were all bankrupt when it came to answering the age-old problem—"How can a man be just before God?" (Job 9:2). There was also a pressing need for the book of Romans in the Christian church. The gospel had been preached in the world for nearly twenty-five years, and the church was rapidly moving away from its Jewish roots to become distinctly Gentile in character. Jewish Christians had many questions: how can God offer forgiveness to filthy Gentiles? What about the teachings of Moses—are they all gone down the drain? What about the promises to Abraham and to the Jewish nation? How do the Hebrew Scriptures fit with what is happening in Christianity? There were also questions about the nature of faith, sin, and grace: why doesn't man need works to be saved—after all, weren't people saved by works before Christ came? If justification is permanent and grace is given freely, does this mean that a Christian can sin freely and get away with it? There was a need for a systematic treatise that would lay out the theological basis for answering these questions, explaining how everything fits together.[2] Although these are questions that were especially in need of an answer in A.D. 56/57, and especially at the church in Rome, they are timeless questions which lift the epistle to the Romans "above the immediacy of the circumstances in which and for which it was written"[3] and give it a timeless significance.

Romans also marked a climax in the life and ministry of the apostle Paul, who was about twenty-one years old as a Christian at the time of writing, and probably in his early fifties physically. Paul had completed the first major phase of his missionary work, having successfully extended the church into the Gentile world by preaching the gospel and establishing churches throughout Asia Minor and Greece. Paul was now at the tail end of his third missionary journey and was preparing to go to Jerusalem, knowing that he faced some sort of hardship when he arrived, perhaps death. At this time of transition in his ministry, and not knowing what would befall him in Jerusalem, Paul wished to set forth a systematic explanation of the Christian gospel for the instruction of the church.

Purpose and Message

The message of the book of Romans is indicated by the thesis statement in 1:16-17—*For I am not ashamed of the gospel: for it is the power of God unto salvation to every one that believeth; to the Jew first, and also to the Greek. For therein is revealed a righteousness of God from faith unto faith: as it is written, But the righteous shall live by faith.* The purpose of Romans is to describe and defend the Christian gospel, which involves explaining the relation between the OT and the NT, and between Israel and the church. Romans explains how the church, the gospel, and the promises to Israel all fit together, and how Jews and Gentiles are to relate to one another in the church. Contrary to some popular views, there is little in Romans on sanctification; the book is mostly about the gospel and dispensational issues. In fact, the major purpose of the book may be to deal with Jew-Gentile/Israel-church/law-grace issues, since the argument of the book builds to the resolution of the relation of Israel to the church in chs. 9–11, and the applicational section builds to a resolution of Jew-Gentile relations in the church in 14:1–15:13. These are issues which are, of course, fundamentally intertwined with the Christian gospel and the controversy over salvation by faith versus works.

Some people have characterized Romans as a systematic theology text, but it really only deals with certain aspects of systematic theology—specifically, the gospel, and how the gospel fits with the OT. Romans seeks to explain the relationship between the OT and the NT, for which reason there are approximately sixty-one direct OT quotes in Romans and seventy-four indirect quotes, from fourteen different OT books. There are more OT quotes in Romans than in all the rest of Paul's epistles combined, and some authors rank Romans as having the largest number of OT quotations of any NT book.

Some commentators affirm that Paul's purpose in writing was to raise money for his trip to Spain. They claim that the entire body of the book, 1:18–15:13, is just padding for his fundraising request. However, there is only one line in the whole book in which Paul mentions that he hopes the Roman church will send him along on his journey to Spain (15:24). Paul did want to collect an offering to send to believers at Jerusalem, but this subject also occupies only a few lines, and the request is not even stated

---

[2] The Roman church in particular had problems with these issues because Rome was the capital of the Gentile world, and yet it had a large Jewish population. Paul indicates that there was some dissention in the Roman church (12:16; 16:17), especially between Jews who were legalistic and Gentiles who despised them (ch. 14). Apparently the dissensions were not vicious, but they were present.

[3] James D. G. Dunn, "Romans, Letter to the" (in *Dictionary of Paul and His Letters*; Downers Grove: IVP, 1993), 841.

directly (15:25-28). Certainly this collection was part of the *occasion* of writing, but fundraising was not Paul's primary *purpose* in writing.[4]

Writing Style

The Greek of Romans is typical Pauline Greek. Romans was obviously a well-planned book. Paul spent some time thinking about the structure of the book and its content before he wrote it. It was not an urgent response to a pressing situation in Rome, nor an emotional appeal, but a well-considered, formal argument.

Textual Base

Romans has a fairly typical textual situation for the Pauline epistles. The strongest witnesses for the book are B and P^{46}, followed by ℵ, A, the Alexandrian minuscules, and the early papyri and uncials.

There are two major textual problems in Romans—the placement of the closing doxology and the omission of "in Rome" in 1:7, 15.

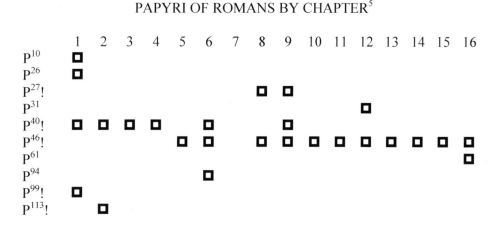

PAPYRI OF ROMANS BY CHAPTER[5]

---

[4] For a full compilation of what people have said over the centuries as to Paul's reasons for writing Romans, see A. J. M. Wedderburn, *The Reasons for Romans* (Studies of the New Testament and Its World, ed. John Riches; Edinburgh: T. & T. Clark, 1988).

[5] Aland's chart mistakenly has P^{27} covering chs. 7–8 instead of 8–9.

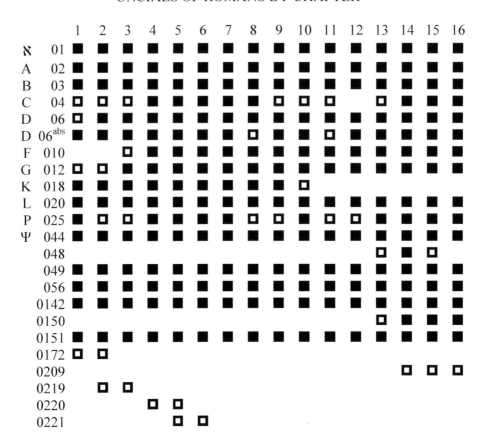

Outline of Romans

Summary Outline

I. Salutation 1:1-7
II. Introduction 1:8-17
III. Universality of Condemnation in Sin Apart from Christ 1:18–3:20
IV. Justification by Faith in Christ as the Solution to Sin 3:21–4:25
V. The Eternal Security of the Justified Believer 5:1–8:39
VI. Israel's Status in the Church Age Explained 9:1–11:36
VII. Service in View of Salvation 12:1–15:13
VIII. Directions regarding Paul's Coming 15:14-33
IX. Conclusion 16:1-27

Expanded Outline

I. Salutation 1:1-7
II. Introduction 1:8-17
    A. Paul's concern for the Roman church 1:8-15

B. Thesis statement 1:16-17
III. Universality of Condemnation in Sin Apart from Christ 1:18–3:20
A. The guilt of Gentiles 1:18-32
B. The guilt of Jews 2:1–3:8
 1. The impartiality of God's judgment 2:1-16
 2. The Jew condemned 2:17-29
 3. The advantage of the Jew 3:1-8
C. Conclusion: all under sin 3:9-20
 1. The sinfulness of all 3:9-18
 2. The impossibility of justification by works 3:19-20
IV. Justification by Faith in Christ as the Solution to Sin 3:21–4:25
A. The good news of justification by faith in Christ 3:21-31
B. Illustration: Abraham's justification 4:1-25
V. The Eternal Security of the Justified Believer 5:1–8:39
A. Glorification as an implication of justification 5:1-11
B. The life-sentence given to those justified by Christ's work 5:12-21
C. Objections to eternal security 6:1–7:25
 1. Objection #1: Shall we continue in sin, that grace may abound? 6:1-14
 2. Objection #2: Shall we sin, because we are not under law, but under grace? 6:15–7:6
  a. The incompatibility of sin and grace 6:15-23
  b. The incompatibility of Law and grace 7:1-6
 3. Objection #3: Is the law sin? 7:7-12
 4. Objection #4: Did then that which is good become death unto me? 7:13-25
D. Assurance and results of eternal security 8:1-39
 1. The spiritual nature of the believer 8:1-11
 2. The adoption of the believer 8:12-17
 3. The inheritance of the believer 8:18-25
 4. The assurance of the believer 8:26-30
 5. The impossibility of a believer losing his salvation 8:31-39
VI. Israel's Status in the Church Age Explained 9:1–11:36
A. Israel's past: national election apart from works 9:1-33
 1. Preface: Paul's love for the Jewish people 9:1-5
 2. Thesis: physical descent insufficient to obtain the promises 9:6-13
 3. Objection #1: God's salvation of Gentiles apart from works is unfair 9:14-18
 4. Objection #2: Israel cannot resist God's hardening 9:19-29
 5. Conclusion: Gentiles being saved by faith, while Israel stumbles 9:30-33
B. Israel's present: national disobedience and responsibility 10:1-21
 1. The universal offer of salvation by faith 10:1-15
 2. Israel's accountability for its rejection of the message 10:16-21
C. Israel's prospect: national obedience and restoration 11:1-36
 1. Israel's hardening only partial 11:1-10
 2. The privilege of Gentiles dependent on faith 11:11-24
 3. Israel's future restoration 11:25-32
 4. Concluding doxology 11:33-36
VII. Service in View of Salvation 12:1–15:13
A. Service in the church 12:1-21
 1. Thesis statement: the imperative for a transformed and dedicated life 12:1-2
 2. The enablement for service 12:3-8
 3. The attitude of service 12:9-21
B. Service in society 13:1-14

1. Service to government 13:1-7
   2. Service to one's neighbor 13:8-10
   3. The attitude of service 13:11-14
  C. Service to weaker brothers 14:1–15:13
   1. The principle of individual responsibility and accountability 14:1-12
   2. The principle of restricting one's lifestyle to avoid offence 14:13-23
   3. The principle of selfless service 15:1-12
   4. Concluding benediction 15:13
VIII. Directions regarding Paul's Coming 15:14-33
  A. Paul's reasons for coming 15:14-21
  B. Paul's route in coming 15:22-29
  C. Paul's request in coming 15:30-33
IX. Conclusion 16:1-27
  A. Commendation of the letter carrier 16:1-2
  B. Salutations to those at Rome 16:3-16
  C. Warning against false teachers 16:17-20
  D. Salutations from those with Paul 16:21-23
  E. Benediction 16:25-27

Argument of Romans

The book of Romans begins with a salutation (1:1-7) and an introduction (1:8-17), and ends with directions regarding Paul's coming (15:14-33) and a conclusion (16:1-27). In between is the body of the epistle (1:18–15:13), which can be divided into a doctrinal section (1:18–11:36) and a hortatory section (12:1–15:13).[6] The doctrinal section is about salvation by faith and God's program for Israel. The climax and central part of the argument is chs. 9–11.[7] This is the section that shows exactly how Jew and Gentile fit together in God's program. Chapters 1–8 build towards chs. 9–11, and chs. 12–15 develop applicational principles from the doctrinal truths established in the first eleven chapters.

Salutation, 1:1-7

The book of Romans opens with a lengthy epistolary salutation which is a single continuous sentence (1:1-7). Paul mentions the gospel of God at the beginning of the salutation (1:1), then expands upon this subject in 1:2-5, which give an encapsulation of the Christian gospel. The comments made in these verses form a seedbed for the rest of the book. Paul then asserts that the Roman Christians are within his jurisdiction as those who have come to faith from among the nations (1:6), and prays for God's blessing upon them (1:7).

---

[6] A common alliterated outline is 1:1-17 Salutation; 1:18–3:20 Sin; 3:21–5:21 Salvation; 6:1–8:39 Sanctification; 9:1–11:36 Sovereignty; 12:1–15:13 Service; 15:14–16:27 Supplement. Using this model, a better outline is 1:1-17 Salutation; 1:18–3:20 Sin; 3:21–4:25 Salvation; 5:1–8:39 Security; 9:1–11:36 Scenario; 12:1–15:13 Service; 15:14–16:27 Supplement. It is clear that there is a major break between ch. 4 and ch. 5, and that chs. 5–8 are a single section. The subject of these chapters is eternal security, not sanctification. In addition, the subject of chs. 9–11 is the relationship between the church and Israel, not God's sovereignty in one's personal faith.

[7] Some say that chs. 9–11 are a parenthetical, since the book would make sense without them. However, major sections of any epistle could be removed, and the rest would still make sense in some way, though a part of the argument would be missing.

Introduction, 1:8-17

Paul follows the salutation with an introduction to the body of the epistle in 1:8-17. First, in 1:8-15, he expresses his heartfelt concern for the Roman church, which he had never personally visited, and yet longed to see. Paul wanted to go to Rome because he was the apostle to the Gentiles, and Rome was the center of the Gentile world; he almost had to extend his ministry to Rome in order to fulfill his apostolic commission. Paul's statement of his desire to preach the gospel at Rome leads into the thesis statement of the book (1:16-17): the gospel is the only means by which God brings salvation to men, whether they are Jewish or Gentile; all are lost and in need of salvation. The gospel reveals the righteousness of God—a righteousness which is imputed to men by faith, who then continue to live by faith.

Universality of Condemnation in Sin Apart from Christ, 1:18–3:20

The guilt of Gentiles, 1:18-32. In the first major division of the book (1:18–8:39), Paul divides men into three classes: Greeks, Jews, and the church (cf. 1 Cor 10:32). In 1:18-32, he deals with unsaved Gentiles, those who act contrary to the knowledge they have about God. Verses 18-19 form the topic sentence of the paragraph which follows. This paragraph is not about why man is lost, but about why men who are already lost in Adam are under the wrath of God: it is because the unsaved Gentile world possesses the truth and consciously disobeys it.[8] In the verses which follow, Paul shows that impiety leads to idolatry (1:20-23), which then leads to immorality (1:24-27) and all manner of wicked deeds and a reprobate mind (1:28-32).[9] The description of pagans in 1:18-32 fits not just the uncivilized savage, but also the erudite Greek, the so-called moral Gentile (cf. 3:9). Homosexuality, which was the norm in ancient Greece, is the mark of being handed over to reprobation for one's rejection of God, since it is a sin which is contrary to nature and dishonors one's own body.

The guilt of Jews, 2:1–3:8. Admittedly, not all unbelievers are idolatrous pagans. The Jews, in particular, appeared to be righteous and to worship the true God. Thus, in ch. 2, Paul argues that the Jew has done just the same thing as the pagan, since he also has the truth and does not obey it (cf. 1:18). The self-righteousness of the Jews, who failed to practice the truth, is just as bad as the sinfulness of the Greeks, who rejected the truth. The argument of this chapter is, for a Jew who is under the Law, the only way he can make it to heaven is by doing it. But no one does it. Therefore both Greeks and Jews stand guilty before God (3:9). Grace is needed.

First, in 2:1-16, Paul lays out the impartiality of God's judgment.[10] The Jew stands self-condemned, since he has condemned the heathen Greek and yet is engaged in the same sinful activities, only in a more

---

[8] According to 1:18-32, paganism does not grow out of a genuine but misguided attempt to search for God, but rather out of a fundamental rejection of natural revelation. Pagan religions, like false religions of every kind, are not a positive response to the light one has, but rather are a rejection of that light. The heathen could neither accept nor ignore the true God, so they exchanged Him for things that are corruptible.

[9] The path of unbelief (where unbelief leads) can be mapped out as follows: failing to glorify and thank the God whom they knew → becoming vain in their reasonings → darkening their hearts → becoming fools → exchanging the true God for idols → dishonoring their bodies → having a reprobate mind → willful condemnation.

[10] The references to Jews in 2:9-10 indicates that the entire paragraph is describing Jews. Also, 3:9 states that Paul has been describing only two groups, Jews and Greeks, and does not include a third group of moral Gentiles. In Paul's thesis statement in 1:16-17, he also divides men into two classes, Jew and Greek, and states that both need to be saved. Some interpreters argue that 2:1-16 describes a moral Gentile, rather than a Jew. This interpretation

refined or religious way (2:1-3). They had hardened themselves to God's offer of grace, resulting in God's judgment for their disobedience to the gospel, without special favoritism (2:4-11). Thus, the superior knowledge of the Jew actually places him at a disadvantage on the judgment day, for he will be judged by a stricter standard (2:12-16).

Paul then gets more specific in 2:17-29, in which he affirms the condemnation of the Jew for squandering their privileges and living hypocritically. Circumcision is only a symbol of what the Jew is supposed to be, and has no power to save in itself.[11]

In response to his condemnation of the Jews, Paul answers in 3:1-8 two arguments posed by a hypothetical Jewish objector. The first objection is given in 3:1—"Hey, what use is it being Jewish if everybody's going to hell anyway?" Paul replies that in fact it is very advantageous to be Jewish, because God gave the Jews special promises and prophecies of the ultimate restoration of their nation through the Messiah's work—promises which God will keep in spite of the rejection of Christ by unbelieving Jews (3:2-4). Paul's Jewish debater then argues that if God's righteousness is demonstrated through His faithfulness to the promises in spite of Israel's unrighteousness in rejecting Christ, then Israel is really bringing God glory, and God would be unrighteous to punish them for it (3:5; cf. 9:19). Paul's first reply to the objector is that if God cannot judge sinners because sin reveals His righteousness, then He could not judge the Gentile world—a preposterous notion (3:6). Paul's second reply is that if sinners cannot be judged because sin showcases God's righteousness, then he could not be judged, either, for preaching a gospel that the Jews claimed was false (3:7). Since the Jews believed Paul should be killed, the objector's argument is self-contradictory. Third, Paul replies that the objection raised in 3:5 would imply that we ought to do as much evil as possible, because that will bring God more glory—as some actually accused Paul of teaching because of his gospel of grace (3:8). Although Paul will deal with this issue more fully in 5:20–6:14, for now he simply notes that those who do evil in order to bring God glory are justly condemned, for they do what they know is evil purposefully and intentionally.

Conclusion: all under sin, 3:9-20. Paul wraps up his argument by demonstrating in 3:9-20 that all are under sin, and no one will be justified by his works. In 3:10-18, Paul strings together five quotations from the OT to nail down his argument by demonstrating its truth from Scripture. Each of these quotations says basically the same thing, which is that all have sinned and all are sinners—including Israel, in 3:15-17 (quoted from Isa 59:7-8).[12] Men are corrupt in their thoughts (3:10-12), in their words (3:13-14), and in their deeds (3:15-18). Such universal and utter depravity shuts the mouth of the Jews as well as that of the

---

originated because some want to believe that moral Gentiles can be saved—in spite of Paul's argument that the person he describes in 2:1-16 is lost. Older commentators wanted to believe that some of the Greek philosophers were saved, especially Socrates, Plato, and Aristotle. However, the Greek philosophers were homosexual, meaning that they fall into the category of 1:26-27, and therefore also 1:20-22. Newer commentators want to believe that moral Muslims are saved, but, again, the man in 2:1-16 is not going to make it to heaven.

[11] Some take 2:28-29 as referring to all believers as spiritual Jews. However, the focus of this entire chapter has been on Jews, and the question arises in 3:1 because of Paul's argument that mere physical ancestry is not enough. Paul never says that Gentiles become Jews when they are saved. He never says the church is spiritual Israel. In fact, the book of Romans argues that Gentiles do not need to become Jews in order to be saved. Contextually, Paul is arguing that being a Jew only in the physical sense is not enough for salvation; it must be accompanied by an internal reality. In 2:25, Paul says that a circumcised ethnic Jew will be reckoned as uncircumcised if he is a transgressor of the law. In 2:28, Paul affirms that Jewishness is not what people think it is; and in 2:29, he says what defines true Jewishness. Paul does not deny that physical descent from Abraham is necessary to be Jewish; he only denies that it is sufficient.

[12] These verses are a description of the unbelieving world. In each case, the OT author refers to those whom he describes in the third person, clearly excluding himself and fellow believers in their redeemed state.

Gentiles, since no Jew can legitimately claim to be just under the Law (3:19-20). Men can only gain condemnation by their works, not justification.

Justification by Faith in Christ as the Solution to Sin, 3:21–4:25

The good news of justification by faith in Christ, 3:21-31. The words Νυνὶ δὲ (*But now*) begin the second major section of Romans.[13] After describing what is wrong with the human race in 1:18–3:20, Paul now brings in the solution, which was already introduced in the salutation (1:1-7) and the thesis statement (1:16-17). The entire OT, the Law included, bears witness to the good news of salvation apart from the Law by which any repentant sinner can obtain God's righteousness through faith in Jesus Christ (3:21-22). Jews and Gentiles cannot take different paths to salvation, because all are sinners who can be justified only by the grace that is offered without price through the propitiatory sacrifice of Jesus Christ on behalf of the human race (3:23-25). The sacrifice of Christ allows God to justify sinners while still being just in His treatment of sin (3:26). No one can boast of his own salvation because justification comes by faith, not by the works of the Law (3:27-28). The Jew does not have an exclusive claim on God, for there is only one God, who must therefore be the God of all peoples, Jews and Gentiles alike (3:29-30). Yet justification by faith apart from the works of the Law is not contrary to the Law; actually, faith in the Person and work of Jesus Christ establishes what was pictured by the ceremonies and ordinances of the Law, thereby fulfilling the Law (3:31; cf. Matt 5:17-19).

Illustration: Abraham's justification, 4:1-25. Chapter 4 concludes Paul's argument for justification by faith by demonstrating it through a historical biblical illustration. In modern times, there is less commentary on this chapter than on the rest of chs. 1–11, but it was likely an important section to Paul's original readers, for whom salvation by Law versus grace was a divisive theological issue.[14] In this chapter, Paul argues from the life of Abraham that justification comes by faith, apart from the works of the Law. The Jews were opposed to Paul's gospel because they believed it contradicted the religion that they had historically been given by God. However, Paul shows that salvation by faith was part of God's program right from the start, using the example of the Jews' first forefather, Abraham.[15] Abraham was justified by faith, apart from works (4:1-8). He was justified before he was circumcised (4:9-12) and before the Law was given (4:13-17), so he certainly was not justified by either. Abraham started out as an uncircumcised Gentile and became a circumcised Jew later in life, and was a believer in both cases. Abraham's faith in God's promises is a model of our justification, since we have believed in the fulfillment of His promise of redemption in Jesus Christ (4:18-25).

The Eternal Security of the Justified Believer, 5:1–8:39

Having proved in 1:18–3:20 that men are lost, and in 3:21–4:25 that they can be justified only through faith in the Person and work of Jesus Christ, Paul proceeds to demonstrate in chs. 5–8 that the justified believer is eternally secure, and will not lose his salvation. Paul makes his basic argument for

---

[13] Νυνὶ δὲ is used to mark a very similar transition in Eph 2:13 and Col 1:22.

[14] In truth, there are still many in the church today who believe in salvation by works, and therefore this chapter probably deserves more attention than it has received.

[15] This chapter raises the issue of how OT saints were saved, and answers it with the assertion that they were saved by faith. However, it was not by faith in Christ's work on the cross *per se*, but by faith in God as He had revealed Himself up to that point in history.

eternal security in ch. 5, handles objections in chs. 6–7, and describes the assurance and results of eternal security in ch. 8.

Glorification as an implication of justification, 5:1-11. Having concluded his argument for justification by faith with ch. 4, Paul now considers it proven and simply states the conclusion in 5:1-2. In 5:3-11, Paul argues that glorification is a natural consequence of justification; that is, all who have been justified will in fact be glorified, and will not drop out along the way. Our hope of sharing God's glory in the resurrection (5:2) produces joy in our present afflictions (5:3-4), because the realization of our hope is guaranteed by the love of God and the presence of the Holy Spirit in us (5:5). God's act in sending His Son to die on our behalf while we were blasphemers and God-haters shows that He loves us with infinite love (5:6-8). If God sent His Son to die for His enemies, surely He will save His friends, i.e., those who have been justified (5:9-10). Thus, our reconciliation to God is reason for us to rejoice in hope of glorification, because we are guaranteed eschatological salvation (5:11).

The life-sentence given to those justified by Christ's work, 5:12-21. Someone may ask how all mankind could be justified by one man's act. The answer is that the act which provided for justification is analogous to the one trespass that plunged the whole world into sin, because Christ is analogous to Adam. Thus, 5:12-21 continues Paul's argument for eternal security by showing that just as all who are in Adam are sentenced to death by Adam's one trespass, so also all who are justified by Christ's one act of righteousness (His sacrificial death) are destined for life as a result. This paragraph is of major doctrinal significance, because it is the basic passage on original sin, and almost all of theology relates to original sin in some way.[16] The argument of 5:12-21 is that one act took care of everything, and guarantees life to those who accept the free gift.[17]

---

[16] Some people think that 1:18-32 explains why man is lost, but it is really 5:12-21 that gives the explanation. Romans 1:18-32 explains why men who are already lost in Adam are under the wrath of God.

The major issue in 5:12 is the imputation of Adam's sin—that is, the question of how it is that all men sinned in Adam and were given credit for Adam's sin. It is normally not automatic that the penalty for one person's sin passes to everyone else in the human race. There are three major views of imputation: federal headship, seminal headship (realistic union), and mediate imputation. Seminal headship and mediate imputation are untenable on both exegetical and theological grounds; only federal headship is taught in Scripture. Federal headship states that all men were given credit for Adam's sin when he committed it, because Adam stood as the federal head (the representative) of the human race. Federal headship is also called immediate imputation, since it states that Adam's sin was imputed to the whole race when he sinned.

The biggest objection to federal headship is that it is unjust to punish one man for the sin of another. However, while this is true in normal circumstances, it is in fact just for us to be punished for Adam's sin if we are part of Adam's race. Adam made a choice for the race in the garden, and the product of that choice was death. It is not possible for a mortal being to beget an immortal being, nor for a sinful man to sire sinless offspring—the offspring take the nature of their parents. However, while physical death and other consequences of the fall are passed to all men from Adam, it is ultimately their own personal rejection of God that condemns men to eternal death. This is illustrated by the doctrine of the age of accountability: an infant who dies due to Adam's imputed guilt, and who has a fallen human nature, and who has committed sins, will still go to heaven because he has not yet developed the faculties that would enable him to make a conscious choice to accept or reject the gospel. Thus, men really only suffer temporal death for Adam's sin; those who will suffer eternal death will do so for their own rejection of God.

In light of the modern evolutionist movement, it is important to note that the argument made in 5:12-21 breaks down if Gen 1–3 is not literally true. If Adam and Eve are not historical, or if sin and death were present in the world before their fall, then there is no need for, nor possibility of, justification through Christ's one act.

[17] In 5:12, Paul begins to boil the whole situation down into a summary by stating the first side of the issue—death and sin entered the world through one man. Verses 13b-14 are a parenthetical supporting the main argument, explaining the phrase "all sinned"—all did not actually commit Adam's transgression, but were given credit for it, which explains why men died before they had violated any specific commandment with a death penalty. Verses 15-

Objections to eternal security, 6:1–7:25. In chs. 6–7, Paul presents objections to the doctrine of eternal security which was established in ch. 5. Chapters 6–7 are structured around four rhetorical questions that a hypothetical Jewish objector is raising against Paul's arguments. The first objection is given in 6:1—are those who have been justified (in the past) free to go on sinning (in the present), since they will not lose their salvation, and God's grace is sufficient to cover their sin? In response to the idea that a Christian can sin freely because he is under grace, Paul replies in 6:2-14 that this is inconsistent with who a Christian is positionally. The doctrine of eternal security does not open the door for believers to sin freely, since what you are should determine how you act—though believers still have a responsibility to be who they are. The second objection responds to Paul's statement in 6:14 that we are not under Law, and asks whether this means we can do whatever we want. Paul replies that grace is a higher standard than Law, and that even on a human level it would be inconsistent for a slave who has been freed from cruel bondage to go back to his old master, to whom he no longer has any obligation or compulsion (6:15-23). Further, believers are not only dead to sin, but also to the Law, and it would make no sense for a believer to go back to the Law, because the Law could not solve man's sin problem (7:1-6).[18] In 7:1-3, Paul changes the analogy from that of slaves and masters to that of husbands and wives. When we were in the flesh, we were bound to serve the Law, like a wife who is under the authority of her husband. But when we were crucified with Christ in fulfillment of the Law, it was as if the Law died, and the believer has married a new Husband, who is Christ.[19] Thus, believers no longer have any obligations to their former husband, the Law.

In response to Paul's argument in 7:1-6 that believers are discharged from the Law, and that the Law only produced sin in our members, the objector says, "Well if we need to be delivered from the Law, does that mean the Law is evil?" (7:7a). Paul's answer is that the Law is a good thing, not a bad thing, because it teaches men God's standards; it was not the Law that made Paul sin, but the sin nature within himself (7:7b-12).[20] The problem is with sin, not with the Law.

---

17 present three contrasts between the trespass and the free gift before the comparison is given in 5:18-19. Verse 15 contrasts Adam and Christ; 5:16 contrasts Adam's one sin and Christ's one act of righteousness; and 5:17 contrasts the result of Adam's sin with the result of Christ's act. Verses 18-19 pick up the main argument from 5:12-13a, presenting the analogy between Adam's one act of disobedience and its consequences, and Christ's one act of obedience and its consequences. Paul then shows how the Law failed to solve man's sin problem (5:20), and how grace through Christ leading to eternal life was needed (5:21).

[18] Most commentators say ch. 7 begins a new subject. But it is better to see the question raised in 6:15 as continuing all the way through to 7:6. This is supported by the use of Ἤ (*Or*) in 7:1, introducing an alternative example. The question raised in 6:15 asked whether believers could sin deliberately because they are under grace instead of Law. Paul spent 6:16-23 arguing that believers have been freed from sin and from sin's domination, and that it would make no sense to go back to our old slave master. In responding to the question of 6:15, however, Paul did not mention the contrast between being under grace and being under Law, which was part of the question. Thus, the Law becomes the chief subject of ch. 7, where the word νόμος (*law*) is used twenty-three times.

[19] Verses 2-3 teach that death alone dissolves a marriage (cf. 1 Cor 7:39). In 7:1, Paul takes it for granted that anyone who knows the Law would recognize this truth and accept it, which is why he uses it as an illustration. Even though this is only intended as an illustration, the illustration nevertheless is assumed to be true, and it teaches important truths about marriage.

[20] Possibly the prevailing view among modern commentators is that 7:7-25 is referring to Israel at Sinai or to Adam, neither of whom are mentioned in chs. 6–7 and therefore are completely read into the text. This is incredible, since Paul continually uses the word "I," and could not be any more clear that he is speaking of himself. The whole passage would have to be interpreted allegorically. Commentators say this is a rhetorical device called prosopopoeia (prosopopoiia). But this rhetorical device is not found anywhere in Scripture, at least not at length. Some point to 1 Cor 6:15, but this is very short and not confusing. Where prosopopoeia is used in Greek literature, it is always clear

The objector now concedes that Paul is not saying that the Law is sinful in itself, but he asks, "Is the Law just an instrument of death, then?" (7:13a). Paul answers in 7:13 that the Law is not an instrument of death, but an instrument of manifesting sin—the true instrument of death—for what it is. In 7:14-25, he uses an autobiographical illustration to explain how the Law does this.[21] The Law reveals what is good and right, but Paul cannot keep the Law even if he wants to, which shows that there is a sin principle within him. It is this sin principle that is the real problem, not the Law. Paul concludes in 7:24-25 by giving the solution to the sin principle, as he looks forward to the day when Jesus Christ will deliver him from the practice of sin in his life. There is nowhere else for the objector to go after this, so there is not another follow-up question after 7:25.

Assurance and results of eternal security, 8:1-39. After dealing with objections in chs. 6–7, 8:1 picks up the main argument from 5:21. Yet the flow of thought is still connected: Paul's wish to be delivered from this body of death (7:24) leads right into ch. 8, in which Paul explains that the redemption of the body will occur in the eschaton. Paul's affirmation in 8:1 that there is no condemnation because God has delivered us from sin and death sums up the preceding argument from 5:1–7:25—those who are in Christ will never be eternally condemned. In 8:2-11, Paul contrasts believers and unbelievers, and argues that while the unsaved mind is in bondage to sin and cannot please God, believers can and do please God because they have the Spirit, who also guarantees that they will obtain resurrection life.

After describing the believer's new nature in 8:1-11, Paul describes the believer's adoption in 8:12-17 as sons of God and joint-heirs with Christ through the Spirit. This paragraph encourages believers not to live as if they are still in the flesh, and also assures them of their eventual inheritance. This inheritance is then described in 8:18-25—believers will receive incorruptible and glorified bodies, which will inhabit a new creation that is unmarred by sin (8:18-25). Paul then assures his readers that everyone who begins the process of salvation is certain to complete it; no one drops out along the way (8:26-30). The Spirit

---

where there is a change in speaker. It is also clear in 7:25 that Paul is speaking of himself. If the passage is read literally, it can only be a reference to Paul—in 7:7-13, to his life before his conversion, and in 7:14-25 to his life afterwards.

[21] It is best to see 7:14-25 as a description of Paul's struggle with sin as a believer, rather than as an unbeliever, for numerous reasons. (1) Paul's shift to the present tense in 7:14 indicates that he is describing a present experience. Wherever Paul describes his past life elsewhere in the epistles, he always does so in the past tense; the so-called "historical present" is only used in the third person in historical narratives. (2) Paul's conclusion in 7:25 thanks God for deliverance through Jesus Christ, yet reaffirms in the same verse his personal struggle as described in 7:14-24. (3) According to 8:7, the unsaved mind is not and cannot be subject to the Law of God. But Paul is very clear throughout 7:14-25 that his mind is subject to the Law of God, though his flesh is not. Those who interpret 7:14-25 as a reference to an unbeliever have to interpret 8:1-11 as contrasting spiritual and fleshly Christians. (4) Paul distinguishes between two natures in him, the flesh (7:18) and the inner man (7:22—cf. 2 Cor 4:16; Eph 3:16), and he affirms that the flesh is not his true nature (7:20). Unbelievers only have the fleshly, sinful nature. (5) Paul says he delights in the Law of God after the inward man (7:22), i.e., his true nature, which indicates he is saved. (6) When reading this passage on their own, most Christians automatically assume that Paul is describing the normal Christian experience, because they feel a deep identification with his conflict. Even Martin Luther, who struggled intensely to keep the Law before his conversion, regarded 7:14-25 as inapplicable to an unsaved man. (7) Romans 8:1 consoles the believer in spite of his struggle, and the rest of ch. 8 argues that believers can have complete confidence in God's faithfulness to complete the work of salvation. Chapter 8 concludes with a very strong affirmation that there is nothing that can separate believers from God's love and prevent them from being glorified, in spite of all their weaknesses, challenges, and struggles. This makes perfect sense on the view that Rom 7:14-25 describes a believer, whereas a discussion of the unbeliever's struggle with sin has no place in a context which discusses the sanctification of the believer and his ultimate glorification.

Some object that Paul could not be describing a believer in 7:14-25 because believers do not need to keep the Law. However, believers are still supposed to obey the moral Law, while not being "under" it in the technical sense of placing oneself under the terms of the Old Covenant (cf. Acts 21:20-26; 25:8; Rom 7:25; 8:7; 13:10).

makes intercession for us to assure our success (8:26-27), and all who are foreknown follow through on each successive step until reaching glorification (8:28-30).[22] As the climax of Paul's argument for the eternal security of the believer, which demonstrates the completeness of the solution to sin offered by Christ, he argues in 8:31-39 that it is absolutely impossible for a believer to lose his salvation before he is glorified. It is impossible for God to fail us (8:31-34), and it is impossible for anyone or anything to make Him fail us (8:35-39). No human or worldly forces can separate us from God's saving love (8:35-37), nor can any supernatural or external forces (8:38-39). Chapter 8 thus ends with the same assertion with which it began—namely, that there is no condemnation to those who are in Christ Jesus. Believers can be completely confident that they are eternally secure.

Israel's Status in the Church Age Explained, 9:1–11:36

The basic soteriological situation has been set forth in 1:18–8:39—the lost condition of all men apart from grace, justification by faith in Jesus Christ, and the eternal security of the justified believer. Now, in chs. 9–11, Paul shows how the Christian gospel fits into God's broader plan in history. Essentially, Paul is handling objections to the gospel in chs. 9–11, since many Jews objected to the concept of a separate people of God and accused Paul of teaching that God has cast off Israel. This was an even more fundamental problem than the issue of Law versus grace. To the first century Jew, the greatest objection to the gospel was the place of the predominantly Gentile church in God's program for Israel. Paul thus explains in chs. 9–11 how the church fits into God's plan for Israel. These chapters are the climax and central part of the book of Romans. The message of chs. 9–11 is that Israel is still elect as a nation, but as long as they reject the gospel and seek salvation through the Law, God will work His program through believing Gentiles.[23]

Israel's past: national election apart from works, 9:1-33. Paul begins his discussion of God's dealings with Israel with a strong affirmation of his love for the Jewish people (9:1-5).[24] He wants his

---

[22] The first step, foreknowledge, is not the same as the second step, foreordination/predestination, since they occur sequentially. Foreknowledge means that God knew in advance who would respond to the offer of salvation; it does not mean "to come into an intimate relationship with someone beforehand" (a nonsensical concept). The second step, predestination, is roughly equivalent to election, and is based on foreknowledge (according to 1 Pet 1:2). The means of predestination consisted of writing the names of believers into the book of life sometime between Gen 1:1 and Gen 1:9 (cf. Eph 1:4; Rev 13:8; 17:8), and the goal of predestination is glorification (being conformed to the image of Christ). The third step, calling, refers to a general call, not an effectual call. Essentially, God makes sure that the gospel goes out to those who are foreknown and predestined. This is the only step that can be experienced by those outside the group that was foreknown. The fourth step, justification, was the subject of 3:21–4:25, in which it was argued that those who place their faith in Jesus Christ for salvation are judicially declared righteous before God based on the imputation of Christ's righteous act to them. The fifth and final step, glorification, is defined in 8:28 as complete conformation to the image of God's Son, and has two aspects: the resurrection of believers with immortal, shining bodies (cf. Matt 13:43; Phil 3:21) and final and perfect sanctification (cf. 1 John 3:2). Paul has already argued in 5:1-11 that those who are justified (in the present) will be glorified (in the eschatological future), though Paul puts the verb in the past tense because it is so sure to happen, it is as good as done.

[23] The election spoken of in these chapters is nowhere individual election to justification/glorification, but is God's choice of Israel as a nation, and the fulfillment of His promises to Israel in the kingdom. The concept of soteriological election is not in Romans 9–11, and was originally read into this chapter historically only by theologians who denied a future for national Israel. It is ironic that the theme of the whole book of Romans is that only those who come to God by faith will be saved, and yet a major section of the book, chs. 9–11, is frequently twisted to mean that salvation comes by God's unconditional election.

readers to know that he is not saying the Jews are unsaved because he hates Jews and wants them to be damned—contrary to modern Jewish portrayals of Christianity, and the traitorous accusations made against Paul himself (cf. Acts 21:20-28). Israel has been given great privileges which make them uniquely suited to be the people of God, but is in rebellion and unbelief—a condition which grieves Paul bitterly (9:4-5).[25] After Paul strongly affirms in 9:4-5 that Israel still has the adoption, the covenants, and the promise of future glory in God's kingdom, he affirms in 9:6 that God's word concerning Israel has not fallen off course (ἐκπίπτω), since He never promised that every individual Israelite would be saved in the present age. God's choice of Isaac over Abraham's other sons shows that not all of Abraham's physical offspring are children of God; by analogy, the Israel of God consists of those who are of Abraham's seed in both a physical and a spiritual sense (9:6-8; cf. 4:11; John 1:47; Gal 6:16).[26] Verses 7-13 explain that the promises never were given to every physical descendant; right from the start, not all the "elect" children of the flesh were children of God. Ishmael was just as much a son of Abraham as Isaac, but the promises were only extended to Isaac.[27] In 9:9-13, Paul is simply making the point that the children of God are not designated as such because of their works, with it being assumed from all that has been said contrasting works with faith in the preceding eight chapters that it is faith that makes an individual a child of God.[28] The next chapter also makes it clear that God is making salvation available through faith, and that Israel has refused to believe. Chapter 9 is simply intended to show that there is nothing unfair or unrighteous about God saving Gentiles.

After establishing that God's choice of people for special privilege is not based on works, a hypothetical Jewish objector claims that it is unfair for God to choose the Gentiles for special privilege without taking works into account (9:14). Paul responds that, on the one hand, God asserted to Moses that since mercy is undeserved, He has the right to show mercy to those to whom He wants to show mercy,[29] while He also has the right to harden those who oppose Him (9:15-18).[30]

---

[24] Paul did not wish to be damned *per se*, or to go to hell, but he did wish that if there was some way he could expiate the sins of his people that he might do so. In one way, this is not a bad wish to make, since this was exactly the desire of Jesus Christ. Christ indeed became a curse in order to save sinners (Gal 3:13). However, Christ, and only Christ, could accomplish redemption, so Paul knew his wish was impossible to fulfill. Christians cannot be accursed, nor could Paul expiate the sins of his people; the Jews simply need to accept Christ's atonement.

[25] Paul specifies in 9:3-4 that he is speaking of ethnic Jews. Throughout chs. 9–11, Paul is consistently talking about ethnic Jews (cf. 11:1).

[26] Verses 7-8 also narrow the definition of Israel rather than expanding it to include believing Gentiles. See also 11:5. This can easily be seen by using a parallel example: the statement, "Not all men are real men" does not mean that some women are men.

[27] Verses 9-12 are not talking about selection for salvation, but for receiving the promises; the word "election" is equivalent to "selection." God selected Isaac and did not select Ishmael, but this did not make either one of them destined to either heaven or hell.

[28] Paul does not say God's choice was unconditional; he only says that it was not based on works. Some basis for the choice must be read into 9:11; contextually, it is more logical to read in foreknowledge of faith than anything else. God knew the future faith of Jacob and Esau.; it is not a coincidence that God happened to pick Isaac's best son. Never in his epistles does Paul contrast works with deterministic election, though he frequently contrasts works with faith.

[29] It should be noted that the will of God is not arbitrary, but is conditioned by His attributes and His character. The condition for receiving God's mercy has already been defined in the book of Romans as faith in Jesus Christ.

[30] Pharaoh was neither created nor damned to display God's glory, but was placed in the position of Pharaoh to display His glory. Further, 9:17 is not talking about displaying God's glory for all eternity, but temporally, through

Paul's hypothetical Jewish disputer responds with a second objection in 9:19—because Israel has been hardened by God, the nation cannot resist what God has planned out.[31] The question posed in 9:19 is not a sincere and honest objection, but an attempt to escape blame—or simply talking back to God. In 9:20, Paul responds by attacking the attitude of the question, affirming with the book of Job (and Isa 29:16; 45:9-10) that God has the right to do things the way He wants, without having to give an account of Himself. In 9:21, Paul, like Jeremiah (Jer 18:6), compares Israel to a lump of clay in a potter's hand, out of which some are being made vessels of honor (i.e., are being saved) while others are being made vessels of dishonor (i.e., are being hardened). In the past—while Israel was the primary manifestation of God's children in the world—God patiently endured disobedient Israelites and displayed His temporal wrath upon the nation,[32] while God is presently making His glory known through those individual believers whom He has called from both the Jews and the Gentiles to form a new people of God (9:23-24). In 9:25-29, Paul presents a biblical basis for what he is saying, proving that the Word of God has not fallen off course (cf. 9:6). In 9:25-26, he quotes Hos 2:23 and Hos 1:10 to show that God has the right to grant sonship and special status to groups that formerly did not have it. In 9:27-28, he quotes Isa 10:22-23 to show that the promises made to the nation of Israel will only be realized by a small remnant. In 9:29, he quotes Isa 1:9 to show that Israel never did respond the way it should have.

Verses 30-33 then summarize the point being made: Gentiles are being saved in the present age because of their faith, while Israel has temporarily lost its position of privilege because they were trying to obtain it by works.

Israel's present: national disobedience and responsibility, 10:1-21. Chapter 9 was about what has historically happened to Israel. Now ch. 10 makes the point that Israel is responsible for its own spiritual condition in the present because the Jews have refused to accept the gospel message. Since this chapter is about salvation, election is never mentioned—the issue is faith. Israel's problem is that they refuse to believe, instead seeking salvation by works (10:1-5).[33] In 10:6-8, Paul alludes to Deut 30:12-14 in order to contrast works righteousness with faith righteousness, which he then describes in 10:9-10.[34] Anyone who

---

the ten plagues, the Exodus, and the crossing of the Red Sea. To harden something is to set it in place, to freeze it where it is—not to essentially change its inclination. Pharaoh was already incredibly hard, and God simply confirmed his hardness. Likewise, at the beginning of the Church Age, Israel was already hard, and God confirmed their hardness. God did not make Pharaoh or Israel essentially different from what they were before, but merely let them go their own way.

[31] Note that the objector would not see any excuse for Pharaoh, and therefore is arguing against the application of this analogy to Israel.

Calvinists believe the essence of this objection is that one has no personal choice concerning his salvation—all is determined by God. But the context is about Israel (9:22); the issue is not about individual salvation, but about the identity of the people of God. The context is speaking of the national hardening of Israel (9:1-5, 18) because they refused to respond to the gospel by faith (9:31-33), in contrast to the Gentiles who were given mercy because of their faith (9:30). Thus, the objection is not about choice concerning individual salvation, but about God's choice of Israel or the Gentiles as His people. Paul's answer is that it is all ultimately based on faith.

[32] It is crucial that ἤνεγκεν (*endured*) is a past tense verb. Verse 22 is talking about something that happened in history, something that is no longer going on today. Also note that 9:22 does not say anything about how one becomes a vessel of wrath or a vessel of mercy; that is not Paul's point in this section. According to 2 Tim 2:20-21, a person has some bearing over whether he is a vessel of honor or dishonor (cf. Rom 2:4-5). The vessels of dishonor are dishonorable by their own choice. But Rom 9:22 says nothing about double predestination.

[33] The view that election of individuals for salvation is the issue in chs. 9 and 11 cannot give an adequate account of how ch. 10 fits in.

believes and calls out to the Lord will be saved, without any regard to race (10:11-13), though of course hearing the message is a prerequisite to believing it (10:14-15).

After demonstrating in 10:1-15 the necessity of believing the gospel for salvation, and noting Israel's failure to believe, Paul then argues in 10:16-21 that because Israel has heard the gospel and rejected it—and they were even warned beforehand by Moses and Isaiah—they are fully accountable for their unbelief. God did His part, but most Jews simply refused to respond.

Israel's prospect: national obedience and restoration, 11:1-36. Paul established in ch. 9 that God can use any instrument He chooses to carry out His purposes, then explained in ch. 10 that God's will is not capricious or arbitrary, but He has a reason for His choices: He has set Israel aside because of their unbelief. Now, in ch. 11, Paul explains that God will restore Israel in the future, whenever they do believe. The Gentiles obtained God's favor by faith, and can lose it by unbelief, just as Israel temporarily lost favor by unbelief, and can regain it by faith.

Paul begins in 11:1-10 by arguing that Israel's hardening is only partial, not total. God's salvation is still coming to some Jews in this age, proving that He has preserved a remnant and has not cast off His people or annulled the promises. Paul then reveals in 11:11-24 that the Gentiles are not receiving God's privileges automatically, but only because of their faith; whenever they lose faith and Israel believes, they will be cut off and Israel will regain its status as the spiritual people of God in this world. He also explains in this section that Israel's temporary fall is not wasted time in God's plan, but is time that God is using to bring salvation to the nations (11:11). Ultimately, it is time that God is using to bring Israel to repentance through the witness of the nations (11:11). Then, when Israel does repent (11:12), their salvation will result in the salvation of countless Gentiles in the tribulation (Rev 7), and even more Gentiles in the kingdom (cf. Isa 66:19). Numerically, there will probably be more Gentiles saved in the tribulation and millennium than in all the previous eras of world history combined. So whether Israel falls or is blessed, it is all for the salvation of the world (11:13-15).

In 11:25-32, Paul shows how it will all end—the Gentiles will indeed be cut out of the olive tree[35] (at the rapture) and Israel will be grafted back in; their hardening will be lifted, the Messiah will return to deliver them, and after the New Covenant is implemented following the second advent, all Jews will be saved in perpetuity, and all of Israel's national sins will be forgiven (11:25-27). Paul summarizes God's plan of the ages in 11:28-32—when the world was slipping into spiritual darkness, God called out Abraham and the Jewish people to preserve a light in the world. When the Jews were slipping into spiritual darkness, God used them to bring the gospel to the nations at great cost. When the nations begin to slip into spiritual darkness, God will use them to bring the gospel back to the Jews, then will use the Jews to bring the gospel back to the nations. In the kingdom, all the Jews will be saved, and will minister blessings to all the nations. God's plan is thus to always preserve a remnant and to save as many as possible. As Paul lays out God's program of the ages and sees how it works out so beautifully, he breaks out in a doxology of praise to God for the wisdom and graciousness of His plan of the ages (11:33-36).

---

[34] Romans 10:9-10 gives as clear a statement on conversion as any passage in the New Testament. Verse 9 states that both confession with the mouth and belief in the heart are necessary to be saved. The confession here is not a public profession, but a calling out to God that occurs at the moment of salvation, according to 10:14. Confession with the mouth refers to a prayer of salvation, wherein a sinner personally calls upon God to save his soul. This is a call that saves (10:12-13), and that follows belief in the gospel (10:10). Romans 10:9 states that one must confess "Jesus as Lord" (though perhaps in different language), which implies both an acknowledgement of His divinity and a realization of one's own responsibility to serve Him and submit to His will. All of this contradicts what the so-called Free Grace movement teaches concerning the mechanics of conversion.

[35] The root of the olive tree is the patriarchs; the nourishment that comes from the roots to the branches is the covenantal blessings; and the branches are the people of God.

Service in View of Salvation, 12:1–15:13

In 12:1–15:13, Paul describes how believers are to relate to one another in the body of Christ, as well as how they are to relate to unbelievers. This flows directly out of the discussion in ch. 11 regarding the relationship between Jews and Gentiles in God's program. The principles Paul gives in 12:1–15:13 are all directed towards fostering unity in the church and living peaceably with the world. In 12:1–13:14, general principles are stated. In ch. 14, principles are stated in terms of "the weak" and "the strong," but it is clear that these categories generally correspond to Jewish Christians and Gentile Christians. As the applicational section concludes in 15:1-13, Paul specifically applies what has been said to the relationship between Jews and Gentiles in the body of Christ.

Service in the church, 12:1-21. The thesis statement for 12:1–15:13 is given in 12:1-2—because God has been so merciful to Christians—both Jews and Gentiles—they ought to respond by giving their all for Him. Following this exhortation, 12:3-8 lists endowments which God has given believers in order to fulfill His commands. Verses 9-21 then give the attitude we are to have as we use our gifts to serve the body of Christ, since if one attempts to use his spiritual gifts with a bad attitude towards others, it will stifle his spiritual effectiveness and usability.

Service in society, 13:1-14. Having described the sort of service believers ought to have in the church, Paul then lays out in 13:1-14 some principles for Christian service in the sphere of general society. The Christian's responsibility of service to government is given in 13:1-7—believers are to submit to the God-ordained governing authorities (including Nero, who was emperor when Paul wrote), and are to pay their taxes faithfully to the government as a means of rendering service to God. Paul then moves from public debts to private debts in 13:8-10, which describes the believer's obligation to love his neighbor and thereby to fulfill all the commandments of the Law. Finally, Paul lays out the attitude we are to have in service, living honorably in view of men, given the fact that each day brings us one day closer to the return of the Lord and the end of the age (13:11-14).

Service to weaker brothers, 14:1–15:13. In 14:1–15:13, Paul returns to the Jew–Gentile issue that was prominent in the first eleven chapters, and describe how stronger brothers (those with Gentile sensibilities) are to relate to weaker brothers (those with Judaizing sensibilities).[36] The point of this section is that if the weaker brother feels guilty about doing something that is morally neutral, the stronger brother is to restrict his behavior in response, in order to avoid leading the weaker brother to violate his conscience.[37]

Paul begins in 14:1-12 by laying out the principle of individual responsibility and accountability. Every man must be sure that what he is doing is right, because each individual will have to answer to God for his own actions. By the same principle, therefore, we do not need to put ourselves in God's place by condemning a brother with a weaker conscience, who may actually be pleasing the Lord by his actions. In 14:13-23, Paul proceeds to set forth the principle that the stronger brother is to restrict his lifestyle to

---

[36] The weak versus strong is probably Jew versus Gentile in most cases. The two outstanding problems the weak brother is said to have are refusing to eat meat (which could have been sacrificed to idols) and the observance of certain holy days.

[37] The weak are people whose consciences are more restrictive than Scripture is. The strong are people whose consciences approximate what the Scripture says. Paul identifies himself with the strong in Rom 14:1 (cf. 1 Cor 9:22). Paul's solution is not to ask the weak to change, but to ask the strong to limit themselves. The bulk of the passage is addressed to the strong.

"Stronger" and "weaker" are often made equivalent to "more spiritual" and "less spiritual." However, since the issues at stake are morally neutral, neither side is inherently more or less spiritual for either doing or not doing them. The terms "stronger" and "weaker" are only about faith concerning certain specific issues.

avoid causing the weaker brother to stumble. The church is to follow the stricter standard, not the more libertine one. Disputed practices are sin, both for the weaker brother (because it violates his conscience), and also for the stronger brother (because it offends a weaker brother). This is a serious issue that could actually end up destroying the wellbeing of the weaker brother if the stronger brother is insensitive. Paul concludes the section in 15:1-13 by arguing that Gentile Christians and Jewish Christians are to serve each other selflessly and accept each other in the body of Christ. Verse 8 is intended to convince Gentiles to accept Jews because Christ has accepted them, while 15:9-12 are intended to convince Jews to accept Gentiles because Christ has accepted them, using four quotations drawn from all three major divisions of the OT. Paul concludes with a short benediction which closes the main body of the book (15:13).

Directions regarding Paul's Coming, 15:14-33

After concluding the discussion of Jew-Gentile relations in 15:13, Paul begins in 15:14 to move to the close of the book by transitioning to a personal note. In 15:14-33, Paul discusses his plans to visit Rome. He first lays out his reasons for coming—he wants to fulfill his commission as a minister of Christ Jesus unto the Gentiles by bringing the gospel to another place where an apostle had not yet ministered, having now covered all the territory between Jerusalem and Rome (15:14-21). Paul next sets out his planned route in coming—he is going to Jerusalem right now to bring an offering to the Jewish church from the Gentile church, and hopes after ministering there to travel to Rome, then on to Spain (15:22-29). Paul concludes with his request in coming—he asks for prayer on his behalf, that he would be delivered from the unbelieving Jews in Judea, that his ministry to the church in Jerusalem in behalf of Gentile Christians would be well received, and that he would afterwards come safely to Rome (15:30-33).

Conclusion, 16:1-27

In ch. 16, Paul moves from the discussion regarding himself to a personal appeal to the Roman church, and thereby concludes the book.

Commendation of the letter carrier, 16:1-2. Paul begins his personal remarks by commending a woman named Phoebe to the church at Rome.[38] Most likely, this is because Paul sent this epistle to Rome with Phoebe. Who in that day would have ever suspected that a letter in that woman's suitcase would change the course of world history some fourteen hundred years later, when it was read by an Augustinian monk named Martin Luther?

Salutations to those at Rome, 16:3-16. Following the commendation of Phoebe, Paul greets a long list of saints in the Roman church, probably because he wants to show that he has a deep personal interest in the church in spite of never having traveled to Rome (16:3-16).[39]

---

[38] The description of Phoebe as a διάκονον in 16:1 is expanded upon in 16:2, which describes how she helps people. This supports the translation of διάκονον as "servant" rather than "deaconess." Of the twenty-eight other occurrences of the term διάκονος in the NT, it is used as a generic reference to a servant or minister twenty-five times, and as a technical term for a person who holds the office of deacon only three times (Phil 1:1; 1 Tim 3:8, 12). There is no other Scriptural evidence for deaconesses; in fact, when the first deacons were appointed, the apostles specifically requested that "males" (ἄνδρας) be nominated (Acts 6:3). In addition, Paul stipulates in 1 Tim 3:12 that deacons must be husbands of one wife, implying that they are males. (The women described in 1 Tim 3:11 are deacons' wives; Greek uses the same word for "wife" and "woman.")

[39] Romans 16:7 is one of the key verses that feminists appeal to in an attempt to justify female clergy. They interpret Ἰουνιαν (*Junias/Junia*) as a female, and then interpret the verse to mean that she is a notable apostle. They

Warning against false teachers, 16:17-20. After the salutations to those at Rome, Paul gives one final warning against false teachers, imploring the church to separate from those who are causing divisions among them and teaching false doctrine (16:17-20). Although this is the first mention of dissention in the church, it is implied that the issues Paul has been explaining throughout the letter are ones that were a problem in Rome. Most likely, the group of troublemakers was the so-called "Judaizers," false teachers who had professed belief in Jesus but insisted that circumcision and observance of the Law were necessary to be saved.

Salutations from those with Paul, 16:21-23. The warning is followed by salutations from those who were with Paul in Corinth when he wrote this epistle (16:21-23). Probably Paul took the pen from Tertius after 16:22 (cf. Gal 6:11; 1 Cor 16:21; 2 Thess 3:17; Phlm 19).

Benediction, 16:25-27. Paul closes the epistle to the Romans with a tremendous doxology which ties together the themes of the book, and which especially relates back to the conclusion of the eleventh chapter (16:25-27).[40]

---

then say this proves that women may legitimately hold positions of prominence in the church. However, "of note among the apostles" does not mean "notable apostles," but "well known to the apostles." See Michael H. Burer and Daniel B. Wallace, "Was Junia Really an Apostle? A Re-Examination of Rom 16:7" *NTS* 47/1 (Jan. 2001): 76-91; David Huttar, "Did Paul Call Andronicus an Apostle in Romans 16:7?" *JETS* 52/4 (Dec. 2009): 747-78.

[40] The placement of the doxology after 14:23, which has very weak manuscript support, probably originated from a time when Marcion and his followers circulated a shortened form of the epistle which lacked 15:1–16:24, as in certain Latin manuscripts.

Bibliography for Romans

As would be expected, there are a huge number of commentaries on Romans. The following bibliography makes no attempt to be exhaustive, only to mention some important works.

Thomas Edgar's work on Romans has been by far the most helpful to me personally. The only chapter where I significantly diverge from his interpretations is ch. 7, especially 7:2-3 and 7:13-25. Edgar did a work on Romans during a year-long partial sabbatical, but has not published his complete notes to date.

Hodge's commentary is one of the best, if not the best, even though he is Reformed. Schreiner is sometimes helpful in spite of being Reformed. Edgar rates Cranfield's two-volume commentary as "good," but I am skeptical because of the series. Moo has at least three commentaries on Romans, with much duplicate material. Edgar rates him as "okay." Some evangelicals are very impressed with Dunn's scholarship, and consider him to be a must read. Whether he can be helpful at times or not, Dunn is liberal and promotes the New Perspective on Paul. He is one of the foremost opponents of the Christian gospel in our day, and is wrong on almost everything he analyzes. He totally misinterprets Paul. Wright's commentary on Romans (not listed) is also a New Perspective work, and is quite underwhelming.

Barnes, Albert. *Romans*. Notes on the New Testament, ed. Robert Frew. Reprint: Grand Rapids: Baker, 1949.

———. *Scenes and Incidents in the Life of the Apostle Paul: Viewed as Illustrating the Nature and Influence of the Christian Religion*. Reprint: Grand Rapids: Baker, 1950.

Befus, Raymond E., Sr. Sermons on Romans from Bethany Bible Church, Grand Rapids, MI. March 6, 1977 to Sept. 2, 1979.

Constable, Thomas L. *Notes on Romans*. 2104 ed. Sonic Light, 2014.

Conybeare, W. J. and J. S. Howson. *The Life and Epistles of the Apostle Paul*. New York: Thomas Y. Crowell, n. d.

Cranfield, C. E. B. *Introduction and Commentary on Romans I–VIII*. Volume 1 of *A Critical and Exegetical Commentary on the Epistle to the Romans*. International Critical Commentary. New York: T & T Clark, 1975.

———. *Commentary on Romans IX–XVI and Essays*. Volume 2 of *A Critical and Exegetical Commentary on the Epistle to the Romans*. International Critical Commentary. New York: T & T Clark, 1979.

———. *Romans: A Shorter Commentary*. Grand Rapids: Eerdmans, 1985.

Dunn, James D. G. *Romans 1–8*. Word Biblical Commentary, vol. 38A. Dallas: Word, 1988.

———. *Romans 9–16*. Word Biblical Commentary, vol. 38B. Dallas: Word, 1988.

Edgar, Thomas R. Course notes from Capital Bible Seminary, Fall 2003.

Fitzmyer, Joseph A. *Romans: A New Translation with Introduction and Commentary*. Anchor Bible, vol. 33. Doubleday, 1993.
Note: Fitzmyer is a liberal Roman Catholic scholar, but his work is still done well. He completely ignores the New Perspective in his commentary.

Gifford, E. H. "Romans." In *The Holy Bible with an Explanatory and Critical Commentary: New Testament*, ed. F. C. Cook, vol. 3, 1-238. New York: Charles Scribner's Sons, 1900.

Godet, Frederic L. *Commentary on Romans*. Reprint: Grand Rapids: Kregel, 1977.
   Note: Originally published as *Commentary on St. Paul's Epistle to the Romans*, 1883. Dr. Edgar required this commentary for his class after writing his commentary. Godet consistently follows the TR over the Critical Text.

Harrison, Everett F. "Romans." In *Expositor's Bible Commentary*, ed. Frank E. Gaebelein et al., vol. 10, 1-171. Grand Rapids: Zondervan, 1976.

Harrison, Everett F. and Donald A. Hagner. "Romans." In *The Expositor's Bible Commentary: Revised Edition*, ed. Tremper Longman III and David E. Garland, vol. 11, 19-237. Grand Rapids: Zondervan, 2008.

Hodge, Charles. *A Commentary on the Epistle to the Romans*. Rev. ed. Philadelphia: William S. & Alfred Martien, 1864.

Jewett, Robert assisted by Roy D. Kotansky. *Romans: A Commentary*. Edited by Eldon Jay Epp. Hermeneia. Minneapolis: Fortress Press, 2007.

MacArthur, John. *Romans 1–8*. The MacArthur New Testament Commentary. Chicago: Moody Press, 1991.

———. *Romans 9–16*. The MacArthur New Testament Commentary. Chicago: Moody Press, 1994.

Moo, Douglas. *Romans*. The NIV Application Commentary. Grand Rapids: Zondervan, 2000.

———. *Romans 1-8*. Wycliffe Exegetical Commentary. Chicago: Moody Press, 1991.

———. *The Epistle to the Romans*. Grand Rapids: Eerdmans, 1996.

Morris, Leon. *The Epistle to the Romans*. Grand Rapids: Eerdmans, 1988.

Moule, H. C. G. *The Epistle of Paul the Apostle to the Romans: With Introduction and Notes*. The Cambridge Bible for Schools and Colleges. Cambridge: Cambridge, 1879.

Mounce, Robert H. *Romans*. New American Commentary, vol. 27. Nashville: Broadman & Holman, 1995.

Ridderbos, Herman. *Paul: An Outline of His Theology*. Translated by John Richard De Witt. Grand Rapids: Eerdmans, 1975.

Riddle, Matthew B. *The Epistle to the Romans*. International Revision Commentary on the New Testament, ed. Philip Schaff, vol. 6. New York: Charles Scribner's Sons, 1884.

Schreiner, Thomas R. *Romans*. Baker Exegetical Commentary on the New Testament. Grand Rapids: Baker, 1998.
   Note: Edgar does not like Schreiner because he is Reformed and teaches perseverance.

Wedderburn, A. J. M. *The Reasons for Romans*. Studies of the New Testament and Its World, ed. John Riches. Edinburgh: T. & T. Clark, 1988.
    Note: Wedderburn describes what people have said over the centuries as to why Romans was written. Wedderburn's view is that there is probably a problem in Rome between the weak and the strong, and that the book is written in part to address that problem. But the book also aims at getting the Romans' prayer support for Paul's trip back to Jerusalem.

Westerholm, Stephen. *Perspectives Old and New on Paul: The "Lutheran" Paul and His Critics*. Grand Rapids: Eerdmans, 2004.

Witmer, John A. "Romans." In *The Bible Knowledge Commentary: New Testament*, ed. John F. Walvoord and Roy B. Zuck, 435-503. Wheaton, IL: SP Publications, 1983.

Interpretive Guide to 1 Corinthians

The book of 1 Corinthians is one of the most popular New Testament epistles, for it deals with common practical problems in the local church. Although many of the believers in Corinth were spiritually immature, and there were numerous significant problems in the church at Corinth, this book is easily applicable to modern churches, since most of today's churches have similar problems. First Corinthians is also popular because its scope is not limited to one specific major problem, but encompasses a wide variety and large number of problems. This epistle has justly been recognized as a key to the health of the local church, and it has frequently been the subject of sermon series.

Churches tend to think well of themselves. They understand that they are not perfect, but if they saw the need for any significant changes, they would make them. I have heard many a preacher characterize Corinth as a church that was beset by serious problems. The reality is, most modern churches are probably worse off than the church at Corinth was. Churches ought to be more introspective when they read 1 Corinthians, instead of turning a blind eye to their own faults. The Corinthian epistles are a wake-up call to complacent, conceited, self-assured Christianity.

Historical Background

Paul founded the church at Corinth on his second missionary journey in A.D. 50–51, and spent an unusually long amount of time working with the Corinthian church—eighteen months (Acts 18:1-18; cf. 1 Cor 3:6, 10; 4:14-15). Paul met Priscilla and Aquila in Corinth and resided with them (Acts 18:2-3). About two years after he left, Apollos traveled to Corinth, and taught the church there while Paul was ministering in Ephesus during his third missionary journey (Acts 18:24–19:1; 1 Cor 3:6), though Apollos had returned to Ephesus by the time Paul wrote 1 Corinthians (1 Cor 16:12).

The church at Corinth was apparently very Hellenistic in its mentality, as indicated by the acceptance by some of incest (1 Cor 5:1), prostitution (1 Cor 6:15-20), fornication (2 Cor 12:21), and eating meat sacrificed to idols (1 Cor 8:9-10). Thus, although Paul founded the church by preaching in the synagogue (Acts 18:4), and Jewish false apostles became prominent in the church (2 Cor 11:22), the Corinthian church was largely Greek in its character.

Most of the problems in Corinth were caused by new Christians retaining a Hellenistic lifestyle and mindset. Greek philosophy viewed matter as evil and resurrection of the body as absurd. The Hellenistic background of the Corinthians also caused them to exalt spiritual experiences that appeared to give a person special knowledge or powers, and to see such things as committing fornication or eating meat sacrificed to idols as bodily actions that do not defile the soul. In addition, since Corinth was a center of oratory and rhetoric, many church leaders had built personality cults and created divisions in the assembly between their disciples and the disciples of other leaders. Paul addresses the problem of divisions in 1 Corinthians, and does not directly attack the sophistic Jewish false teachers who were causing many of the problems in Corinth until 2 Corinthians. In 1 Cor 4:18-19, he simply promises to deal with them when he comes to Corinth.

The city of Corinth was situated on an isthmus in the province of Achaia in southern Greece.[1] This isthmus connected Peloponnese with the mainland of Greece. Since the isthmus was narrow (about four miles wide), a grooved and paved road was constructed around 600 B.C. to facilitate the portage of light ships across the isthmus, as a shortcut between the Aegean and Adriatic Seas.[2] Ships which could not

---

[1] For detailed historical and archeological information on the city of Corinth, see Jerome Murphy–O'Connor, *St. Paul's Corinth: Texts and Archaeology* (3rd ed.; Collegeville, MN: Liturgical Press, 2002).

[2] A canal across the isthmus was begun by Nero, but was not ultimately completed until 1893.

cross the isthmus would often unload their cargo on one side, and have it transported overland to a ship waiting on the other side. Corinth, which was situated in the middle of the isthmus, thus became a major center of commerce in the Roman world. It controlled both east-west trade and travel by sea, and north-south trade and travel by land, and was a much more significant city than its two ports of Cenchrae and Lechem.

Corinth was mostly destroyed in 146 B.C. by Roman armies after a rebellion, although there was a remnant population which continued to live in the area; Cicero records a visit to the city between 79 and 77 B.C. (*Tusc.* 3.53). In 44 B.C., Corinth "was re-founded by Julius Caesar as a Roman colony, after which it quickly rose to prominence once again (cf. Appian *Rom. Hist.* 8.136)."[3] Corinth was a cultural center in the region, and it served as the main junction connecting Europe and Asia. By New Testament times, it was more of a Roman city than a Greek one. It was the capital of Achaia and the third most important city in the Roman Empire, after Rome and Alexandria.

In Paul's day, Corinth had a population of approximately 200,000 free citizens and 400,000 slaves. It contained ample elements of the motley crowd that is typical of seaports and commercial centers. There is much written in ancient Greek literature about the terrible vices of Corinth; although most of these sources refer to the pre-Roman city that was destroyed in 146 B.C., historians who described the Roman city of Paul's day—notably, Strabo and Pausanius—note the same type of corruption, including rampant temple prostitution (cf. 1 Cor 6:12-20).

Dio Chrysostom gives an account of the atmosphere in old Corinth as he describes the fourth-century B.C. Cynic philosopher Diogenes' residence in Corinth during the Isthmian games:

> After Antisthenes' death [Diogenes] moved to Corinth, since he considered none of the others worth associating with, and there he lived without renting a house or staying with a friend, but camping out in the Craneion. For he observed that large numbers gathered at Corinth on account of the harbors and the courtesans, and because the city was situated as it were at the crossroads of Greece. Accordingly, just as the good physician should go and offer his services where the sick are most numerous, so, said he, the man of wisdom should take up his abode where fools are thickest in order to convict them of their folly and reprove them.
>
> So, when the time for the Isthmian games arrived, and everybody was at the Isthmus, he went down also....
>
> That was the time, too, when one could hear crowds of wretched sophists around Poseidon's temple shouting and reviling one another, and their disciples, as they were called, fighting with one another, many writers reading aloud their stupid works, many poets reciting their poems while others applauded them, many jugglers showing their tricks, many fortune-tellers interpreting fortunes, lawyers innumerable perverting judgment, and peddlers not a few peddling whatever they happened to have.[4]

Author

In 1:1, both Paul and Sosthenes are names as authors, though it is clear from the contents of the book that Paul is the speaker and primary author throughout. Sosthenes is apparently named as a person who agrees with what Paul is writing. Acts 18:17 refers to a Sosthenes who was a Jewish opponent of Paul at Corinth; it is possible that this man was later saved and became one of Paul's companions, although this cannot be known with certainty. "The Pauline authorship of 1 Corinthians has never been disputed and

---

[3] S. J. Hafemann, "Corinthians, Letters to the" (*Dictionary of Paul and His Letters*; Downers Grove: IVP, 1993), 172.

[4] Dio Chrysostom *Oration* 8.4-10. From the Loeb translation by J. W. Cohoon (slightly modified).

the letter is already attested in the 90s by Clement of Rome (cf. *1 Clem.* 35:5; 47:1-3; 49:5) and in the first decade of the second century by Ignatius (cf. Ignatius *Eph.* 16:1; 18:1; *Rom.* 5:1, etc.)."[5]

Date and Occasion of Writing

According to 16:8, Paul wrote 1 Corinthians from Ephesus near the end of his three-year stay there during his third missionary journey (cf. Acts 20:31). Since Paul informs the Corinthians in 16:8 that he intends to remain in Ephesus until Pentecost (June 13), 1 Corinthians must have been sent early in the year A.D. 56.

The occasion of writing can be deduced from the contents of the letter. While Paul was in Ephesus in A.D. 55/56, a delegation came from the church at Corinth to consult him about various problems in the church and issues that the church was debating. The delegation carried a letter from the church which posed questions about marriage and meat sacrificed to idols (7:1, 25; 8:1).[6] Paul also heard from various people, probably those in the delegation, about divisions in the church (1:11), immorality in the church (5:1), and abuses in the Lord's Supper (11:18). He does not say so specifically, but he evidently heard about believers suing other believers, disorder in the assembly, abuse of spiritual gifts, disregard of head coverings, and disbelief in the resurrection. Paul therefore wrote a letter (1 Corinthians) as a corrective to these problems, sending it back to Corinth with the delegation that came to Ephesus—and, apparently, with Titus as his own personal representative (2 Cor 7:6-16). In the letter, he also stated his intent to visit Corinth in person in order to follow up on the problems, and also to receive the Corinthians' offering for the church in Jerusalem and to give the church more detailed instruction in person (4:18-21; 11:34; 16:1-7).

Purpose and Message

The content of 1 Corinthians shows clearly that the epistle was written to instruct and correct the Corinthian church in response to the prevalence of various sins and doctrinal errors. The problems addressed in 1 Corinthians, unlike those in 2 Corinthians, are primarily problems within the church itself, and not tensions between the church and Paul. Thus, Paul's purpose in writing 1 Corinthians is not apologetic but didactic. Due to the variety of problems in Corinth, the message of 1 Corinthians is multifaceted: stop your divisions, your toleration of incest, and your immorality; go about marriage God's way, and enter into it thoughtfully; avoid giving offense by knowingly eating meat sacrificed to idols; return to apostolic traditions regarding head coverings and the Lord's Supper; exercise spiritual gifts in an orderly manner, and do not place undue focus on tongues; get over your hang-ups about bodily resurrection; and make preparations for my upcoming visit. The theme of unity/singlemindedness in love is the thread which ties this multifaceted message together.

---

[5] Hafemann, "Corinthians," 175.

[6] Some take all of the "Now concerning. . ." (Περὶ δὲ) statements as Paul's responses to things the Corinthians had written. Περὶ δὲ is certainly used in this way in 7:1, and likely in 7:25 and 8:1. However, it would appear that the section of the book in which Paul responds to questions raised in the Corinthians' letter ends at 11:1, and that Περὶ δὲ is used in 12:1, 16:1, and 16:12 merely to begin a new section (cf. 1 Thess 4:9; 5:1). The fact that Paul addresses the questions which the Corinthians posed to him in the middle of the book indicates that they were not the most important reason for writing the epistle, even if they were the immediate impetus for it.

Outline of 1 Corinthians

Summary Outline

I. Introduction 1:1-9
II. Redress of Divisions in the Church 1:10–4:21
III. Redress of Scandals in the Church 5:1–6:20
IV. Responses to Questions Sent by the Church 7:1–11:1
V. Exhortation to Hold Fast to Apostolic Traditions 11:2-34
VI. Corrective on Spiritual Gifts 12:1–14:40
VII. Corrective on the Resurrection 15:1-58
VIII. Closing Remarks 16:1-24

Expanded Outline

I. Introduction 1:1-9
    A. Salutation 1:1-3
    B. Expression of thanksgiving 1:4-9

II. Redress of Divisions in the Church 1:10–4:21
    A. Heading: Rebuke of the Corinthians for following men 1:10-17
    B. Premise: The opposition between man's wisdom and God's wisdom 1:18–2:16
        1. The foolishness of the gospel to the world 1:18-25
        2. The ignobility of the church in the world 1:26-31
        3. The simplicity of Paul's gospel presentation 2:1-5
        4. The inability of the natural mind to accept God's wisdom 2:6-16
    C. First application: Warning against ministry in the flesh 3:1-23
        1. Man's inability to produce spiritual results on his own 3:1-9
        2. Man's inability to build the church on his own 3:10-15
        3. Warning against harming the church 3:16-17
        4. Warning against valuing the world's wisdom 3:18-23
    D. Second application: Warning against judging the apostles by man's standards 4:1-21
        1. Man's inability to judge man 4:1-5
        2. The humility of the apostles 4:6-13
        3. Warning against despising the apostles 4:14-21

III. Redress of Scandals in the Church 5:1–6:20
    A. Scandal of tolerating incest 5:1-13
        1. The application of discipline to the sinning so-called brother 5:1-8
        2. The application of discipline to any sinning so-called brother 5:9-13
    B. Scandal of lawsuits between believers 6:1-11
    C. Scandal of fornication with prostitutes 6:12-20

IV. Responses to Questions Sent by the Church 7:1–11:1
    A. Response to questions about marriage 7:1-40
        1. Directions regarding marital relations 7:1-7
        2. Directions regarding marital status 7:8-24
        3. Directions regarding singleness 7:25-40
    B. Response to questions about meat sacrificed to idols 8:1–11:1
        1. Exhortation to give up one's rights for the sake of love 8:1-13
        2. Paul's example of giving up rights for the sake of ministry 9:1-27

   3. Lesson from the historical judgment of idolatry 10:1-13
   4. Warning against participation in idolatry 10:14-22
   5. Resolution: live to edify others and glorify God 10:23–11:1
V. Exhortation to Hold Fast to Apostolic Traditions 11:2-34
 A. Head coverings 11:2-16
 B. The Lord's Supper 11:17-34
VI. Corrective on Spiritual Gifts 12:1–14:40
 A. Introduction: the nature of spiritual gifts 12:1-3
 B. The source of spiritual gifts 12:4-11
 C. The relative significance of gifts 12:12-31
 D. The superiority of love to the gifts 13:1-13
 E. The superiority of prophecy to tongues 14:1-19
 F. The purpose of tongues and prophecy 14:20-25
 G. The practice of tongues and prophecy in the assembly 14:26-36
   1. The order of speaking 14:26-33a
   2. The exclusion of women 14:33b-35
 H. Exhortation to submit to apostolic authority in the use of tongues and prophecy 14:36-38
 I. Conclusion: exercise spiritual gifts decently and in order 14:39-40
VII. Corrective on the Resurrection 15:1-58
 A. The centrality of Christ's resurrection to the gospel message 15:1-11
 B. The dependence of Christianity on the truth of the resurrection 15:12-19
 C. The fact of Christ's resurrection and ours 15:20-28
 D. Practical reasons to believe in the resurrection 15:29-34
 E. The nature of the resurrection body 15:35-49
 F. The nature of the resurrection event 15:50-58
VIII. Closing Remarks 16:1-24
 A. Instructions regarding Paul's upcoming visit 16:1-9
 B. Instructions regarding the visit of Timothy and Apollos 16:10-12
 C. Summary exhortation 16:13-14
 D. Exhortation to acknowledge Paul's fellow-laborers 16:15-18
 E. Final salutations 16:19-21
 F. Closing benediction 16:22-24

Argument of 1 Corinthians

First Corinthians is arranged topically in response to numerous specific problems in the Corinthian church, and thus tends to have more abrupt transitions than other epistles. After a brief introduction (1:1-9), Paul deals with divisions in the church in 1:10–4:21 and scandals in the church in 5:1–6:20, then responds to questions sent to him by the Corinthians in 7:1–11:1, exhorts the church to hold fast to apostolic traditions with regard to head coverings and the Lord's Supper in 11:2-34, sets out the proper view and use of sign gifts in 12:1–14:40, presents an argument for the fact and importance of bodily resurrection in 15:1-58, then closes the epistle with personal remarks in 16:1-24.

Introduction, 1:1-9

First Corinthians opens with a standard epistolary salutation which emphasizes the call of believers to sanctification and the unity of the church through its one Lord (1:1-3). Paul thanks God for the good things about the church in Corinth before criticizing them for their problems (1:4-9). The thanksgiving shows that most of the Corinthians were genuine believers, that they were an exceptionally gifted assembly, and that they were progressing in their Christian walk in spite of their problems. Unlike in Galatia, the corruption of the gospel by the idea of works-salvation was apparently not a significant issue in Corinth.

Redress of Divisions in the Church, 1:10–4:21

In the first major section of the book, from 1:10 to 4:21, Paul deals with the problem of divisions in the church. Probably this issue is addressed first because it was a fundamental problem which lay behind the disputes mentioned through the rest of the book. The church at Corinth was characterized by disunity. The basic reason for the disunity was that they had exalted human wisdom and human glory and neglected God's wisdom and God's glory.

Heading: Rebuke of the Corinthians for following men, 1:10-17. The proposition statement for the first unit is given in 1:10, in which Paul calls the church to singlemindedness in Christ.[7] The reason for this call is given in 1:11-12—the Corinthian church had divided up into factions on the basis of personality cults that grew up around leaders in their church, probably pastors of house churches.[8] Paul then rebukes the Corinthians for following men (1:13-17), noting that he himself had intentionally tried to avoid the development of a personality cult when he founded the church at Corinth.[9]

Premise: The opposition between man's wisdom and God's wisdom, 1:18–2:16. Following the rebuke of the Corinthians for following men, Paul argues in 1:18–2:16 that man's wisdom is fundamentally opposed to God's wisdom. The Corinthians did not get saved by human wisdom, so why would they follow it for their sanctification? In 1:18-25, Paul argues that the gospel by which they were saved bypasses human wisdom, and actually appears as foolishness to unbelievers, because it violates their basic understanding of reality. Paul then argues in 1:26-31 that the Corinthians can tell that the gospel is not based on human wisdom just by looking at the makeup of their church. The bulk of those who make up the church—including the Corinthian church—are just "average" or below average in the world's eyes, just plain, ordinary people, and yet the divisions in the Corinthian church were caused by pursuing human wisdom and greatness. However, God has set things up so that the gospel primarily bypasses those who have worldly prominence and abilities, so that He can display His power by using people who are obviously inadequate in themselves to do His work in the world. This glorifies God by showing that the success of His program comes through His power, not man's.

In ch. 2, Paul sets forth his own practice of preaching and teaching wisdom. When he preached the gospel in Corinth, he did so with a simple message, without crafty argumentation, sophisticated philosophy, dynamic oratory, or entertaining gimmickry (2:1-5). However, while unbelievers can

---

[7] Importantly, Paul does not call for unity through acceptance of doctrinal differences, and in fact states in 11:19 that divisions are ultimately necessary in order to separate those who are approved from those who are apostate.

[8] A comparison of 1:12 and 3:4 with 4:6 and 4:15 shows that Paul uses the names of himself, Apollos, Cephas, and Christ as representative of leaders at Corinth, so as to avoid naming specific leaders in the Corinthian assembly. According to 4:15, the problem with the church was that they were following their ten thousand custodians, rather than following Paul, Cephas, Apollos, and Christ.

[9] Verses 13-17 teach two important principles regarding baptism: first, 1:13 implies that all of the Corinthians were baptized, and therefore that all Christians should be baptized; second, 1:17 implies that baptism does not save, for if baptism were necessary for regeneration, then Paul would have been sent to baptize as well as to preach the gospel.

understand the simple gospel, there is a more advanced wisdom which cannot be understood by unbelievers, but which is understood by mature believers (2:6-16).[10] This explains why man's wisdom is of no value for sanctification—the unsaved mind does not have God's wisdom and cannot give it, for it comes only through the Spirit of God.

First application: Warning against ministry in the flesh, 3:1-23. After setting out the basic opposition between man's wisdom and God's wisdom, Paul applies this principle in chs. 3–4 to the ministry of the leaders of the church in Corinth, and to the Corinthians' view of the apostles' ministry. First, in ch. 3, he warns the Corinthians against attempting to do ministry in the flesh. In spite of the capacity which all believers have for obtaining God's wisdom, the Corinthians have failed to use this capacity because they are fleshly-minded (3:1-3). Their allegiance to human leaders shows that they attribute success to human ability, whereas in fact spiritual leaders are like farmers who can sow seeds and pour water on them, but have no ability to make a plant grow; the results can only be produced by God (3:4-9). Paul laid the foundation of the church at Corinth, which rests on the gospel of Jesus Christ; therefore if any man tries to build up the church in the flesh, his work will be burned as worthless on the judgment day, whereas those who renounce human wisdom and human methods and instead edify the church through the Spirit and the Word will have great and abiding reward (3:10-15). Paul then warns the leaders of the Corinthian church directly in 3:16-17 that their division of the church into factions due to their self-promotion and exaltation of the things of this world was destroying the church, and that God would destroy them in response.[11] Finally, Paul warns the Corinthians against valuing the world's wisdom, since the only way to truly be wise is to reject everything the world thinks is right and reorient one's entire way of thinking to God's Word, which means becoming foolish in the eyes of the world (3:18-20). Those who are wise in the world's wisdom need to junk it in order to have real wisdom, replacing the wind-blown reed of academic opinion with simple faith in the Word of God. Paul concludes by warning the Corinthians against bragging about their exalted leaders, since believers have all things in Christ.

---

[10] This is not to say that unbelievers cannot understand at some level what Christians believe, only that they cannot recognize this wisdom for what it is, and accept it.

Never let anybody tell you that Christianity is a religion for the unintellectual. There is nothing more intellectually challenging than understanding the Bible properly. Anybody with sufficient mental acumen and diligence can learn advanced calculus or physics or biology. Anybody with sufficient ability can learn Greek or Hebrew or church history. But ability and study alone are insufficient to find the right interpretation of Romans or Revelation or Genesis, or of any other portion of Scripture. There are men who have great natural gifts of intellect, who study with great diligence, and yet misinterpret the Bible the whole way through. Most pastors, most theologians, and most Bible scholars truly understand very little of Scripture, even if they think they understand it (cf. 1 Tim 1:7).

Biblical studies is thus different from every other academic discipline in that natural intellectual ability and diligent study do not guarantee successful comprehension of the subject matter; they do not even make successful comprehension likely. You could take the best-respected physicist in the world, give him a passage from the Bible, ask him to interpret it, and he would get it all wrong. You could put that physicist through seminary with a major in Old Testament, and he could do his doctoral dissertation on the book of Daniel, and he would still misinterpret Daniel the whole way through the book. After all this, someone who knows the right interpretation could sit down with him and teach him the book of Daniel, and he still would not get it. Not only would he not get it, he would think it is all ridiculous, and he would pity your ignorance. That is how intellectually difficult the Bible is.

It may also be noted that the spiritual ignorance of unbelievers prevents them from properly understanding any academic discipline, though not to the same extent as it prevents him from understanding the Bible directly.

[11] It was common for ancient temples to have a plaque on them saying, "Whoever destroys this, this god will destroy him" (cf. Ezra 6:12). Paul latches onto this common concept, and shows that it is applicable to the church as the temple of God in a very real and true sense. All believers are part of God's temple because the Spirit of God dwells in them.

Second application: Warning against judging the apostles by man's standards, 4:1-21. In ch. 4, Paul applies the opposition between man's wisdom and God's wisdom to the Corinthians' view of the apostles. In 4:1-5, Paul warns the Corinthians against judging the apostles prematurely, since the Lord is the ultimate judge, not man. Success in ministry is not defined by human results, but by one's faithfulness to his calling, and man lacks the proper knowledge needed to definitively evaluate another man's service for the Lord. Paul then contrasts the humility and ignobility of the apostles with the high status which the Corinthians claimed for themselves, the message being that they should humble themselves and imitate the apostles since they obviously are not more spiritual than the apostles (4:6-13). Paul concludes the section by warning against despising the apostles, especially himself (4:14-21). Paul is coming to Corinth, and he will use his apostolic authority to discipline those who fail to heed his instruction.

Redress of Scandals in the Church, 5:1–6:20

After dealing with the problem of divisions in the church in 1:10–4:21, Paul addresses three serious scandals (moral problems) in the church in 5:1–6:20: the scandal of tolerating incest (5:1-13), the scandal of lawsuits between believers (6:1-11), and the scandal of fornication with prostitutes (6:12-20).

Scandal of tolerating incest, 5:1-13. The first scandal Paul which addresses involved the ugly case of a man who had taken his father's wife (5:1-13). Presumably, his father had died, and he had married (or simply begun living with) his stepmother. The church had totally failed to discipline the man for committing a sin of such enormity, but Paul already had done so, and commanded the church to join him in disciplining the man, both to protect the purity of the church, and to protect the erring brother (5:1-8). Paul then moves from this specific case to general principles, warning the Corinthians not to associate with any wicked professing believer (5:9-13).[12]

Scandal of lawsuits between believers, 6:1-11. The mention of judging at the close of ch. 5 leads Paul to address another scandal, that of lawsuits between believers (6:1-11). The basic principle is that believers should not sue other believers in secular courts, as the Corinthians were doing, since this is a bad testimony, and leaders in church are better qualified to resolve these disputes anyway.[13]

Scandal of fornication with prostitutes, 6:12-20. The mention of sexual immorality at the close of the previous paragraph leads Paul into a discussion of a third scandal, that of believers committing fornication with prostitutes (6:12-20). Some Corinthians were claiming that deeds done in the body are inconsequential, and were using this to claim that they could freely commit fornication with prostitutes

---

[12] ἔγραψα in 5:9, 11 should be taken as an epistolary aorist, "I write," as in 9:15 (cf. Rom 15:15; Gal 6:11; Phlm 19, 21; 1 John 2:13-14). Paul is not making reference to a previous "lost" epistle. Verse 11 makes this especially clear. It is obvious that the Corinthians had not separated themselves from fornicators. In addition, it is unthinkable that the early church would have destroyed or lost some apostolic writings. This is especially unthinkable for the Corinthian church, which preserved two of Paul's epistles in spite of their quite negative portrayal of the church.

[13] Paul limits these principles to believer vs. believer (cf. 5:13) and civil matters. There is therefore no prohibition on taking unbelievers to court. I think there are even exceptional cases where a believer could take another professing believer to court. For example, if a Christian business owner does $1,000,000 worth of work for another Christian business, and the second business never pays, the first one can sue the second to get his money back. What Paul is talking about is more disputable cases involving a manageable loss, most of which would probably be settled in small claims court.

(6:12-13a).[14] Paul's counter to this is that we cannot have only the here and now in view, since our bodies will be raised immortal, and they belong to the Lord (6:13b-14). Paul then issues a strong warning against sexual immorality, and explains that physical adultery is also spiritual adultery (6:15-20).

Responses to Questions Sent by the Church, 7:1–11:1

Having addressed the most pressing and urgent problems in the church at Corinth in 1:10–6:20, Paul proceeds to answer the questions sent to him by the church at Corinth in 7:1–11:1. Predictably, these were questions regarding two very practical situations that the Corinthian Christians were dealing with.

Response to questions about marriage, 7:1-40. The first subject that the Corinthians had asked Paul about was marriage. In 7:1-7, Paul addresses the issue of marital relations, and affirms that although celibacy is a good thing, those who are in the married state should not withhold marital relations from the other partner. He next sets out guidelines regarding marital status (7:8-24). It is better for those who are widowed and those who have never been married to remain single, though it is fine for them to get married if they are burning with the desire to do so (7:8-9). Paul, summarizing Jesus' teaching in the Gospels, then addresses the issue of divorce and remarriage, issuing a blanket prohibition on divorce, as well as a blanket prohibition on remarriage to a different spouse after divorce (7:10-11). Regarding those who had been saved after marriage, and were married to an unbelieving spouse, Paul advises them to remain in the marriage to be a spiritual blessing to their family, though if the unbelieving spouse divorces the believer, the believer should not remarry the unbeliever (7:12-16). Paul summarizes in 7:17-24 the general principle he is giving, which is to maintain your present marital status, or the position you held in life when you were saved. Paul then hones in specifically on the issue of singleness in 7:25-40. Although marriage was established at creation as the ideal for all men, because of the present evil condition of the world, singleness is actually better for most people than marriage, because it will allow a believer to be undivided in his service to the Lord and will spare him from added problems and pressures in life. Marriage is still a good thing, and those who marry do a good deed and do not sin, but those who remain single do better and in most cases will actually be happier.[15]

Response to questions about meat sacrificed to idols, 8:1–11:1. In 8:1–11:1 Paul responds to the second question posed by the Corinthians in their letter, which was about eating meat sacrificed to idols. He begins by laying down principles which were to guide believers' actions on this issue. First, in ch. 8, he argues that we ought to be willing give up our rights out of love. Meat sacrificed to an idol is nothing in reality, but if it offends a brother it is necessary to avoid eating it in order to avoid causing a brother to stumble. Paul proceeds in ch. 9 to present his own life as an example of someone who has given up things for the edification of the church. The things he has given up are big things, things people normally do not give up—most notably, marriage and a salary. These are things that Paul had every right to have, but he would not take them for the good of the church.[16] Since Paul has personally followed the principles he has

---

[14] Verses 12-13a apparently set forth a slogan the Corinthians had coined, rather than Paul's own instruction.

[15] First Corinthians 7 is an important passage, because if it were not in the Bible, many Christians would say it is a sin to be single by choice—as some affirm anyway.

[16] Verses 20-23 are grossly misinterpreted by many in the church today. There is a very common attitude that says the only way to reach a subculture is to actually join that subculture and participate in it. For example, there are people who go to bars and drink and dance and smoke and listen to secular music in order to reach people who have that lifestyle. The problem is, the gospel calls men to repentance, and a person who is evangelized by someone who lives and acts just like him will not repent of his lifestyle, even if he supposedly "gets saved." This chapter is actually exhorting believers to restrict their liberties, rather than exercising them to the full.

laid out in chs. 7–8, he then exhorts the Corinthian church to follow these same principles. First, in 10:1-13, he uses the historical example of God's judgment of Israel in the wilderness to warn the Corinthians against taking their liberty and knowledge too far in the mistaken confidence that one is strong enough not to have to worry about falling into sin. Paul explains what he means in 10:14-22—one who takes the freedom to eat meat sacrificed to idols too far will actually participate in the worship of idols, which represent demons. Paul finally gives the resolution in 10:23–11:1. Rather than doing whatever is expedient, as the Corinthian slogan claimed (10:23a), believers are to do whatever edifies (10:23b-24). Go ahead and eat meat that is sold in the market or served to you at a dinner or feast, without asking whether it has been sacrificed to an idol (10:24-27). However, if someone tells you it has been offered to an idol, refuse to eat it (10:28-29). The basic principle is, live to edify others and glorify God (10:30–11:1).

Exhortation to Hold Fast to Apostolic Traditions, 11:2-34

After dealing with the questions sent to him by the Corinthians, Paul then addresses other problematic matters in the church at Corinth. The first two matters, discussed in 11:2-34, were problems that arose through the Corinthians' failure to follow apostolic tradition in the use of head coverings (11:2-16) and the observance of the Lord's Supper (11:17-34).

Head coverings, 11:2-16. Paul begins his discussion in 11:2-3 by laying down the general principles that the church should abide by apostolic traditions and by the hierarchy of authority established by God. In general, the Corinthians were doing this. But as 11:4-16 make clear, many of the Corinthian women were violating the traditions by not wearing head coverings (as a sign of being under male authority) when they worship.[17] All of the reasons Paul gives in 11:3-16 for women wearing head coverings while they worship and men not doing so appeal to universal principles; they are not cultural, and still apply today.[18]

The Lord's Supper, 11:17-34. After dealing with the matter of head coverings, Paul rebukes the Corinthian church for not following apostolic tradition in their manner of observing the Lord's Supper (11:17-34). The Corinthians had turned the Lord's Supper into a riotous feast, in which rich believers drank themselves drunk and ate gluttonously, while poor believers went hungry.[19] As a result, the Lord

---

[17] The reference to women praying and prophesying in 11:5 cannot refer to praying or prophesying in the assembly, since that would contradict 14:34-35. Note that 11:2-16 do not mention the assembly or meeting together. In fact, the whole of chs. 1–10 is not about problems in the assembly, either. The section about the assembly begins with 11:17, which makes a clear transition to speaking about the assembly. The remainder of the chapter contains repeated references to "coming together."

The mere mention of praying and prophesying does not imply that Paul is speaking of the assembly. It is obvious that prayer is often done privately, outside of official church gatherings. Most examples of prophesying in both the OT and the NT occur outside of the assembly as well. There is no reason why a female prophet would have to prophesy in the assembly.

[18] Roman men and women both covered their heads when praying or sacrificing in the Roman religion. Conversely, Greek women *un*covered their heads in religious ceremonies. So the cultural data is a wash. In Judaism prior to the destruction of the second temple, men always worshipped with their heads uncovered, and women with their heads covered. It was only after the second temple was destroyed that Jewish men began to cover their heads as a sign that the nation had lost its covering (by losing the altar of burnt-offering to make atonement).

[19] There is no sin that disqualifies a believer from partaking of communion except the sin of eating the bread or drinking the cup in an improper manner, as the Corinthians were doing in the manner just described. Notice Paul

had killed many of the Corinthians in judgment, while smiting many others with illnesses. The way to repent was to observe the bread and cup ceremonially together, to feast at home, and when eating a shared meal, not to grab all the food before someone else gets it.

Corrective on Spiritual Gifts, 12:1–14:40

The main body of 1 Corinthians closes with two sections of correctives regarding doctrinal problems in the Corinthian church. The first issue which Paul addresses is that of spiritual gifts (12:1–14:40). The Corinthians were placing undue stress on the showy sign gifts, especially tongues (languages), even though tongues was actually one of the least important gifts for the edification of the body of Christ.

Before giving practical instruction regarding the practice of tongues and prophecy in the Corinthian assembly, Paul lays the theological groundwork for this instruction in chs. 12–13. He introduces the section in 12:1-3 by contrasting the former religious practice of the Corinthians in following non-speaking idols with the doctrinally sound utterances given by the Holy Spirit. The Holy Spirit is the source of all spiritual gifts, which He distributes to different believers for the edification of the body according to His will (12:4-11).[20] In 12:12-31, Paul then warns against viewing some gifts as unimportant, since all are necessary for the body of Christ to function, and no gift can function independently of the others. The claim that those who do not speak in tongues are not part of the body is simply wrong (12:16). In fact, if one were to list the gifts in order of priority, tongues would actually rank last, and therefore should not be the one gift that all the Corinthians wished to have (12:28-31).

Before giving instructions regarding the use of sign gifts, Paul gives one more theological principle in ch. 13, which is that the exercise of love is more important than, and necessary to, the exercise of spiritual gifts—implying that the Corinthians' practice of gifts was being done without love. A spiritual gift which is exercised to a hypothetical extreme, but is done without love, is worthless (13:1-3). Paul lists

---

does not say that you are better off not taking communion than partaking with unconfessed sin in your life, nor does he say, "confess your sin before taking communion." He only warns against sinning in the actual manner in which communion is taken. This is about partaking in an unworthy manner, not in an unworthy state, or as an unworthy man. Verses 20-23 and 33-34 shows that the issue is that some were not waiting for others to get their food, and thereby allowing them to go hungry. In spite of all the moral problems in Corinth, Paul never tells people in this paragraph that they need to repent of their immoralities before they take communion.

Misinterpretation of this verse has caused great anguish for countless Christians through the ages, and it has caused many to needlessly refuse to partake of this ordinance when they could have and should have. Some people wonder if they are good enough to take communion, and those with a more sensitive conscience often conclude they cannot. But the communion ordinance is open to all (adult) believers, no matter whether they have "unconfessed sin" in their life or not.

On the other hand, many real and true forms of partaking in an unworthy manner are not condemned today because this phrase has been misinterpreted as a reference to unconfessed sin in the life of a believer. Eating the Lord's Supper with chips and Coke, as some do, is a way of partaking unworthily, as is using alcoholic wine. Any manner of partaking that is inherently sinful and unholy is unworthy of Christ. The teaching of some denominational churches that one cannot eat for a certain number of hours before or after communion is also clearly contrary to the practice of the Lord's Supper which Paul presents in this passage.

[20] All of the gifts listed in 12:8-10 are sign gifts, since these were the problem in Corinth. The issue of the cessation of sign gifts is not directly addressed in 1 Cor 12–14, since sign gifts were still functioning at the time. However, Heb 2:4 indicates that the function of sign gifts was to confirm the message of the gospel at the beginning of the Church Age, and were mainly a thing of the past by the time that epistle was written. The early church fathers also state that the sign gifts ended at the end of the apostolic age. Claims that the sign gifts are still operational today can be disproved simply by defining the gifts the way the Bible defines them, and comparing them to what is claimed to be the operation of these same gifts today. It may also be noted that modern Charismatic churches violate all the rules for the use of and attitude towards the sign gifts given in 1 Cor 12–14.

the fruits of love in 13:4-7, which shows that the exercise of love would correct all of the problems in the Corinthian church. The spiritual gifts are temporary, but love is permanent (13:8-12). In the eternal state, all prophecy will be fulfilled, the multiplicity of languages will be eliminated, and no one will have special knowledge because all will know fully, but the operation of love will continue. Love is even superior to faith and hope, though all three of these continue throughout the age, since faith and hope will be realized in the eternal state but love will continue (13:13).

Following the parenthetical in ch. 13, Paul explains in 14:1-19 why prophecy is superior to tongues—it is because prophecy can be understood without an explanation, and therefore edifies the church, whereas speaking in tongues (i.e., foreign languages) is useless without an interpretation because it is not understandable, and therefore does not edify the church.[21] The Corinthians should revel in edifying the church, not in putting on a miraculous show. This gives rise to the question as to what the purpose of the gift of tongues is, if it does not edify the church. Paul gives the answer in 14:20-22a—tongues are a sign to unbelievers, and are meant to be spoken outside the assembly to unbelievers who can understand the language being spoken (cf. Acts 2:5-13). Prophecy, on the other hand, is a sign to believers, and is to be used within the assembly to show that God is among the assembled group (14:22b-25).

Paul finally sets down rules for the practice of tongues and prophecy in the assembly in 14:26-36. Everything should be done in an orderly manner, with the goal of edification (14:26). No more than two or three tongue-utterances should be allowed per service, and only if there is an interpreter present (14:27-28). Likewise, there should be no more than two or three prophetic utterances per service, and these utterances should be critically evaluated (14:29). Those who receive an utterance from the Spirit during the assembly are to speak one by one, with each one waiting for the previous speaker to finish before beginning (14:30-33a). Further, only male prophets, male tongue-speakers, and male tongue-interpreters are to speak, since women are not permitted to speak in the assembly (14:33b-35).[22] The Corinthians cannot create their own customs in the use of spiritual gifts, and are being highhanded and arrogant if they do so, since the Word of God did not originate with them or come to them uniquely, but rather came to them from others (14:36). If the Corinthians are genuinely spiritual, they will not create their own rules, but will recognize that the things Paul writes are from the Lord (14:37). Those who disregard Paul's instruction are willingly ignorant (14:38).

---

[21] Throughout this passage, both "a tongue" (singular) and "tongues" (plural) refer to known languages, spoken through the gift of the Holy Spirit. "Tongues" refers in general to the gift, since many different languages could be spoken. "A tongue" refers to a specific manifestation of the gift, since only one tongue could be spoken at a time. There is nothing in this passage which points to a qualitative distinction between "tongues" and "a tongue." Those who say that "a tongue" refers to gibberish encounter a substantial difficulty in 14:26-27, where the term clearly refers to the gift given by the Holy Spirit. Note that the Greek word γλῶσσα (*tongue*) means "language," and is never used anywhere in all of Greek literature with reference to anything other than a known language.

[22] This is a custom that applies cross-culturally, "in all the churches of the saints" (14:33b). If there is a different culture in the church at Corinth, they need to change. "All the churches of the saints" indicates that the principle given is universal, not cultural.

This is not just a random command. Verse 34 states that women are to keep silence in the churches for two reasons: they would be usurping male authority if they spoke, and they would be violating the Law. Another reason could be inferred from 1 Tim 2:11-12: women must not speak in the assembly because men are there.

Verse 34 forbids women from speaking any of the things noted in 14:26: a psalm, a teaching, a revelation, a tongue, or an interpretation. Specifically, they are forbidden to do this in the assembly, either as an individual speaker, or as part of a small group of speakers. Women may not sing solos in church, and perhaps should not even be part of the choir. Verse 35 also forbids women from asking questions in church—a principle which would apply to Sunday School classes as well, since such classes are a public assembly of men and women.

The conclusion is given in 14:39-40—emphasize prophecy, but do not completely forbid use of the (genuine) gift of tongues as an overreaction, and conduct your church services in a decent and orderly manner (as described in 14:26-35).

Corrective on the Resurrection, 15:1-58

The final theological corrective Paul gives in 1 Corinthians is on the subject of the resurrection (15:1-58). Some of the Corinthians were denying that believers would be raised with a physical body, due to the influence of Greek philosophy, which viewed matter as evil and bodily resurrection as absurd (cf. Acts 17:32; 26:8, 23-24). They were apparently not explicitly denying the resurrection of Christ, but this was a logical implication of their thinking.

Paul begins his apology by reminding the Corinthians of the basic gospel message which he preached to them, of which the resurrection was a central part and was attested by all the apostles and over five hundred other witnesses, most of whom were still alive and could be interviewed (15:1-7). Paul himself was also a witness of the resurrection, and in fact his vision of the risen Christ was the entire basis for his conversion and ministry (15:8-11). Paul then argues that a denial of resurrection destroys the gospel, since it implies that Christ was not raised, thereby making Him powerless, making the apostles false witnesses, and falsifying the hope of life after death (15:12-19). However, in fact Christ has been raised, and His resurrection guarantees the resurrection of all who are in Christ, along with the ultimate restoration of all things and the ultimate consummation of God's rule (15:20-28). Paul then presents practical reasons to believe in the resurrection in 15:29-34. First, he points out that the Greeks' practice was inconsistent with their profession: the denial of the resurrection by some in Corinth was due to the influence of the prevailing secular philosophy, and yet in the pagan rites of that city, pagan priests performed immersions for the dead—perhaps not unlike Mormon (LDS) rituals today (15:29). Paul is saying, "If you Greeks really don't believe in the resurrection of the body, then why are people in your culture doing something on behalf of dead people?"[23] In addition, the things that Paul himself is doing make no sense if there is no resurrection, since there would be no reason to risk dying or suffer hardship without the hope of life after death (15:30-32). The Corinthians are to separate themselves from those who are opposing the Christian doctrine of resurrection, since these people have no knowledge of God and will corrupt the rest of the assembly if allowed to remain in it (15:33-34).

Paul then presents as an objection two mocking questions that a typical Greek would raise to make belief in a bodily resurrection look stupid: "How are the dead raised? And with what type of body do they come?" (15:35). Paul's answer is that it is actually these questions that are stupid, because the objector does not realize that the resurrection body is part of a realm of an entirely different kind (15:36-49). The resurrection body will still be a physical body, and its shape and functionality will not be radically different, but it will be designed for a glorified, immortal existence rather than a temporal one.[24]

---

[23] Notice how Paul refers to those who are immersed for the dead in the third person ("they"), whereas in the next verse, he refers to his ministry team in the first person ("we"). Paul thereby distinguishes himself from those who are immersed for the dead. Note that Paul does not say these immersions will result in the salvation of the dead, or will do any good at all for the dead.

[24] The word that is used for "spiritual" in 15:44 is πνευματικός, which means "pertaining to the spirit," or "having characteristics of the spirit." A different adjectival ending (-ινος) would have to be used for the word to mean "made of the spirit." A comparison could be made to the words σάρκινος and σαρκικός, both of which are translated "fleshly," though the first means "made of flesh," and second "having characteristics of the flesh." In English, a "fleshly" person could refer either to a person who has a body that is made of flesh or to a person who is dominated by sinful passions, but in Greek two different words for "fleshly" would be used for these different senses. Paul uses the same word for "spiritual" that is used in 15:44, πνευματικός, to say in 10:3-4 that the Israelites ate spiritual food and drank spiritual drink from a spiritual rock, even though the food, drink, and rock were all

Having described the nature of the resurrection body in 15:35-49, Paul then reveals the nature of the resurrection event in 15:50-58. All Church Age believers, both deceased and alive, will have their physical bodies transformed in an instant into glorified, immortal bodies that are suitable for life in the kingdom of God, and will thereby experience the ultimate victory over sin and its penalty.[25] This great hope is a reason for believers to remain steadfast in their faith and diligent in their labor for the Lord, knowing that it all will be rewarded by and by.

Closing Remarks, 16:1-24

Paul has now finished addressing the matters that he felt required a written response, and in ch. 16 he closes the letter with a few final items of business and salutations. He begins by giving instructions concerning his upcoming visit, explaining what the Corinthians are to do before he arrives (16:1-4), and when and from where he will be coming (16:5-9). He then gives instructions regarding the plans of Timothy to visit Corinth, exhorting the church to receive him with gentleness (16:10-11). Paul finally explains that Apollos will visit when he has an opportunity to do so, but was unable to do so immediately in spite of Paul's urging (16:12). Paul then summarizes the thrust of his exhortations in the entire letter, urging the Corinthian Christians to stand fast in the faith and to do all things in love (16:13-14). He next exhorts the Corinthian church to acknowledge and submit themselves to various fellow-laborers of Paul's in Corinth (16:15-18). The letter closes with final salutations (16:19-21) and a closing benediction (16:22-24).

---

material objects. In 2:15, Paul refers to a "spiritual" (πνευματικός) person, without meaning that the person is spiritual in substance. Likewise, the word "natural" in 15:44 is ψυχικός, which has the same adjectival ending and means "pertaining to the soul," i.e., "pertaining to this life." It does not mean "made of the soul," and such a meaning would not make sense, for our current bodies are not made of the same substance as our souls, but are physical.

Paul's point is therefore not that our physical bodies are lost in the resurrection, but that the substance of the old body is transformed and glorified rather than simply being reanimated in the same way in which the body presently exists. It is made immortal, glorified, no longer subject to decay or dependent upon food for nutrition, and so forth. Paul explains in 15:45 that the "natural body" is like Adam's body, while the "spiritual body" is like Christ's body. While the pre-resurrection body ultimately traces its origins to Adam, it is Christ who gives life to the resurrection body. All the references to Christ's resurrection in Scripture show that Christ was raised with a physical body.

[25] The "mystery" revealed by Paul in 1 Cor 15:51-52 is not the second advent, which was spoken of throughout the OT and by Jesus, but is the rapture of the church. The rapture was not revealed in the OT, even if it could be deduced by implication, because it is something that is specifically for the church, and not for Israel. Thus, the translation of living saints is never revealed in the OT, either. Verses 51-52 also add the important detail that both dead and living believers will be raised at the rapture, which creates a serious problem for posttribulationism—there would be no one left to enter the millennium in a mortal body if the rapture were posttribulational. Thus, there are three major reasons why 1 Cor 15:51-52 must be regarded as speaking of the rapture: (1) it is "a mystery" that was not revealed before the Church Age; (2) it includes the resurrection of Church Age saints ("we"); and (3) it includes the resurrection both of the living and the dead ("all").

Note that "the last trumpet" does not refer to the last trumpet in a series (i.e., the seventh trumpet of Rev 11:15-19, which is different from the trumpet of Matt 24:31), but to the last trumpet in the present age, the one which closes this age, and therefore the last trumpet for Christian believers. Trumpets were commonly used as a summons both in ancient Israel and in classical Greece, so that the term "last trumpet" would be similar to our idea of a "last call" for a police officer or fireman.

Bibliography for 1 Corinthians

Some articles on slogans are noted in the following bibliography due to the exegetical importance of discerning whether a particular statement is an affirmation of Paul's or a false affirmation of the Corinthians'.

Barnes, Albert. *1 Corinthians*. Notes on the New Testament, ed. Robert Frew. Reprint: Grand Rapids: Baker, 1949.

Bray, Gerald, ed. *1–2 Corinthians*. Ancient Christian Commentary on Scripture: New Testament, vol. 7, ed. Thomas C. Oden. Downers Grove, IL: InterVarsity Press, 1999.

Bruce, F. F. *1 and 2 Corinthians*. New Century Bible Commentary. Grand Rapids: Eerdmans, 1971.

Burk, Denny. "Discerning Corinthian Slogans through Paul's Use of the Diatribe in 1 Corinthians 6:12-20." *Bulletin for Biblical Research* 18, no. 1 (2008): 99-121.

Constable, Thomas L. *Notes on 1 Corinthians*. 2104 ed. Sonic Light, 2014.

Evans, [Rev. Canon]. "1 Corinthians." In *The Holy Bible with an Explanatory and Critical Commentary: New Testament*, ed. F. C. Cook, vol. 3, 239-376. New York: Charles Scribner's Sons, 1900.

Fee, Gordon D. *The First Epistle to the Corinthians*. New International Commentary on the New Testament. Grand Rapids: Eerdmans, 1987.
  Note: Fee's commentary is recommended by many, but he is Assemblies of God and therefore totally misinterprets the passages on spiritual gifts and the role of women.

Grosheide, F. W. *Commentary on the First Epistle to the Corinthians: The English Text with Introduction, Exposition and Notes*. New International Commentary on the New Testament. Grand Rapids: Eerdmans, 1953.

Hodge, Charles. *1 Corinthians*. Crossway Classic Commentaries, ed. Alister McGrath and J. I. Packer. Wheaton, IL: Crossway, 1995.

Keener, Craig S. *1–2 Corinthians*. New Cambridge Bible Commentary. Cambridge: Cambridge, 2005.

Lias, J. J. *The First Epistle to the Corinthians: With Notes, Map and Introduction*. Cambridge Bible for Schools and Colleges. Cambridge: Cambridge, 1878.

Lowery, David K. "1 Corinthians." In *The Bible Knowledge Commentary: New Testament*, ed. John F. Walvoord and Roy B. Zuck, 505-49. Wheaton, IL: SP Publications, 1983.

MacArthur, John, Jr. *1 Corinthians*. The MacArthur New Testament Commentary. Chicago: Moody Press, 1984.

Mare, W. Harold. "1 Corinthians." In *Expositor's Bible Commentary*, ed. Frank E. Gaebelein et al., vol. 10, 173-297. Grand Rapids: Zondervan, 1976.

McGee, J. Vernon. *1 Corinthians–Revelation*. Volume 5 of *Thru the Bible with J. Vernon McGee*. Nashville: Thomas Nelson, 1983.

Murphy–O'Connor, Jerome. *St. Paul's Corinth: Texts and Archaeology*. 3rd ed. Collegeville, MN: Liturgical Press, 2002.

Plummer, Alfred and Archibald Robertson. *A Critical and Exegetical Commentary on the First Epistle of St Paul to the Corinthians*. 2nd ed. International Critical Commentary. Edinburgh: T. & T. Clark, 1914.

Smith, Jay E. "The Roots of a 'Libertine' Slogan in I Corinthians 6:18." *The Journal of Theological Studies* 59, no. 1 (April 2008): 63-95.

——— "Slogans in 1 Corinthians." *Bibliotheca Sacra* 167 (January–March 2010): 68-88.

Thistleton, Anthony C. *The First Epistle to the Corinthians: A Commentary on the Greek Text*. New International Greek Testament Commentary. Grand Rapids: Eerdmans, 2000.
  Note: Thistleton's much-touted NIGTC commentary is basically a clearinghouse for the various views that are taken in other commentaries. Thistleton quotes all the secondary literature and describes their positions, but does not have a strong analysis of his own. It seems that in many instances he did not even look up the primary source references he cites from other commentaries. The value of this commentary is in the amount of material it contains, but this is also its weakness. Overall, it is very weak as a commentary.

Verbrugge, Verlyn D. "1 Corinthians." In *The Expositor's Bible Commentary: Revised Edition*, ed. Tremper Longman III and David E. Garland, vol. 11, 239-414. Grand Rapids: Zondervan, 2008.

Witherington, Ben III. *Conflict and Community in Corinth: A Socio-Rhetorical Commentary on 1 and 2 Corinthians*. Grand Rapids: Eerdmans, 1995.

Interpretive Guide to 2 Corinthians

Second Corinthians is a rare Pauline epistle which is largely neglected by most Christians and churches, in spite of its length. Most Christians know very little about 2 Corinthians, aside from the two chapters on giving (chs. 8–9). In part, this is because the book deals largely with a personal issue between Paul and the Corinthian church which is not as obviously applicable to modern situations as epistles which deal directly with timeless principles and doctrines. But 2 Corinthians is also neglected because it is a difficult book to understand. One cannot make sense of the epistle without knowledge of the historical situation which gave rise to it, to which Paul continually refers as he writes. Second Corinthians is the least systematically arranged of all of Paul's epistles, and has the most conversational Greek. It is free-flowing, emotional, personal, and autobiographical. This epistle which was written for such a specific place and time does, however, have enormous relevance to today; perhaps this relevance is not immediately acknowledged because the attitudes at Corinth which Paul condemns so sharply are uncomfortably akin to our own.

Author

Both Paul and Timothy are named as authors in 1:1, but for the most part the letter is a personal appeal of Paul to the Corinthians, and Paul is the primary author (cf. 10:1).[1] In addition to the letter's self-claim, the personal, historical, and geographical references in 2 Corinthians fit with what is known from Acts, Romans, and 1 Corinthians concerning Paul's companions and travels. Since 2 Corinthians is the most autobiographical of Paul's epistles, it contains a significant amount of personal detail. Further, there would be no reason for a forger to invent such an obviously impassioned and personal letter, for it was uniquely suited to a specific historical occasion in the life and ministry of the apostle Paul. For these reasons, even most liberals do not challenge the Pauline authorship of 2 Corinthians. Some have objected to the unity of the letter, but there is no textual evidence to support dividing 2 Corinthians into two or more separate letters, nor is there so much as a hint from the church fathers that 2 Corinthians was originally two letters. The unity of 2 Corinthians is demonstrated in that it has a unified argument and logical flow of thought. For example, the list of Paul's qualifications in 6:3-10 is expanded upon in ch. 11. Any claim that 2 Corinthians is not a unity is therefore baseless speculation.

Date and Occasion of Writing

Second Corinthians is a sequel to 1 Corinthians, and therefore a familiarity with 1 Corinthians and its occasion is a prerequisite for understanding 2 Corinthians.[2] Paul had mentioned several times in 1 Corinthians his intent to visit Corinth (1 Cor 4:18-21; 11:34; 16:1-7). However, he says in 2 Cor 1:15–2:4 that he delayed his visit because of the problems he had heard about in order to give the church more time and another warning to repent. He left Ephesus around Pentecost (June 13, A.D. 56; cf. 1 Cor 16:8), then traveled to the city of Troas on the northwest coast of Asia Minor (2 Cor 2:12), where he had planned to meet Titus, who had delivered 1 Corinthians and was supposed to bring a report back to Paul. In spite of an open door for ministry, Paul was distressed because Titus had not yet come to Troas, and therefore he went into Macedonia to look for him (2 Cor 2:13). Titus met Paul in Macedonia after visiting Corinth,

---

[1] In 1 Cor 4:17 and 16:10, Paul says he was going to send Timothy to Corinth. Probably Timothy is named as a coauthor of 2 Corinthians because he had gone to Corinth and brought a report back to Paul (cf. Acts 19:22).

[2] For historical background regarding the church at Corinth, see the introduction to 1 Corinthians.

and reported that Paul's letter (1 Corinthians) had grieved the Corinthian church because of Paul's harsh reproof of their sin, but that the majority had repented and still longed to see Paul (2 Cor 7:5-16; cf. 2:1-11).[3] In fact, Paul's change of plans in delaying his visit to Corinth had caused some Corinthians to accuse Paul of deceit, fickleness, or lack of care for the church (1:15–2:4). Titus also reported that the brother who had been living in incest had repented but remained under severe discipline (2:5-11; cf. 1 Cor 5:1-8). In addition, Jewish false teachers in Corinth, who billed themselves as "superapostles," had rejected Paul's apostolic authority and were pressing the Corinthian Christians to do the same (chs. 10–12). They derided Paul's physical appearance, challenged his qualifications, and denied his power. These false apostles were evidently extraordinarily gifted rhetoricians and had impressive human credentials; the Corinthians' loyalties were divided, and many appeared on the verge of rejecting Paul's position as an apostle.

The problems at Corinth were severe enough so that if Paul were to come to Corinth immediately, a disaster would blow up in his face.[4] Another letter was needed to clarify his relationship with the church, to defend his credentials, and to give the Corinthians adequate time to prepare for his visit, so as to ensure that they would accept him when he came and would not force him to use his apostolic authority to strike down large numbers of unrepentant sinners in the church (cf. 1:23–2:4; 12:13–13:10; 1 Cor 4:18-21). Thus, Paul wrote 2 Corinthians and sent Titus back to Corinth with an unnamed brother, possibly Luke, to deliver the letter (8:16-24). Apparently the Corinthians responded well to Paul's second letter, for when he traveled to Corinth, he stayed with them for three months (Acts 20:3; 1 Cor 16:6). He also wrote the epistle to the Romans from Corinth (cf. Rom 16:1-2, 23), in which he notes that the saints at Corinth had indeed collected an offering for the saints in Jerusalem (Rom 15:26), and he gives every indication that the relationship between himself and the Corinthian Christians is now quite harmonious.

Second Corinthians can be dated within a narrow historical window. Paul wrote 2 Corinthians after he had left Ephesus (around June 13, A.D. 56) and traveled to Troas and into Macedonia, where he received a report from Titus concerning the problems at the church in Corinth. Paul's tone in 2 Corinthians makes it sound as if he is coming to Corinth soon after the epistle arrives—long enough to be

---

[3] The theory that there are one or two "lost letters" which Paul wrote to Corinth is based on a misunderstanding of various passages in 1 & 2 Corinthians. There is no evidence from extant MSS or the church fathers for lost letters, and Peter affirms in 2 Pet 3:15-16 that all of Paul's epistles are canonical Scripture. The church did not reject any of the writings of any of the apostles as non-canonical.

Note that ἔγραψα in 1 Cor 5:9, 11 should be understood as an epistolary aorist, "I write," as in 1 Cor 9:15 (cf. Rom 15:15; Gal 6:11; Phlm 19, 21; 1 John 2:13-14). Paul is not making reference to a previous "lost" epistle. Verse 11 makes this especially clear. It is obvious that the Corinthians had not separated themselves from fornicators. In addition, it is unthinkable that the early church would have destroyed or lost some apostolic writings. This is especially unthinkable for the Corinthian church, which preserved two of Paul's epistles in spite of their quite negative portrayal of the church.

There is no reason why the letter which caused sorrow in Corinth, mentioned in 2 Cor 7:8-23 (cf. 10:9-10), cannot be 1 Corinthians; the situation described fits perfectly with the contents of 1 Corinthians. Likewise, the situation described in 2 Cor 2:5-11 fits perfectly with the discipline prescribed in 1 Cor 5. It would be strange if Paul said nothing at all in 2 Corinthians about the church's response to 1 Corinthians, given the short gap of time between the two epistles. Finally, while the sorrowful letter mentioned in 2 Cor 2:4 could be 1 Corinthians, it is more likely 2 Corinthians, with ἔγραψα again to be understood as an epistolary aorist.

[4] Paul says in 12:14 "this is the third time I am ready to come to you" (cf. 1:15; 12:14). This probably means that this was the third time he was purposing to come to Corinth, since only two visits are recorded in the book of Acts. Paul says in 1:15-16 that he had canceled his second visit to Corinth. Probably 13:2 should be translated "as if I were present the second time," not "when I was present the second time." Compare 1 Cor 5:3-5. The theory advanced by some commentators that Paul made an unsuccessful visit to Corinth between 1 Corinthians and 2 Corinthians, in which he was rebuffed, is contradicted by the contents of both books, as well as by Paul's promise in both books that he would use his apostolic power to strike down all who opposed him and were unrepentant when he arrived (1 Cor 4:18-21; 2 Cor 1:23–2:4; 12:13–13:10).

sure the church has had time to repent and to resolve the problem with the false teachers, but not so long as to require the writing of another epistle. Since Paul spent three months in Corinth in the winter of A.D. 56–57 (Acts 20:3; 1 Cor 16:6), 2 Corinthians must have been written in the late summer or early fall of 56, perhaps in September. The place of writing was Macedonia (northern Greece), near the end of Paul's third missionary journey.

Purpose and Message

The purpose of 2 Corinthians is defined by the letter's occasion of writing. As has already been stated, Paul's purpose in writing 2 Corinthians was to clarify his relationship with the church, to instruct the church to forgive a repentant brother, to defend his credentials, and to give the Corinthians adequate time to prepare for his visit, so as to ensure that they would accept him when he came and would not force him to use his apostolic authority to strike down large numbers of unrepentant sinners in the church (cf. 1:23–2:4; 12:13–13:10; 1 Cor 4:18-21). The message of 2 Corinthians, like that of 1 Corinthians, is multifaceted, but the theme which ties the epistle together is Paul's status as a special ambassador of Christ Jesus to the Corinthian church, and the need for the Corinthians to recognize and accept him as such.

Outline of 2 Corinthians

Summary Outline

I. The Basis of Paul's Relationship with the Corinthians 1:1–7:16
II. Preparation for Paul's Upcoming Visit to Corinth 8:1–13:14

Expanded Outline

I. The Basis of Paul's Relationship with the Corinthians 1:1–7:16
  A. Salutation 1:1-2
  B. Paul's sincerity demonstrated by his conduct 1:3–2:13
     1. Paul's thanksgiving for deliverance in affliction 1:3-11
     2. Paul's assertion of pure motives 1:12-14
     3. Paul's change of plans 1:15-22
     4. The reason for the change of plans 1:23–2:4
     5. Paul's tender concern for the sinning brother 2:5-11
     6. Paul's anxiety for the Corinthians' state 2:12-13
  C. Paul's sincerity demonstrated by the nature of his ministry 2:14–5:19
     1. Heading: Paul's sincerity as a minister of God in Christ 2:14-17
     2. The definition of Paul's ministry by the New Covenant 3:1-18
        a. Contrast between the nature of Paul's ministry and the nature of Moses' 3:1-11
        b. Contrast between the glory of Paul's ministry and the glory of Moses' 3:12-18
     3. The openness of the New Covenant ministry 4:1-6
     4. The sufferings of the New Covenant ministry 4:7-15
     5. The hope of the New Covenant ministry 4:16–5:10
     6. The aim of the New Covenant ministry 5:11-19
  D. Appeal based on the preceding demonstration 5:20–7:16
     1. Appeal to be saved 5:20–6:13

        a. Appeal based on Paul's status as an ambassador of Christ 5:20–6:10
        b. Appeal based on Paul's affection for the Corinthians 6:11-13
    2. Appeal to separate from unbelievers 6:14–7:1
    3. Appeal to receive Paul 7:2-16
        a. Appeal on the basis of Paul's innocence towards the Corinthians 7:2-3
        b. Appeal on the basis of Paul's comfort from the Corinthians 7:4-16

II. Preparation for Paul's Upcoming Visit to Corinth 8:1–13:14
    A. Collection of the offering 8:1–9:15
        1. The example of the Macedonian saints 8:1-6
        2. The encouragement to give 8:7-15
        3. Commendation of those collecting the offering 8:16-24
        4. The purpose of the delegation 9:1-5
        5. The blessings of liberal giving 9:6-15
    B. Warning based on apostolic authority 10:1–13:10
        1. Statement of Paul's authority regarding the Corinthians 10:1-18
        2. Paul's qualifications on the human level 11:1–12:10
            a. The reason for Paul's lowly demeanor 11:1-15
            b. Paul's human qualifications as an apostle 11:16-33
            c. Paul's spiritual qualifications as an apostle 12:1-10
        3. Concluding warnings concerning Paul's coming 12:11–13:10
            a. Assessment of Paul's defense of himself in view of his past relationship with the Corinthians 12:11-13
            b. Assessment of Paul's defense of himself in view of his future coming to the Corinthians 12:14-18
            c. Assessment of the reason for Paul's defense 12:19-21
            d. Procedures to be followed when Paul arrives 13:1-10
    C. Farewell and benediction 13:11-14

Argument of 2 Corinthians

Second Corinthians has a well defined two-part division: chs. 1–7, dealing with the basis of Paul's relationship to the Corinthians, form the body of the epistle, and chs. 8–13, in which Paul gives instructions concerning his upcoming visit, forms the conclusion. The conclusion is greatly exaggerated in length because of the problems that potentially await Paul when he comes. Both parts of the epistle assume as background the problems noted in 1 Corinthians and the challenge to Paul's authority by false teachers in Corinth, since 2 Corinthians is a response to these issues.

The Basis of Paul's Relationship with the Corinthians, 1:1–7:16

In the main body of 2 Corinthians, chs. 1–7, Paul argues that his relationship with the Corinthians (and with all men) is based on godly sincerity rather than fleshly goals and concerns. His sincerity is demonstrated by his conduct (1:3–2:13) and by the nature of his ministry (2:14–5:19), and as a result the Corinthians need to be reconciled to God if they are not (5:20–6:13), to separate themselves from the unbelievers who refuse to repent in their midst (6:14–7:1), and to receive Paul and his associates (7:2-16).

Salutation, 1:1-2. Second Corinthians opens with a typical, though brief, epistolary salutation which stresses the legitimacy of Paul's apostleship (1:1-2).

Paul's sincerity demonstrated by his conduct, 1:3–2:13. Paul begins the body of the epistle, as he often does, with a thanksgiving to God (1:3-11). However, the focus of this thanksgiving is specifically relevant to the situation of the Corinthians—Paul thanks God for delivering him in affliction, the greatness and ubiquitousness of which proves that his ministry is not self-interested but is done in service of others. Paul is also beginning an autobiographical narrative of his activities between 1 & 2 Corinthians, starting with the afflictions which befell him while he tarried in Asia (1:8). Paul then asserts directly the purity of his motives towards the Corinthians (1:12-14). His behavior towards them has been based on godly sincerity, not fleshly wisdom, as they will be able to see for themselves from what he writes. The issue regarding his behavior is explained in 1:15-22: Paul had said repeatedly in 1 Corinthians that he was coming to Corinth (1 Cor 4:18-21; 11:34; 16:1-7), but had delayed coming and had actually cancelled a planned second visit (1:15-16). Some in Corinth had taken this as a sign of fleshly instability or lack of concern (1:17), though they should have known better because of the faithfulness and truthfulness of God who established, anointed, and irrevocably sealed Paul and his coworkers (1:18-22). The actual reason for Paul's change of plans was his genuine concern for the spiritual well-being of the Corinthians (1:23-24). He was afraid that if he came immediately, while many were unrepentant and hostile, his visit would be sorrowful, and he would be forced to use his apostolic power to discipline many in Corinth, rather than rejoicing with them over their repentance (2:1-3). For this reason, he wrote a second epistle first, in much anguish, so that the Corinthians would recognize the sincere love which he has for them (2:4; translate ἔγραψα as "I write" or "I have written").

Paul's repeated mention of sorrow in 2:1-4 leads him to address a matter in which a sinning brother had caused sorrow to the Corinthian assembly, and now was being made sorrowful by them (2:5-11)—a reference to the discipline Paul prescribed in 1 Cor 5:1-13 for a man living in an incestuous relationship. The Corinthians had applied exactly the sort of harsh discipline which Paul had prescribed, handing the man over to Satan and totally disassociating themselves from him. However, the man had unexpectedly repented, and the Corinthians had failed to forgive and restore him. Paul commands them to forgive him and restore him in love immediately, before he is overwhelmed with grief over his sin. Paul brings this matter up partly because it was a pressing issue which needed immediate redress, but also to show the Corinthians his tender concern for them and his eagerness to forgive them.

Having addressed this matter, Paul then returns in 2:12-13 to the narrative of his activities since writing 1 Corinthians. After leaving Ephesus, he went to Troas, and in spite of a great door being opened to him there for the gospel of Christ, Paul could not stay because he was anxious to hear the report from Titus concerning the state of the church in Corinth. Paul therefore traveled into Macedonia to find Titus—an act which demonstrates how greatly and sincerely Paul cares for the Corinthian believers.

Paul's sincerity demonstrated by the nature of his ministry, 2:14–5:19. Having demonstrated his sincerity by his conduct in 1:3–2:13, Paul proceeds to defend the nature of his ministry (and that of the other apostles), which was under assault by the false teachers in Corinth. His argument in 2:14–5:19 is that he (and his coworkers) have been given a New Covenant ministry which brings men reconciliation with God through Jesus Christ. His credentials have been given by God, not man, and his ministry operates through the Spirit, not through the flesh.

After speaking of his travels in 2:12-13, Paul gives thanks to God in 2:14-17 for making him sufficient as a minister wherever he goes. He sets forth in these verses the basic premise for which he is arguing, which is that he is a genuine minister of God in Christ who is used by God to bring the message of gospel to the world, resulting in life to those who believe and in death to those who disbelieve. To Paul's Corinthian opponents, this was exactly the sort of self-commendation which they had previously seized upon to challenge his qualifications (3:1). Paul responds by appealing to the conversion of the Corinthians under his ministry as proof of his authenticity as a New Covenant minister (3:2-3). The very nature of Paul's ministry necessitates that his sufficiency comes from God rather than men, for Paul is a minister of the New Covenant through the Spirit, not a minister of the flesh (3:4-6).[5] Being a minister of the New Covenant means to have a ministry of the Spirit,[6] rather than a ministry of the letter, i.e., of the Law. The Law kills, because no one can keep it. The Law can only condemn, not save. It is the Spirit who regenerates men and gives them spiritual life. Thus, 3:7-9 contrasts Moses, who, as a minister of the Old Covenant, was a minister of death (3:7) and condemnation (3:9), with Paul, who, as a minister of the New Covenant, is a minister of the Spirit (3:8) and righteousness (3:9).[7] Since Moses' ministry under a temporary covenant came with glory, how much more glory does Paul's ministry have under an eternal covenant? Paul then expands on this, contrasting the veiled and faded glory of Moses' Old Covenant ministry with the open, transforming, and permanent glory of the apostles' New Covenant ministry (3:12-18).[8]

After contrasting his ministry to the church under the New Covenant with Moses' ministry to Israel under the Old Covenant in ch. 3, Paul continues to explain what it means to be a minister of the New Covenant in ch. 4 ("Therefore, seeing we have this ministry. . ."). The openness of the New Covenant ministry is defined in 4:1-6—in contrast to the false apostles who were walking in craftiness, handling the word of God deceitfully, and preaching themselves, Paul and his coworkers were engaged in the open, straightforward proclamation of "Christ Jesus as Lord, and ourselves as your servants for Jesus' sake," though the truth of this message is unrecognized by those who are perishing because the devil has blinded

---

[5] Second Corinthians 3:6 clearly affirms that Christians are living under a New Covenant system, but it does so without affirming that the church is fulfilling the promises of Jer 31:31-34 or that the covenant has already been cut (made). Logically, it is possible for "fringe benefits" of the covenant to be operative after the dedicatory sacrifice, which is the grounds for its fulfillment, has been made. While many would prefer to read 2 Cor 3:6 as a statement that the New Covenant has already been cut with the church and is already being fulfilled, this is not stated in 2 Cor 3:6 and is not a logical implication of the text. Further, if the New Covenant is cut with the church and fulfilled in this age, this does not fulfill the original promise that the New Covenant was to be cut with Israel in the millennium, nor does it fulfill any of the provisions stated in Jer 31:31-34. The only consistent reading of the biblical text is to accept that Jer 31:31-34 will be cut and fulfilled as originally stated, and that the New Covenant has only been dedicated in the present age.

[6] This is a better interpretation than the view that πνεύματος refers to the internalization of the external letter ("the spirit of the law"). Second Corinthians 3:6 is saying that the Law ("the letter") kills men (cf. Rom 7:9-11), whereas the Holy Spirit gives men life (cf. Rom 8:6). This fits with the uses of πνεῦμα in 2 Cor 3:3, 17, and also fits with parallels in Rom 7:6 and 8:2.

[7] Paul appears to portray Moses as the sole minister of the Old Covenant. By analogy, only the apostles and their close associates would be ministers of the New Covenant. Throughout ch. 3, "we" refers to Paul and the other apostles, while "you" refers to the Corinthians (except for "we all" in 3:18). Thus, when Paul says that God made "us" ministers of a New Covenant, this is not, in context, a statement about Christians in general. The apostles were given the ministry of delivering to the world the good news about Jesus in a special way that other Christians are not—just as Moses was given the ministry of the Old Covenant in a way that subsequent Israelite clergy were not—since they were witnesses of the resurrection and were designated by Jesus to found His church. They were heralds of a new era, announcing the end of the Old Covenant through its fulfillment in the Person and work of Jesus Christ, whose atoning death was the dedicatory sacrifice of the New Covenant and made possible the fulfillment of all the New Covenant promises. Although the Spirit is not mentioned in Jer 31:31-34, His indwelling presence is implied, and is mentioned specifically in other New Covenant texts (Isa 59:21; Ezek 36:27). The death of Christ made possible the coming of the Spirit to regenerate all who accept the gospel.

[8] It is a common misconception that Moses put a veil on his face so Israel would not be frightened by his shining skin. Actually, he wore the veil so that they would be. According to Exod 34:34-35, Moses took the veil off when he spoke with God, and left it off when he came back out to the people immediately afterward, while his face was still reflecting God's glory. But as the glory began to fade, Moses veiled his face, so Israel would not be able to see that it was no longer shining. Essentially, Moses tricked Israel into thinking his face was shining all the time, when it had actually faded. Paul says Israel is still fooled by Moses' veil, since they think the glory of the Law is still present, when in reality it has been done away in Christ.

their minds. But the New Covenant ministry is also a ministry of suffering, for the treasure of the gospel had to be brought to the world by mortal, weak, and downtrodden men in order to make it obvious that the power of the gospel comes from God, and not from men (4:7-15). The reason why the apostles minister faithfully through suffering is because of the hope of the New Covenant ministry—they are working by faith for an eternal reward which is incalculably more significant than the sufferings of this life, and they have the hope of resurrection in an immortal body, while being sobered by the knowledge that they will be held accountable by the Lord in a future day of judgment (4:16–5:10). The aim of the apostles under the New Covenant ministry is to persuade men to be reconciled to God and to become new creatures in Christ, no longer knowing men after the flesh or living unto themselves or unto the flesh (5:11-19).

Appeal based on the preceding demonstration, 5:20–7:16. In 5:20–7:16, Paul proceeds to make three appeals on the basis of the preceding demonstration of his sincerity and of his status as a New Covenant minister. As a representative of God who has been given a ministry of reconciliation, Paul issues a general call to be reconciled to God in 5:20–6:13, indicating that many in the Corinthian church were not genuinely saved (cf. 13:5). He appeals to them on the basis of his status as an ambassador of Christ (5:20–6:10), and on the basis of his affection for the Corinthians (6:11-13). Since Paul is Christ's representative, the Corinthians cannot reject Paul and accept Christ at the same time. Paul then appeals to the Corinthians to separate themselves from unbelievers in their midst who have rejected the appeal to accept Paul and his gospel (6:14–7:1)—an appeal which seems to have primary reference to the Jewish false teachers in Corinth and their disciples, who openly opposed Paul yet had been received by the Corinthians. Paul closes the body of the epistle by making a direct appeal to the Corinthian church to receive him (7:2-16). Paul has defrauded no one in Corinth and does not seek to take advantage of them, but rather to benefit them (7:2-3). He has great boldness toward the Corinthians, because their response to his first letter comforted him and leads him to expect that they will also respond positively to his second letter as well (7:4-16). In 7:5, Paul finally returns to the narrative of his personal activities since writing 1 Corinthians, which he left off after 2:13. Titus reported that the Corinthians had been grieved by Paul's rebukes for their failures, which initially caused Paul grief over the hurt he had caused, but upon reflection made him joyful because the Corinthians were made sorry for their sins and had therefore repented. This repentance, in conjunction with other events, showed that the Corinthians truly cared about Paul and his coworkers and were zealous to minister to them and to receive them.

Preparation for Paul's Upcoming Visit to Corinth, 8:1–13:14

In the concluding section of 2 Corinthians, chs. 8–13, Paul gives instructions regarding the collection of an offering for the saints at Jerusalem (chs. 8–9), and warns the Corinthians to be ready when he comes, so he will not have to use his apostolic authority to discipline them (chs. 10–13).

Collection of the offering, 8:1–9:15. The main body of 2 Corinthians ends at 7:16, and the lengthy conclusion begins in 8:1. Commentators sometimes leave the impression that chs. 8–9 have little relation to the contents of the rest of the book. However, these chapters introduce the section in which Paul gives instructions concerning his visit. In Romans and 1 Corinthians, Paul puts the section on raising money for the saints at Jerusalem after the body of the epistle and before the closing exhortations. He does the same in 2 Corinthians, except that both sections of the conclusion are much longer due to the unusual problems he is facing. In 2 Corinthians, the conclusion of the epistle is almost as long as the body. The section on preparing the offering has to go somewhere, and Paul wants to end the epistle with an uninterrupted personal appeal that deals specifically with his relationship to the Corinthians and his battle against the false apostles in Corinth.

In 8:1-6, Paul moves from the past (Titus' visit) to the present, which is the offering that the Macedonian churches have taken for the saints in Jerusalem. After setting forth the example of their liberality, Paul encourages the Corinthian church to voluntarily give in like manner, because this will demonstrate their spiritual fruitfulness (8:7), it will follow the example set by the Macedonians (8:8) and by Jesus Christ (8:9), it will prove their sincerity (8:10-12), and it will be a means of ensuring that other churches provide for them in their own time of need (8:13-15). Paul then commends the brethren who have been appointed to collect the offering, in order to show that they are regarded as trustworthy by all and were appointed by the other churches for this purpose (8:16-24). The reason why they are coming to Corinth ahead of Paul is so that Paul would not be ashamed if he came and found that they had not already prepared the offering (9:1-5). Paul concludes the longest single passage on money in the Bible by describing the blessings of liberal giving, in order to show the Corinthians why it is expedient for them to give generously (9:6-15).

Warning based on apostolic authority, 10:1–13:10. In 10:1, Paul moves from the present (the collection of the offering) to the future, which is his coming to Corinth. In 10:1–13:10, Paul issues a warning to Corinthians on the basis of his apostolic authority to repent before he comes. The primary thrust of Paul's entreaty is that the Corinthians must accept him and his teaching over the false apostles and their teaching. If the church does not reject the false apostles and recognize Paul as a genuine apostle, he will be forced to apply severe discipline to the church when he comes.[9] Apparently Jewish opponents of Paul had become more active in Corinth between 1 Corinthians and 2 Corinthians, since 1 Corinthians was a direct challenge to their authority. They had rejected Paul's instruction in 1 Corinthians and were attempting to get the Corinthian church to transfer their allegiance before Paul arrived.[10]

Paul begins his warning in ch. 10 by setting forth his authority with regard to the Corinthians, in contrast to the fleshly usurpation of authority by the false teachers.[11] In addition, the false apostles are self-commended, whereas Paul's commendation comes from the Lord. However, because the Corinthians

---

[9] This warning is addressed to the church in general, not to the false apostles. The fate of the latter has already been sealed—they will not repent and are destined for judgment. Paul is addressing the people who are sitting on the fence, trying to decide whom to follow. Paul rarely names enemies and never appeals to them directly—he only addresses those in the church who are following the troublemakers (cf. Gal 6:12-13; Phil 3:18-19).

Note that Paul is not angry in chs. 10–13, but is anxious and affectionate. He argues strongly, and uses biting sarcasm, but only to move the church to repent. As someone who is humble and does not wish to promote himself, he is not stung by any damage to his self-image inflicted by the Corinthians' diminished view of himself; he argues not out of an insecure, egoistic need to defend himself in the court of human opinion, but to protect the Corinthians' own well-being.

[10] On Paul's opponents in this letter, see P. W. Barnett, "Opponents of Paul" (in *Dictionary of Paul and His Letters*; Downers Grove, IL: IVP, 1993), 646-47. They were Jewish (11:22), and claimed to be ministers of Christ (11:23) and apostles of Christ (11:13), but were actually ministers of Satan (11:14-15). They had impressive human credentials (3:1) and rhetorical skills (10:10), but had come to Corinth preaching a different gospel (11:3-5), where they had been received and salaried (11:4, 20). They presented themselves as significant people, and boasted of themselves, and were respected by the Corinthians for this reason, whereas Paul, who had come in meekness and humility and simplicity, was easily despised. Although the message of the false apostles is not specifically delineated, Paul says that they had fashioned themselves as "ministers of righteousness" (11:15), which indicates that they were preaching the message of righteousness through the works of the Law, while still professing to believe in Jesus in some way. This is thus the same group of "Judaizers" who had plagued Paul from his very first missionary journey as he spread the gospel in Gentile lands.

[11] The tone of the letter changes dramatically in 10:1, as Paul zeros in on the issue. However, the difference in style is way overblown by the critical commentators, some of whom are convinced that chs. 10–13 are a different letter or were written at a different time than chs. 1–9. In reality, chs. 1–9 do not make sense without chs. 10–13 following. There is no conclusion after ch. 9, no benediction, and no statement of what Paul will do when he gets to Corinth. The arguments in chs. 1–7 are designed to demonstrate that Paul is sincere in his ministry to the Corinthians, and chs. 8–9 are designed to prepare the Corinthians for Paul's visit.

had been wowed by the human qualifications of the false apostles, Paul is forced in 11:1–12:10 to present his own qualifications on the human level. Unlike the false apostles, who took money from the Corinthians and are seeking to destroy them, Paul's selfless love for the church was demonstrated by his refusal to charge them for his teaching (11:1-15). Paul's lowly demeanor is entirely voluntary, done for the Corinthians' sake, and is not due to a lack of qualification or authority. From any human aspect, he has greater apostolic and ministry qualifications than do the Judaizers, though it is foolish for him to boast of how great he is in the flesh (11:16-23). He has far greater labor for Christ and greater sufferings for Christ than any of the self-styled "superapostles" who had come to Corinth (11:24-33). Not only does Paul have incredible credentials on the human level, he also has spiritual credentials that far surpass those of the false apostles (12:1-10). He was actually caught up to the highest heaven, and experienced sights and sounds of Paradise which were beyond his ability to translate (12:1-4). This and other revelatory experiences were so great that God had to give him a "thorn in the flesh" to keep him humble and reliant on God's grace, and to show the world that the church was built through God's power, not man's—thereby explaining the paradoxical balance between Paul's exalted position and lowly manner (12:5-10). Paul's glorying in his weaknesses is glorying in Christ on whom he depends. His weakness in the flesh therefore does not signify lack of authority, but rather demonstrates God's power in him.

Having concluded his boasting, Paul proceeds to issue direct warnings and exhortations to the Corinthian church in 12:11–13:10. He first reflects on his defense of himself in view of his past relationship with the Corinthians—the Corinthians compelled him to foolishly boast of himself in order to show that he is not inferior to the "superapostles," as they should have known from his past demonstration of apostolic signs and wonders among them and his long ministry in Corinth (12:11-13). Paul then applies his defense of himself to his plans to come to Corinth, protesting that he is not coming to get anything from them, but rather to give of himself for them—just as he and his coworkers have done in the past (12:14-18). The reason for Paul's defense of his integrity and qualifications is not, as they think, to protect Paul's ego, but rather to protect the Corinthian church from discipline, should Paul come and find that they are still divided into factions on the basis of human leaders, and have disregarded Paul's authoritative warnings (12:19-21). Paul then outlines the procedures which will be followed when he arrives—he will hold court with the Corinthian church, and will use his apostolic power to discipline all who are unrepentant (13:1-4).[12] He warns the Corinthians to evaluate their spiritual readiness to meet him as Christ's representative, and to examine whether they are genuinely saved, lest they suffer from a demonstration of Paul's power (13:5-6). Paul's desire, however, is that the church repent, and that he use his authority to build up rather than to cast down when he arrives—which is why he has written this second letter (13:7-10).

Farewell and benediction, 13:11-14. Paul concludes 2 Corinthians appropriately with a typical epistolary farewell and benediction in which he prays for love, peace, unity, and maturity in the church at Corinth (13:11-14).

---

[12] The apostles had authority to kill and to raise to life, as the Spirit led. Apostolic authority killed Ananias and Sapphira; it raised to life Dorcas and Eutychus. Paul used his apostolic authority to blind Elymas (Acts 13:8-11), to cast out demons (Acts 16:18), and to perform extraordinary miracles (Acts 19:11-12; 28:4-9). Apostolic authority gave Peter the ability to discern when Ananias and Sapphira lied, and likely gave extraordinary insight in other situations as well. The apostles' special authority and power was due to their foundational role in the building of Christ's church (cf. Matt 16:18-19; Lao 2:20).

Bibliography for 2 Corinthians

Barnes, Albert. *II Corinthians and Galatians*. Notes on the New Testament, ed. Robert Frew. Reprint: Grand Rapids: Baker, 1949.

Barnett, Paul. *The Second Epistle to the Corinthians*. New International Commentary on the New Testament. Grand Rapids: Eerdmans, 1997.

Barrett, C. K. *The Second Epistle to the Corinthians*. Black's New Testament Commentary. Peabody, MA: Hendrickson, 1973.

Bray, Gerald, ed. *1–2 Corinthians*. Ancient Christian Commentary on Scripture: New Testament, vol. 7, ed. Thomas C. Oden. Downers Grove, IL: InterVarsity Press, 1999.

Bruce, F. F. *1 and 2 Corinthians*. New Century Bible Commentary. Grand Rapids: Eerdmans, 1971.

Constable, Thomas L. *Notes on 2 Corinthians*. 2104 ed. Sonic Light, 2014.

Danker, Frederick W. *II Corinthians*. Augsburg Commentary on the New Testament. Minneapolis: Augsburg, 1989.

Furnish, Victor Paul. *II Corinthians: Translated with Introduction, Notes and Commentary*. Anchor Bible, vol. 32A. Garden City, NY: Doubleday, 1984.

Garland, David E. *2 Corinthians*. New American Commentary, vol. 29. Nashville: Broadman & Holman, 1999.

Harris, Murray J. "2 Corinthians." In *Expositor's Bible Commentary*, ed. Frank E. Gaebelein et al., vol. 10, 299-406. Grand Rapids: Zondervan, 1976.

———. "2 Corinthians." In *The Expositor's Bible Commentary: Revised Edition*, ed. Tremper Longman III and David E. Garland, vol. 11, 415-545. Grand Rapids: Zondervan, 2008.

———. *The Second Epistle to the Corinthians: A Commentary on the Greek Text*. New International Greek Testament Commentary. Grand Rapids: Eerdmans, 2005.

Hodge, Charles. *2 Corinthians*. Crossway Classic Commentaries, ed. Alister McGrath and J. I. Packer. Wheaton, IL: Crossway, 1995.

Hughes, Philip Edgcumbe. *Paul's Second Epistle to the Corinthians: The English Text with Introduction, Exposition and Notes*. New International Commentary on the New Testament. Grand Rapids: Eerdmans, 1962.
    Note: Hughes was once used a textbook for 2 Corinthians at Dallas Theological Seminary. Stanley Toussaint thinks Hughes is excellent.

Keener, Craig S. *1–2 Corinthians*. New Cambridge Bible Commentary. Cambridge: Cambridge, 2005.

Kruse, Colin G. *The Second Epistle of Paul to the Corinthians: An Introduction and Commentary*. Tyndale New Testament Commentaries. Grand Rapids: Eerdmans, 1987.

Lias, J. J. *The Second Epistle to the Corinthians: With Notes, Map and Introduction*. Cambridge Bible for Schools and Colleges. Cambridge: Cambridge, 1879.

Lowery, David K. "2 Corinthians." In *The Bible Knowledge Commentary: New Testament*, ed. John F. Walvoord and Roy B. Zuck, 551-86. Wheaton, IL: SP Publications, 1983.

Martin, Ralph P. *2 Corinthians*. Word Biblical Commentary, vol. 40. Nashville: Thomas Nelson, 1986.

McGee, J. Vernon. *1 Corinthians–Revelation*. Volume 5 of *Thru the Bible with J. Vernon McGee*. Nashville: Thomas Nelson, 1983.

Naylor, Peter. *2 Corinthians 8–13*. Volume 2 of *A Study Commentary on 2 Corinthians*. Auburn, MA: Evangelical Press, 2002.

Plummer, Alfred. *A Critical and Exegetical Commentary on the Second Epistle of St Paul to the Corinthians*. International Critical Commentary. Edinburgh: T. & T. Clark, 1915.

Scott, James M. *2 Corinthians*. New International Biblical Commentary. Peabody, MA: Hendrickson, 1998.

Waite, Joseph. "2 Corinthians." In *The Holy Bible with an Explanatory and Critical Commentary: New Testament*, ed. F. C. Cook, vol. 3, 377-481. New York: Charles Scribner's Sons, 1900.

Witherington, Ben III. *Conflict and Community in Corinth: A Socio-Rhetorical Commentary on 1 and 2 Corinthians*. Grand Rapids: Eerdmans, 1995.

Interpretive Guide to Galatians

As the first epistle of the apostle Paul, the great missionary and teacher of the early church, the epistle to the Galatians lays out the themes and doctrines which were central to Paul's ministry. It is a classic statement on justification by faith alone, apart from the works of the Law, for which reason it was a favorite book of Martin Luther and was called the cornerstone of the Protestant Reformation. Galatians is a book of fundamental importance for Christian theology, since it explains and defends the core of the gospel. It is primarily about justification, although issues regarding sanctification arose because of Jewish false teachers who claimed that Christians had to be circumcised and keep the Law in order to be saved in the end. They were teaching that justification was a process rather than a point in time, essentially no different than sanctification. The book of Galatians clearly and forcefully refutes these claims.

Not only is Galatians a crucial book for understanding the gospel, it is also a book of great importance for understanding the role of the Mosaic Law. Galatians 3 is perhaps the most significant chapter in the Bible for understanding the purpose of the Law. According to Gal 3:24-25, the purpose of the Law in the OT period was to keep Israel separate from pagan nations and pagan influences until the Messiah came. Paul argues strenuously in Galatians that the purpose of the Law was neither justification (2:16) nor sanctification (5:18), two common misconceptions.

The book of Galatians has never ceased to be relevant, since there have always been large numbers of people under the broad umbrella of what is called "Christianity" who have held to a works-based system of justification. Obvious contemporary examples of theological systems which advocate a return to the Law include forms of Messianic Judaism, dual-covenant theology, reconstructionism (theonomy), and, in some instances, covenant theology. The New Perspective on Paul (represented by N. T. Wright, James D. G. Dunn, E. P. Sanders, and probably the majority of NT scholars as of 2010) teaches essentially the same thing as the Judaizers against whom Paul is arguing in this book—namely, that one must keep the Law in this life in order to be justified in the eschaton. This is also, as Luther correctly observed, the essential teaching of the Roman Catholic Church. The RCC does not teach adherence to the Mosaic Law, but replaces it with an alternative legalistic works system, so the same arguments apply. The RCC teaches that there is no difference between justification and sanctification, and that a person is not ultimately *declared* righteous until he has *become* fully righteous and has suffered temporal punishments for post-baptismal sins.

Author

Paul names himself as the author of the epistle in the heading of 1:1, and he uses the first person singular throughout, though he notes that there were others with him as he wrote (1:2; cf. 1:8-9).[1] Galatians is one of those rare books for which liberal scholars have chosen not to dispute authorship, which saves believers the trouble of having to argue for its authenticity in response to skeptics. In truth, though, this would be a particularly difficult letter to dispute, since it is focused on the themes that Paul was known for and is an intensely personal letter with significant autobiographical detail.

Although Paul was the sole author of the epistle, he had an anonymous amanuensis, as shown by 6:11.[2] This amanuensis seems to have had little effect on Paul's writing style in the book, which is about at the mean for Paul's epistles.

---

[1] It is interesting that Barnabas is not named as a cosender of this epistle, since the Galatian churches had been planted by both Paul and Barnabas. Even in epistles where Paul does name one of his ministry partners as a cosender, such as Silvanus or Timothy, Paul clearly remains the primary author. The Galatians would have recognized Paul as the leader of the ministry team.

Addressees

This epistle was written to believers in the churches Paul had planted on his first missionary journey, which were in southern Galatia. However, most patristic commentators believed that Paul wrote to northern Galatia because southern Galatia was merged with other provinces later in Roman history, and called by another name. The specific cities of Asia Minor which Paul and Barnabas visited in Acts 13–14 are Pisidian Antioch, Iconium, Lystra, Derbe, Perga, and Attalia, though the latter two were not part of Galatia.

According to Gal 3:2, the Galatians had received the Spirit, and therefore were, in spite of their acute confusion on the gospel, mainly saved (cf. 5:1; 6:18). They had not explicitly denied the gospel or rejected Christ; they were genuinely saved and sincere, but misguided. They apparently did not have a problem with immorality or other works-related issues, outside of works that are a direct product of legalism. Paul does not rebuke them for major moral problems, only for doctrinal ones. They did not fall for the Judaizers in order to rein in their sinful condition, but for other reasons. Were they just deceived? Did they wish to boast of their self-righteousness?

One wonders what happened when epistles such as Galatians were first read in the churches to which they were sent. Were there debates? Did people get up and walk out? Did they take sides? Were they offended? In Galatia, at least, the people apparently got on their knees and repented, then threw out the Judaizing false teachers. When Paul returned to the area in Acts 16:1-5, the churches received him well.

Historical Background, Date, and Occasion of Writing

In their first missionary journey (A.D. 47–48), Paul and Barnabas sailed from their base of operations in Syrian Antioch to Cyprus and then traveled through various towns in the southern part of the province of Galatia, preaching the gospel and planting churches (Acts 13:1–14:28). They did not go beyond Galatia on this journey; instead, after Paul was stoned at Derbe, they retraced their steps so as to establish the churches they had planted earlier in their mission. After returning to Syrian Antioch, they gave the church a report, telling them in particular that many Gentiles had been saved through their ministry (Acts 14:27-28). The church at Antioch received Paul and Barnabas warmly, but some Jewish Christians from Judea were less enthusiastic about the conversion of Gentiles and the gospel of justification by faith which Paul preached. A group of these men came to Antioch and argued that Gentiles cannot be saved unless they are circumcised and keep the Law of Moses (Acts 15:1). The Antiochene church sent Paul and Barnabas to Jerusalem to settle the matter. Apparently the Jews who disputed with Paul in Antioch traveled on to Galatia when Paul left for Jerusalem, and taught the Galatians that they had to keep the Law in order to be saved (cf. Acts 15:23-24). When Paul and Barnabas arrived at Jerusalem, they were opposed by certain Christian Pharisees who insisted that the Galatian converts be circumcised and keep the Law of Moses (Acts 15:5). James and the apostles sided with Paul and Barnabas, and sent out a circular letter to affirm their position. Paul then returned to Antioch (Acts 15:30), where, following a visit by Peter (Gal 2:11), he heard that the Judaizing false teachers had traveled to Galatia and successfully convinced the new Christians that they had to bring themselves under the Law in order to be saved. This was a problem of the severest sort: a direct attack on the gospel of justification by faith. An immediate and forceful response was required, so Paul wrote his epistle to the Galatians to defend his gospel. Sometime later,

---

[2] The use of an amanuensis is well attested in ancient literature, as is the custom of the actual author writing the ending to the letter in his own hand. See Everett Ferguson, *Backgrounds of Early Christianity* (3rd ed.; Grand Rapids: Eerdmans, 2003), 131, for a picture of a papyrus letter, dated August 24, A.D. 66, which shows the careful book hand of the amanuensis at the top and a conclusion scrawled by the author in cursive script at the bottom.

probably within a matter of months, Paul traveled to Galatia with Silas to revisit the Galatian churches in person and deliver the letter from the Jerusalem Council which stated the apostles' and elders' approval of Paul's gospel (Acts 16:4). It appears that the Galatian churches repented when they received Paul's epistle, and his revisit of these churches went smoothly. Paul thus wrote Galatians between the Jerusalem Council of Acts 15 and his second missionary journey, probably early in A.D. 49.[3]

Purpose and Message

The purpose of the book of Galatians is to defend the gospel of justification by faith against a group of Jewish false teachers who claimed that Christians must be circumcised and keep the Law of Moses in order to be saved.[4] The message of Galatians is that justification is by faith in Jesus Christ alone, apart from the works of the Law. Law and grace are mutually exclusive: if you have one, you cannot have the other. Anyone who puts himself under the Law, even as a method of sanctification, has put himself under a system of salvation that is essentially works based, thereby denying practically the provision of grace through faith in Christ.

Chronology of the Ministry of Paul

The chronology of the ministry of Paul is a major issue in the study of Galatians due to the account of Paul's early life as a Christian in 1:15-24 and the reference to "fourteen years" in 2:1. To facilitate discussion of these passages, the chart below presents major events in the life of Paul and their chronological relation.[5]

Date (A.D.)	Event and Reference
May 22, 33	Church begins at Pentecost (Acts 2:1-41)
35	Conversion on the road to Damascus (Acts 9:1-19a)
35–38	Paul in Damascus and Arabia for three years (Acts 9:19-25; Gal 1:15-17)
38	Plot in Damascus (Acts 9:23-25)
38	Paul's 15-day Jerusalem visit (Gal 1:18; Acts 9:26-29)
38	Paul sent to Tarsus (Acts 9:30; Gal 1:21)
42–43	Paul and Barnabas in Antioch for one year (Acts 11:25-26; Gal 1:21)[6]
43–44	Paul and Barnabas make a famine relief visit to Judea (Acts 11:27-30; 12:25)
44–47	Paul, Mark, & Barnabas in Antioch (Acts 12:25–13:1)

---

[3] Galatians is the only one of Paul's epistles associated with his first missionary journey. There are two epistles associated with Paul's second journey (1 & 2 Thessalonians), and three with his third (1 & 2 Corinthians, Romans). The Prison Epistles (Ephesians, Philippians, Colossians, Philemon) were written during Paul's first Roman imprisonment, and the Pastoral Epistles (1 & 2 Timothy, Titus) were written afterwards.

[4] Circumcision was the biggest issue, because it was the prerequisite for and the sign of putting oneself under the Law.

[5] See also my presentation of these dates and events in a timeline.

[6] According to Acts 11:26, Paul was in Antioch for one year before traveling to Jerusalem with the money for famine relief. This famine occurred during the reign of Claudius, and near the time of Herod Agrippa I's death (so Acts 12:1). Claudius reigned from 41 to 54; Herod Agrippa reigned over Judea from 41 to 44, and died in 44.

47–48	First missionary journey (Acts 13:4–14:26)
49	Jerusalem Council, fourteen years after Paul's conversion (Gal 2:1-10; Acts 15:1-29)
49	Peter at Antioch (Gal 2:11ff.; Acts 15:35)
49–52	Second missionary journey (Acts 15:36–18:22)
53–57	Third missionary journey (Acts 18:23–21:16)
57	Arrest and defense in Jerusalem (Acts 21:17–23:24)
57–59	Imprisonment in Caesarea (Acts 23:25–26:32)
fall 59–spring 60	Journey to Rome (Acts 27:1–28:15)
60–62	First Roman imprisonment (Acts 28:16-31)
62–65	Further ministry (1 Timothy; Titus)
summer–winter 65	Second Roman imprisonment (2 Timothy)
winter 65/66	Martyrdom[7]

There are two key points where events in the life of Paul can be dated fairly precisely according to extrabiblical historical data. The first point is the trial before Gallio. Near the end of Paul's stay in Corinth, he was brought before Gallio, who is said in Acts 18:12 to be proconsul of Achaia. According to an inscription found at Delphi, Gallio became proconsul on July 1, A.D. 51, and he probably left in mid-September of the same year.[8] Paul embarked on his second missionary journey sometime after the Jerusalem Council of Acts 15, and after visiting several cities in Asia Minor spent eighteen months in Corinth (Acts 18:11). This means that Paul must have arrived in Corinth between January and April A.D. 50. This, in turn, means that the Jerusalem Council of Acts 15 could not have occurred later than A.D. 49. Since the crucifixion occurred on April 3, 33, the visit to Jerusalem which Paul describes in Gal 2:1-10 must be the Jerusalem Council, and Paul must have been saved in A.D. 35.

The second key date in the life of Paul is the transition between the procuratorships of Felix and Festus, since Acts 24:27 states that Paul was imprisoned in Caesarea for two years, and he began his journey to Rome in autumn (Acts 27:9), shortly after Festus succeeded Felix as procurator of Judea. Festus most likely succeeded Felix in the summer of A.D. 59.[9]

The Relationship of the Law to the Church

The book of Galatians and other NT writings maintain that Christians are not under the Law as a system of living, but are under grace (Rom 6:14-15)—yet we are not without law in the sense of not being bound by specific commands from God (1 Cor 9:21). The New Testament is replete with such commands, and universal moral principles in the Law still apply (cf. Gal 6:2; James 2:8). We are still supposed to obey the moral Law, but are not "under" it in the technical sense of placing oneself under the terms of the Old Covenant (Rom 6:14-15; 1 Cor 15:55-57), because anyone who is under one part of the Law is under the whole thing (Gal 5:1-4). Everyone who is under the law is under a curse (Gal 3:10), and Christians are not under a curse (Gal 3:13). The blessings and curses of Deut 27–28 were given to OT Israel, not to the church. Further, the Law was a means of regulating approach to a holy God by sinful men, and the whole

---

[7] On the date of Paul's martyrdom, see comments regarding the date of Hebrews, the date of 2 Peter, and the date of 2 Timothy.

[8] See J. Murphy-O'Connor, "Paul and Gallio" *JBL* 112 (1993): 315-17; Craig A. Evans, *Ancient Texts for New Testament Studies* (Peabody, MA: Hendrickson, 2005), 314.

[9] See the excellent discussion of this chronological problem in Joel B. Green, "Festus, Porcius," in *The Anchor Bible Dictionary*, vol. 2 (New York: Doubleday, 1992), 795.

priestly and sacrificial system has been replaced by Jesus Christ's high priesthood. Galatians and Hebrews are both very clear on the fact of the cessation of the Law (Gal 2:19, 21; 3:13, 19, 23-25; 4:5; 5:1-4, 18; Heb 7:18; 8:13).

It should be emphasized, against dual-covenant theology, that modern-day Jews are not under the Law, and keeping the Law does not do any good for them. No Christian is under the Law; all are saved by grace through faith. Paul said he is not under the Law, and he was a Jew. When Jesus Christ dedicated the New Covenant with His blood, the Old Covenant ceased to operate. Both Jews and Gentiles live under a New Covenant system today.

It should also be emphasized that Paul does not present the Law itself negatively in any of his epistles. The Law is always spoken of positively in the Bible, and never negatively. The Law was given for Israel's benefit, not to degrade Israel. It was good, and holy, and true. What Paul presents as negative is putting oneself back under the Law after we have been freed from it in Christ. Paul's basic point in portraying the Law as a παιδαγωγός in Gal 3:24-25 is to show that while it had a legitimate function of guardianship for a period of time, this function ceased after a point of maturity was reached. The Law was not a bad thing in itself, but it was not complete in itself, either; it was only a bridge to the end product, to the time when the guardian is no longer needed (cf. Gal 4:4-7).

Outline of Galatians

I. Greeting 1:1-5
II. The Divine Origin of Paul's Gospel 1:6–2:21
    A. The immutability of the gospel 1:6-9
    B. Paul's conversion possible only by direct revelation 1:10-17
    C. Paul's lack of contact with the apostles 1:18-24
    D. The commonality of the apostolic gospel 2:1-10
    E. The authority of Paul's gospel over human authority 2:11-21
III. Defense of Justification by Faith, Apart from the Works of the Law 3:1–5:12
    A. The inability of the Law to save 3:1-14
    B. The disassociation of Law and promise 3:15-22
    C. The new identity of God's people in Christ 3:23-29
    D. The release from the Law through Christ 4:1-7
    E. The senselessness of the return to Law 4:8-11
    F. Appeal return to Paul and his teaching 4:12-20
    G. Illustration of the need to cast off the Law 4:21-31
    H. Admonition to the Galatians not to place themselves under the Law 5:1-12
IV. The Nature of Life in the Spirit, Free from the Law 5:13–6:10
    A. The guiding principle of Christian freedom 5:13-15
    B. The superiority of trust in the Spirit rather than the flesh 5:16-24
    C. Exhortation to walk by the Spirit and love 5:25-26
    D. Instruction on living by the principle of love 6:1-10
        1. Instruction on restoring a sinning brother 6:1-5
        2. Instruction on sowing to the Spirit 6:6-10
V. Closing Remarks 6:11-18
    A. Personal appeal not to glory in the flesh 6:11-16
    B. Proof of Paul's motives 6:17
    C. Benediction 6:18

Argument of Galatians

The body of the epistle of Galatians contains three major sections: a defense of the divine origin of Paul's gospel (1:6–2:21), a defense of justification by faith, apart from the works of the Law (3:1–5:12), and an explanation of the nature of life by the Spirit, free from the Law (5:13–6:10). The body of the book is bracketed by a greeting (1:1-5), and a section of closing remarks (6:11-18).

Greeting, 1:1-5

The book of Galatians opens with a typical epistolary greeting (1:1-5). There are two key points in this greeting. First, Paul emphasizes the divine origin of his apostleship (1:1), as a prelude to his argument for the divine origin of his gospel (1:6–2:21). His apostleship gave him the authority to define the gospel, because he got the message directly from the Lord Jesus and was appointed by Him to proclaim it. The second notable aspect of the greeting is its complete lack of any commendation. The contrast with 1 Cor 1:4-9 shows that the Galatians' tampering with the gospel was even more serious than the Corinthians' moral problems.

The Divine Origin of Paul's Gospel, 1:6–2:21

In 1:6–2:21, Paul defends the divine origin of his gospel, since the Judaizers had clearly challenged Paul's authority to define the gospel. First, in 1:6-9, Paul asserts in the strongest language that the gospel which he preached in Galatia cannot and does not change, and is not valid in any other form. Those in Galatia who are teaching a different gospel stand condemned. In 1:10-17, Paul presents a powerful proof of the divine origin of his gospel: he was so strongly committed to Judaism, and so violently opposed to Christianity, that only a direct revelation from Jesus Christ could have been powerful enough to convert him from his former lifestyle. In fact, after seeing the Lord directly on the road to Damascus, Paul was given further teaching about Jesus directly by the Holy Spirit in Arabia, rather than by the apostles in Jerusalem (1:16-17). In 1:18-24, Paul explains that after his conversion, he had very little contact with the apostles and very little contact with Jerusalem and Judea, thereby excluding the possibility that he could have taken his gospel from them. When Paul finally did have significant contact with the apostles and laid out his gospel before them, they agreed that his gospel was the same as theirs, and recognized that he was the apostle to the Gentiles (2:1-10).[10] However, Paul's gospel was so independent of human authority that he subsequently rebuked the leading apostle in public when the latter began to live as if he were under the Law, in contradiction of the gospel (2:11-21).

Defense of Justification by Faith, Apart from the Works of the Law, 3:1–5:12

After defending the divine origin of his gospel, Paul lays out in 3:1–5:12 the main argument of the book, which is a defense of the gospel of justification by faith, apart from the works of the Law. The Law

---

[10] The visit of Paul to Jerusalem recorded in 2:1-10 must be the Acts 15 visit, not the famine relief visit of Acts 11:29-30. The arguments pro and con are too extensive to list here, but one significant problem is the chronology. Herod Agrippa I died in A.D. 44, which according to Acts 12:1 occurred at about the same time as the famine relief visit. There are only eleven years between the crucifixion (April 3, 33) and the death of Herod, and no room for the fourteen years of Gal 2:1. Most likely, Paul does not list the famine relief visit because he only saw the elders of Judea, and did not have any significant contact with the apostles.

is actually slavery from which the Galatians were released. It makes no sense to go back under it, since inheritance is not through Law, and the Law's slavery is total.

Paul opens his argument in 3:1-14 with a demonstration that the Law was not given to save. He appeals to the Galatians' own conversion experience, in which they received the Holy Spirit—as attested by sign gifts—through belief of the gospel, not by doing the works of the Law (3:1-5). The fact that they had begun their Christian life in the Spirit implies that their salvation will be consummated by the Spirit, not by keeping the Law. Paul then appeals in 3:6-9 to the example of Abraham in order to show that faith is the sole condition for partaking of the blessings promised to Abraham. In 3:10-14, Paul contrasts the blessings which come through faith with the curse which comes through the Law, showing that Jesus suffered this curse on our behalf so that we could obtain salvation through faith. In the next paragraph, 3:15-22, Paul shows that the Law neither nullifies nor contradicts the promise which is obtained by faith, but was a separate entity which temporarily existed alongside it until the Messiah's advent. This gives rise to a question: if the Law cannot save, why was it given? The answer comes in 3:23-29: the Law functioned in the Mosaic dispensation like the guardian (παιδαγωγός) of a minor which kept Israel separate from pagan nations and pagan influences until the Messiah came.[11] Its purpose was essentially to define and maintain Israel's national identity. However, when a point of maturity is reached, the guardian must be removed to allow the grown child to live as a man. In the present age, the church is one new people of God defined by faith in Christ, not by the identity markers of the Law—most notably, circumcision and the observance of special days (cf. 4:10; 5:2-3). It is those who are in Christ who are heirs of the promises given to Abraham, not those who have identified themselves with Israel through the signs of the Old Covenant (3:29). In 4:1-7, Paul explains that God's people were released from the Law's guardianship when Christ came and redeemed us, making us free sons and heirs of God rather than slaves of the guardian. In 4:8-11, Paul then applies what he has been saying to the situation of the Galatians, arguing that by identifying themselves with the signs of the Old Covenant they are seeking the status of slaves rather than sons. They are essentially turning away from the offer of redemption in Christ and participating in a competing system of salvation which, like idolatry, seeks justification by works. In 4:12-20, Paul makes a personal appeal to the Galatians, rebuking them for turning away from his example and teaching, and puzzling over what has happened to their relationship. He concludes the argument in 4:21-31 with an analogy which makes the point that those who are under the law are in bondage, while those who are in Christ are free. Although this paragraph has sometimes been used as justification for use of the allegorical hermeneutic, what Paul does is far different from the allegorizing of Philo, Origen, or Augustine. Paul affirms the literal historical truth of the Genesis narrative, and he tells his readers explicitly that he is making an analogy.[12] Caird's explanation is excellent:

> The underlying debate is whether Jews or Christians have the better claim to be called children of Abraham and heirs to his inheritance. The Jewish case rests on physical descent traced through the free-born wife, with the implication that the repudiated son of the slave-woman represents the Gentiles. Paul's answer is that by physical descent Ishmael is just as much a son of Abraham as Isaac, and that those who rely on physical descent, and the legalistic interpretation of the Old Testament that goes with it, symbolised by Mount Sinai, might just as well be the slave-woman's

---

[11] My suggested translation for Gal 3:23-25 is, *But before faith came, we were confined under the law, shut up until the faith which was coming should be revealed. So then the law has been our guardian until Christ, that we might be justified by faith. But now that faith is come, we are no longer under a guardian.* The temporal use of εἰς is rare, but examples include Phil 1:10, 1 Thess 4:15, and 2 Tim 1:12. That εἰς is intended to be understood temporally in 3:23 is shown by its pairing with Πρὸ (*before*). This increases the likelihood of understanding εἰς temporally in 3:24. The context has to do with the role of the Law for a fixed period of time in salvation history, and the temporal understanding of εἰς is the only one which fits.

[12] The verb ἀλληγορέω is not necessarily equivalent to the English word "allegorize." It is a compound formed from ἄλλος + λέγω/εἴρω, meaning "something other than what is said."

children, since they are in fact in bondage. The real difference between Isaac and Ishmael is that Isaac was the son of God's promise, so that those who live by faith in that promise are the true children of Abraham and his free-born wife.[13]

Thus, the Galatians are in a situation analogous to that of Abraham and Sarah in Gen 21, and ought to do exactly the same thing that Abraham was commanded to do in that chapter—they are to cast out the earthly Jerusalem and religious Judaism.

In the final paragraph in the section, 5:1-12, Paul applies everything that has been said in an appeal to the Galatians not to place themselves under the Law. The Law is an all-or-nothing proposition: those who receive circumcision, which is the sign of identification with the Old Covenant, have placed themselves under the terms of that covenant, thereby obliging them to do all the works of the Law and exposing them to the curse for disobedience (5:2-3; cf. 3:10).[14]

The Nature of Life in the Spirit, Free from the Law, 5:13–6:10

Having made the argument that the Galatians should seek justification by faith, apart from the Law, Paul concludes the epistle with an applicational section which answers the question of how Christians can be expected to live righteously without the Law (5:13–6:10). He argues that Christians not only are free from the Law, but do not need the Law, since those who are led by the Spirit and walking in love will naturally lead a holy life in accordance with the principles of the Law. In 5:13-15, Paul states that the guiding principle for the use of freedom in Christ is love for one other. The message of 5:16-24 is, do not put your confidence in the flesh, because the flesh is weak. "A life under law is a life subject to the desires of the flesh. The works of the flesh, then, are to be seen as the result of living under the Law rather than under the guidance of the Spirit."[15] Unlike the Law, the Spirit gives power to produce His fruit in our lives and mortify the flesh. Paul then exhorts the Galatians to walk in accordance with the Spirit and love, given the fact of their new life in the Spirit (5:25-26).

In 6:1-10, Paul gives examples of how Christians can live in accordance with love for each other—in contrast to legalism, which attempts to destroy those who do not keep the law. First, Paul deals with the issue of restoration (6:1-5). Rather than condemning a struggling brother, Christians should participate in his struggle and help him overcome, realizing that we are all susceptible to the same temptations. In 6:6-10, Paul exhorts the Galatians to do works which fall into the category of sowing to the Spirit, rather than legalistically sowing to the flesh—which, specifically, means doing good towards fellow believers.

Closing Remarks, 6:11-18

At 6:11, Paul takes the pen from his amanuensis to close the letter in his own handwriting. In 6:11-16, Paul appeals to the Galatians to glory in the cross of Christ, and not in their flesh. The Judaizers are motivated by a desire to avoid persecution and look good, whereas the only true ground of boasting is identification with the cross of Christ, thereby bringing suffering and ostracism (6:11-14). The only thing

---

[13] G. B. Caird, *The Language and Imagery of the Bible* (London: Duckworth, 1980), 171.

[14] Verse 4 is not speaking of loss of salvation, but of the removal from grace as a system of living. Verse 6 states that circumcision means nothing, so certainly the act of circumcision would not cancel out a confused Christian's salvation. Loss of salvation is not an issue in this epistle, and the rest of the NT frequently and categorically affirms assurance of salvation.

[15] G. W. Hansen, "Galatians, Letter to the" (*Dictionary of Paul and His Letters*; Downers Grove: IVP, 1993), 334.

that makes any difference in the world is regeneration of the inner man through faith in Christ, since this alone defines membership in Christ's body (6:15). Paul then pronounces a blessing upon those who live by the principle of faith, as a balance to the negative statements he has made (6:16). The final phrase in 6:16, "the Israel of God," has become a major battleground for Protestant theological debates, though it was almost certainly a non-issue for the original readers.[16] In 6:17, Paul offers a powerful proof of the purity of his own motives: his scars from persecution. This was something of which none of the Judaizers could boast. The book concludes with a short benediction (6:18).

---

[16] Some (e.g., RSV, NIV, TNIV) translate the final καὶ as "even," in which case the verse would be saying that the church is the true Israel (the NLT makes this explicit). Probably this interpretation did not even occur to the original readers. In context, it makes perfect sense to take "the Israel of God" as a references to Jewish Christians, those Israelites who are Israelites indeed. Paul has been wishing harm upon Jews who teach Christians to be saved through the Law, so here he wishes peace upon the Jews who have found and practiced salvation through faith in Christ. He distinguishes between the Israel of the flesh, which includes all the physical descendants of Jacob, and the Israel of God, which is that part of Israel that is born of God (cf. Rom 9:6-8).

Bibliography for Galatians

Barnes, Albert. *II Corinthians and Galatians*. Notes on the New Testament, ed. Robert Frew. Reprint: Grand Rapids: Baker, 1949.

Betz, Hans Dieter. *A Commentary on Paul's Letter to the Churches in Galatia*. Hermeneia. Philadelphia: Fortress Press, 1979.

Boice, James Montgomery. "Galatians." In *Expositor's Bible Commentary*, ed. Frank E. Gaebelein et al., vol. 10, 407-508. Grand Rapids: Zondervan, 1976.

Bruce, F. F. *The Epistle to the Galatians: A Commentary on the Greek Text*. New International Greek Testament Commentary. Grand Rapids: Eerdmans, 1982.

Burton, Ernest De Witt. *A Critical and Exegetical Commentary on The Epistle to the Galatians*. International Critical Commentary. Edinburgh: T. & T. Clark, 1921.

Campbell, Donald K. "Galatians." In *The Bible Knowledge Commentary: New Testament*, ed. John F. Walvoord and Roy B. Zuck, 587-612. Wheaton, IL: SP Publications, 1983.

Campbell, Ernest R. *Galatians*. Silverton, OR: Canyonview Press, 1981.

Cole, R. A. *The Epistle of Paul to the Galatians: An Introduction and Commentary*. Tyndale New Testament Commentary. Grand Rapids: Eerdmans, 1965.

Constable, Thomas L. *Notes on Galatians*. 2104 ed. Sonic Light, 2014.

Criswell, W. A. *Expository Sermons on Galatians*. Grand Rapids: Zondervan, 1973.

Eadie, John. *Commentary on the Epistle of Paul to the Galatians*. Edinburgh: T. and T. Clark, 1884. Reprint, Minneapolis: James and Klock, 1977.

Edwards, Mark J., ed. *Galatians, Ephesians, Philippians*. Ancient Christian Commentary on Scripture, ed. Thomas C. Oden. Downers Grove, IL: InterVarsity Press, 1999.

Ellicott, Charles J. *A Critical and Grammatical Commentary on St. Paul's Epistle to the Galatians*. Andover: Warren F. Draper, 1896.

Fee, Gordon D. *Galatians*. Pentecostal Commentary Series, ed. John Christopher Thomas. Blandford Forum, UK: Deo, 2007.

Fung, Ronald Y. K. *The Epistle to the Galatians*. New International Commentary on the New Testament. Grand Rapids: Eerdmans, 1988.

George, Timothy. *Galatians*. New American Commentary, ed. E. Ray Clendenen and David S. Dockery, vol. 30. Nashville: Broadman & Holman, 1994.

Guthrie, Donald. *Galatians*. New Century Bible Commentary. Grand Rapids: Eerdmans, 1973.

Hansen, G. Walter. *Galatians*. IVP New Testament Commentary Series, ed. Grant R. Osborne. Downers Grove, IL: InterVarsity Press, 1994.

Hendriksen, William. *Exposition of Galatians*. New Testament Commentary. Grand Rapids: Baker, 1968.

Howson, J. S. "Galatians." In *The Holy Bible with an Explanatory and Critical Commentary: New Testament*, ed. F. C. Cook, vol. 3, 483-536. New York: Charles Scribner's Sons, 1900.

Lenski, R. C. H. *The Interpretation of St. Paul's Epistles to the Galatians and to the Ephesians and to the Philippians*. Columbus, OH: Lutheran Book Concern, 1937.

Lightfoot, J. B. *Saint Paul's Epistle to the Galatians: A Revised Text with Introduction, Notes, and Dissertations*. 8th ed. London: MacMillan and Co., 1884.

Longenecker, Richard N. *Galatians*. Word Biblical Commentary, ed. David A. Hubbard, Glenn W. Barker, and Ralph P. Martin, vol. 41. Dallas: Word Books, 1990.

Lührmann, Dieter. *Galatians*. Translated by O. C. Dean, Jr. Continental Commentaries. Minneapolis: Fortress Press, 1992.

Luther, Martin. *A Commentary on St. Paul's Epistle to the Galatians*. Westwood, NJ: Revell, 1953.

MacArthur, John F. *Galatians*. MacArthur New Testament Commentary. Chicago: Moody Press, 1987.

Martyn, J. Louis. *Galatians*. Anchor Bible, ed. David Noel Freedman, vol. 33A. New York: Doubleday, 1992.

Matera, Frank J. *Galatians*. Sacra Pagina, ed. Daniel J. Harrington, vol. 9. Collegeville, MN: Liturgical Press, 1992.

McGee, J. Vernon. *1 Corinthians–Revelation*. Volume 5 of *Thru the Bible with J. Vernon McGee*. Nashville: Thomas Nelson, 1983

Meyer, Heinrich August Wilhelm. *Critical and Exegetical Handbook to the Epistle to the Galatians*. Translated by G. H. Venables. 2nd ed. Edinburgh: T. and T. Clark, 1884.

Perowne, E. H. *The Epistle to the Galatians*. Cambridge Bible for Schools and Colleges, ed. J. J. S. Perowne. Cambridge: Cambridge, 1900.

Rapa, Robert K. "Galatians." In *The Expositor's Bible Commentary: Revised Edition*, ed. Tremper Longman III and David E. Garland, vol. 11, 547-640. Grand Rapids: Zondervan, 2008.

Ridderbos, Herman N. *The Epistle of Paul to the Churches of Galatia*. New International Commentary on the New Testament. Grand Rapids: Eerdmans, 1953.

Witherington, Ben, III. *Grace in Galatia: A Commentary on St Paul's Letter to the Galatians*. Grand Rapids: Eerdmans, 1998.

Interpretive Guide to Ephesians

Ephesians has long been a favorite epistle of Bible teachers, preachers, and commentators. It is easy to see why. Although every NT epistle is relevant to all Christians, most address specific situations in the life of the early church. Ephesians, however, presents timeless principles which apply universally, and says virtually nothing about issues specific to a single place and time. In fact, Ephesians is the least personal of all of Paul's epistles. There is no list of names and salutations that the pastor must work through; there are no personal references within the book; and there is no complex historical situation in the background which must be pieced together before the book can be interpreted. The well-marked structure of Ephesians makes it easy for the pastor to follow the flow of thought for himself and his congregation, and to divide the book into sections for sermons and outlines. There is little eschatology in the book, which many pastors like. There are no major problems in the church that Paul is specifically addressing in Ephesians, making its tone is more gentle and positive. Ephesians is a very well planned book which presents rich doctrinal truths in picturesque prose, then applies these truths to the Christian life.

Title and Destination

When the books of the Bible were first written, they did not contain titles, just as ordinary letters today do not have titles. The common title of this epistle, "To the Ephesians" (ΠΡΟΣ ΕΦΕΣΙΟΥΣ), is supported by the single reference to a specific destination in this epistle, which is in 1:1. However, the words ἐν Ἐφέσῳ (*at Ephesus*) in that verse are not found in some early manuscripts. This is a significant problem, for if there is no destination stated in the book, this would cast doubt on the correctness of the common title, and would open up the question of the original destination. The analysis below will first consider the textual variant ἐν Ἐφέσῳ in 1:1 before addressing the question of the title and destination. It will be concluded that "Ephesians" is more properly called "Laodiceans," since the true destination of the epistle was not Ephesus, but Laodicea.

Evaluation of the Authenticity of ἐν Ἐφέσῳ in 1:1

Evidence for including ἐν Ἐφέσῳ: $\aleph^2$ A B^2 D F G Ψ^c 0278. 33. 1881 *Byz* latt sy co

Evidence for not including ἐν Ἐφέσῳ: P^{46} $\aleph$* B* 6. 424^c. 1739; Or^{vid} ($Mcion^{T, E}$)

The words ἐν Ἐφέσῳ (*at Ephesus*) are not read by P^{46} and the original hands of Sinaiticus ($\aleph$) and Vaticanus (B). P^{46} is an early third century manuscript which has, on the whole, preserved a very good text and many original readings. It does not show signs of major editing or have a tendency to wild readings, which the omission of ἐν Ἐφέσῳ would be if these words were original. Sinaiticus and Vaticanus are even more mainstream manuscripts. If it is accepted that they are two of Constantine's fifty officially-ordered copies of the Bible, then they represent the best text of the New Testament as it was known in Constantinople ca. 330. They are not characterized by wildness or major editorial work. If such an important reading as the address to the Ephesians were in common circulation early in the fourth century, it would certainly be present in both $\aleph$ and B.

Since the three earliest and most reliable manuscripts of this epistle do not include ἐν Ἐφέσῳ (*at Ephesus*), it at least must be acknowledged that the shorter reading was in wide circulation at a very early date. The other manuscripts which do not read ἐν Ἐφέσῳ are also important witnesses: ms. 6 is classified as a Category III manuscript in the epistles, containing many readings which are independent of the Byzantine text; ms. 424 is strictly a Byzantine text, but was corrected against an early manuscript of high quality; ms. 1739 is one of the most valuable minuscules in the epistles, containing a very early and reliable text. The text used by Origen (early third century) did not contain ἐν Ἐφέσῳ, and neither did manuscripts mentioned by Basil (fourth century). Tertullian (early third century) and Ephraem also fail to quote these words.

According to Tertullian and Epiphanius, Marcion called this epistle "To the Laodiceans." Marcion's title implies that the words ἐν Ἐφέσῳ were not present in his text. Admittedly, Marcion was a heretic who intentionally altered Scripture, and yet he is an early (second century) witness to the text. Heretics often quoted Scripture accurately, and some of Marcion's citations do preserve original readings. Further, it seems that most of Marcion's editing was done in the Gospel of Luke, and there is no obvious reason why altering the title of this epistle would advance the Marcionite heresy. All of the witnesses which normally reflect distinctively Marcionite readings (i.e., the Old Latin and other Western witnesses) contain the words "at Ephesus."

Internal evidence strongly favors the shorter reading, for if these words are original, how can their omission be accounted for in the main stream of the early manuscript tradition? This point is especially compelling given the title ΠΡΟΣ ΕΦΕΣΙΟΥΣ in each of the manuscripts with the shorter reading. These are not manuscripts of a tradition which was opposed to identifying the destination of this letter as the Ephesian church, as would be expected if the words ἐν Ἐφέσῳ in 1:1 were original. On the other hand, if originally there was no explicit reference to Ephesus in the book, and yet the title "To the Ephesians" was added at some point, it would be very natural for a scribe to place a reference to Ephesus in the introduction. The only surprising thing is that that this reference does not appear earlier in the textual history of the epistle. Once it was added, it became well known as a significant reading, and one which the church would automatically favor because it accords with the common title of the book—which is why almost all later manuscripts contain it. Any manuscript evidence for the omission is therefore favored by strong intrinsic probabilities.

It is sometimes argued that the shorter reading creates an awkward Greek construction, but this is purely subjective. It could be argued just the same that the words ἐν Ἐφέσῳ also create an awkward translation, if done according to the literal sense of the words: "Paul, an apostle of Christ Jesus through the will of God, to the saints that are in Ephesus, and to faithful ones in Christ Jesus." In other verses where Paul follows οὖσιν with the name of the epistle's destination, he never follows the destination by καὶ, as this is awkward and splits the description of the recipients (Rom 1:7; 2 Cor 1:1-2; Phil 1:1; cf. 1 Cor 1:2). With the shorter reading, the following translation of Eph 1:1 results: "Paul, an apostle of Christ Jesus through the will of God, to the saints who are also faithful in Christ Jesus." This certainly sounds like a more natural reading, though of course some may not agree. It is natural for Paul to use a substantival participle from εἰμί to refer to his recipients, and it is in no way necessary that this be followed by a place name. Also, it should not be assumed that the location of the recipients must be mentioned in the epistle, since no location is stated in Hebrews, James, 2 Peter, 1, 2, & 3 John, or Jude, and is not mentioned in the preface of the Pastoral Epistles or Philemon.

Thus, the alleged omission of ἐν Ἐφέσῳ cannot be accounted for through any ordinary transcriptional blunder, and the deliberate excision of these words from the text would be nothing short of a major editorial job, for reasons which cannot be adequately adduced. Anyone who accepts sound principles of textual criticism must concede that the shorter reading is strongly favored on both internal and external grounds. It is therefore certain that the words ἐν Ἐφέσῳ (*at Ephesus*) should not be read in the text of 1:1.

Evaluation of the Title, "To the Ephesians"

Since it is clear that the words "at Ephesus" in 1:1 are spurious, and there are no other references to Ephesus or to the Ephesians in the epistle, it must be asked whether the title "To the Ephesians" (ΠΡΟΣ

ΕΦΕΣΙΟΥΣ) is erroneous. This is not purely a question of textual criticism, since the titles of New Testament books were not part of the original text, but were added by the church. All of the Pauline Epistles are titled after their recipients (rather than 1 Paul, 2 Paul, etc.), while the General Epistles are titled after their authors. There are only two problems with this nomenclature: in Hebrews, the author is not named, and in Ephesians the recipients are not named. The problem was solved for Hebrews by naming it after the recipients rather than the author. But Ephesians could hardly be named "The Epistle of Paul," since Paul wrote twelve other epistles.

It cannot be known for certain how copies of this epistle were titled early in the history of its circulation, but it seems that more than one group of recipients were identified. The title ΠΡΟΣ ΕΦΕΣΙΟΥΣ (*To the Ephesians*) was in circulation at least as early as P^{46} (ca. 200), and yet the title *ad Laodicenses* (*To the Laodiceans*) was in circulation even earlier, while Marcion was active (ca. 150). Although, as already noted, Marcion was a heretic, there is no obvious reason to suspect that he contrived this title to advance his heresy, nor is there evidence that he considered it an unusual title for the letter. It seems that the title *To the Laodiceans* was once in common circulation with this epistle, at least in some copies.

A variety of explanations might be proposed to account for the early appearance of both of these titles. In any case, it is clear that the books of the New Testament originally circulated without titles, and that these were added sometime in the second century. By that point in time, the recipients of this epistle, along with the author of Hebrews, had been forgotten in some parts of the church. Hence, when titles began to be added, scribes wished to call this epistle by the name of its recipients to identify it as an epistle of Paul, but the text of the book did not state who the recipients were. Since Ephesus was a prominent church in the apostolic age, and both Paul and Timothy had spent considerable time ministering there, someone probably guessed that Paul must have written this epistle to Ephesus. (It is known from the later subscriptions and expanded titles of most New Testament books that scribes did frequently guess about the historical details surrounding the epistles and inserted their guesses into the text of the epistles.) A minority of scribes put down "Laodiceans," on the basis of tradition and/or of the exegetical evidence outlined below; but these were quickly outnumbered by those manuscripts which were titled "Ephesians," perhaps because of Marcion's association with the former title, perhaps because of the negative portrayal of the Laodicean church in Rev 3:14-21, and so the latter title was standardized.

Regardless of which supposition might correctly explain all the details as to how these two titles came about, it is apparent that in fact the epistle must have originally been sent to Laodicea, and not to Ephesus. The primary evidence for a Laodicean destination comes from the book of Colossians, which refers to an epistle to the Laodiceans (Col 4:16). It has long been recognized that Ephesians and Colossians are in some ways twin epistles, based on a distinct similarity in content, structure, and even phraseology. Since Col 4:16 states that Paul had sent an epistle to Laodicea at the same time that he wrote his epistle to Colossae, it would not be surprising if these two epistles bore similarities to each other, as Ephesians and Colossians obviously do. Paul mentions Laodicea in connection with the Colossians five times (Col 2:1; 4:13, 15, 16), and commands each epistle to be read in the other's church—alongside the other Scriptures. Although some have claimed that this epistle to the Laodiceans was non-canonical, Col 4:16 puts the epistle to the Colossians on exactly the same level as an epistle to the Laodiceans, indicating that they had the same authoritative status, and 2 Pet 3:15-16 states directly that all of Paul's epistles are inspired Scripture. Ephesians is the only NT epistle which could be the epistle to the Laodiceans mentioned in Col 4:16.

There are several other connections which indicate a Laodicean destination for "Ephesians." The reference to Tychicus making Paul's affairs known to the church is found in both Eph 6:21 and Col 4:7, indicating that he delivered both letters, and at the same time—therefore making Ephesians the epistle to the Laodiceans mentioned in Col 4:16. Paul's instruction for the Colossians to greet the Laodiceans (Col 4:15) also indicates a connection to Laodicea in this other epistle that Tychicus was delivering, and perhaps implies that he had not sent a personal greeting to the Laodiceans, whom he did not personally know. If "Ephesians" were written to the church at Ephesus during Paul's first Roman imprisonment, on the other hand, it is most remarkable that it completely lacks any personal references or greetings, even though Paul spend three years ministering in Ephesus (Acts 20:31), and he was very close friends with many of the Ephesians (cf. Acts 20:36-38). If Paul were writing to the Ephesians, we would expect him to warmly greet many individuals by name and to refer to his personal experiences with them, as he does in his other epistles. But in this letter, Paul never shows personal knowledge of any of the recipients, nor does he recall a time when he had been among them; instead, he indicates in 1:15 that he knows of their faith on a secondhand basis. Indeed, Ephesians is recognized as the least personal of all the Pauline epistles—hardly what would be expected were the letter sent to Ephesus. On the other hand, the impersonal tone of Ephesians makes sense for an epistle to a church Paul had never visited. Since Colossae and Laodicea were quite close to each other, and Paul intended for both letters to be read at both churches, it seems he decided to place all his salutations in the second of the two letters, rather than duplicating them.

Thus, the circumstances of writing are apparently similar for both Ephesians and Colossians, as they were both written near the end of Paul's first Roman imprisonment, share similar themes and structure, were both delivered by Tychicus, and were delivered to the same geographical area. Ephesians contains no mention of the "savage wolves," the threat from false teachers which was the major thrust of Paul's emotional exhortation to the Ephesian elders in Acts 20:28-31. The tone of Ephesians, with its exhortations to lowliness and meekness and longsuffering (4:1-2) and against greed (4:19), seems to fit better with the wealthy, comfortable Laodiceans than with the persecuted Ephesians. Paul speaks of possessing spiritual riches in Christ (2:7; 3:16), in contrast to material wealth. The epistle also contains repeated exhortations to separate from the world and from a worldly lifestyle (4:17–5:20), which would best fit with a wealthy, complacent church that was in danger of being sucked into a materialistic, worldly lifestyle—or that perhaps had never left such a lifestyle. Likewise, the address to slaves in 6:5-9 is natural for a wealthy city, which would have a disproportionately large population of slaves. The instruction on how to relate to each other in the body of Christ (4:1-16) and in the home (5:22–6:4) also fits a Laodicean setting. Those in a persecuted church would naturally be bound together by the opposition, helping and encouraging one another, whereas those in a comfortable setting could easily divide over class, race, power struggles, and the like. The only references to persecution in the epistle are to Paul's suffering (3:1; 4:1), not to the recipients'. Likewise, the readers are presented in 2:11ff. as exclusively Gentile, whereas the church at Ephesus began in a Jewish synagogue, with Jewish believers (Acts 19:1-9).[1] Every indication is that "Ephesians" is really the epistle to the Laodiceans.

In an irrational attempt to preserve the traditional title, some commentators speculate that Ephesians could have been an encyclical letter that was perhaps first delivered to Ephesus, but was intended to be circulated in other churches as well, including Laodicea.[2] In one sense, all of the New Testament epistles

---

[1] Throughout Ephesians, "you" refers to the Gentile readers, while "we" refers to Jews.

[2] As part of this hypothesis, some scholars actually propose that Paul left a blank space in 1:1 where churches could fill in their own name when making copies of the manuscript or reading it. It is apparent that this suggestion is both totally unsupported and totally unsupportable, for several reasons: (1) There is no manuscript evidence for a blank space in 1:1, nor is there any precedent in other books of the Bible—or even secular correspondence—for leaving a blank space to be filled in later. (2) This theory denies the immutability of God's Word, since it suggests that a single book of Scripture could be produced in many different editions, all of which would be valid. (3) If originally there were a blank space in 1:1, one would expect to find no manuscripts without a name, and manuscripts with a variety of names other than Ephesus. (4) If a blank space were left in the text, it should only be for the proper name, and the word ἐν should be present in the text of all manuscripts. (5) Why would a church need to fill in its name on the address label in order to know the epistle was sent to them? This theory is tautological to the point of absurdity. The more obvious way to address an encyclical letter is to address it to all the saints in a particular region, as in Gal 1:2 and 1 Pet 1:1-2.

If, as Wallace suggests, Tychicus stopped at Ephesus before going on to Laodicea and Colossae and left a copy of Ephesians there, he should also have left a copy of Colossians and Philemon there, meaning that Colossians and Philemon would be epistles to the Ephesians just as much as "Ephesians."

were intended as encyclicals, since they were all written as Scripture, with the intent that they would be copied and circulated throughout all the churches. Yet the epistles are also *letters*, and letters are *sent* to a particular destination, with content that is particularly for the recipients at that destination—though in the New Testament this instruction is obviously profitable for others as well due to the nature of these letters as the Word of God. The "Epistle to the Ephesians" was evidently intended for a specific destination, because Paul continually refers to the recipients as if they are a specific group of people that he has in mind, and not a variety of churches in a variety of locales (cf. 1:15-16; 2:11; 3:1; 4:20-24; 6:21-22). In particular, Paul's prayer for these people (1:16) sounds like a prayer on behalf of a specific local assembly, and not a general prayer for all believers. Colossians 4:16 identifies this local assembly as the church of the Laodiceans.

The reason why commentators propose the idea that Ephesians was an "encyclical" letter is that they simply are not willing to deny that this epistle was sent to Ephesus. They frankly do not have a sincere desire to find and follow God's truth, and desire to keep their own traditions instead. For the same reason, most laymen instinctively fight any attempt to suggest that this epistle was written to Laodicea, rather than Ephesus. Translations, commentaries, pastors, and laymen alike are much more willing to accept readings of the Critical Text when they are apparently insignificant than in passages where they obviously make a big difference, as with the longer ending of Mark (Mark 16:9-20), the pericope of the adulteress (John 7:53–8:11), and such verse omissions as Luke 22:43-44, Luke 23:34a, and John 5:3b-4.[3] Yet it is actually more important to find and follow the correct readings in the more significant variants—the ones in which men have corrupted the Word of God most radically—than in the smaller variants. The significant variants are also the easiest ones to analyze, and to distinguish between original and spurious readings. The church's forceful and irrational rejection of the original readings in these variants is a mark of spiritual insincerity, for one's treatment of the Word of God parallels his treatment of the God of the Word.

In conclusion, therefore, "Ephesians" should really be called "Laodiceans." The evidence for the Laodicean destination corroborates the independent evidence for the omission of ἐν Ἐφέσῳ in 1:1, while the evidence that these words are a secondary addition to the text of 1:1 naturally casts doubt on the authenticity of the title ΠΡΟΣ ΕΦΕΣΙΟΥΣ, corroborating the independent evidence for a Laodicean destination. Nevertheless, for now we shall continue to refer to Paul's epistle to the Laodiceans by the name of "Ephesians," in spite of the patent incorrectness of this title, simply because it is the name by which the church knows this book.

Historical Background

Laodicea, sometimes called Laodicea ad Lycum to distinguish it from other towns of the same name, was a wealthy city located in Asia Minor, in what is now southwestern Turkey. It was situated in the Lycus River valley near Hierapolis (six miles NE) and Colossae (ten miles SE), about forty-five miles southeast of Philadelphia and a hundred miles east of Ephesus. An important political and commercial center, it was the capital of the province of Phrygia, and lay on an important junction on the great trade route through Asia. Much of its trade consisted in the exchange of money, i.e., banking. It was also home to a thriving cloth and garment industry famous for its soft black wool, and to a medical school which produced a widely-renowned eyesalve. The combination of these industries, along with a history of loyalty to Rome, made Laodicea an exceptionally wealthy city.

---

[3] Many people think it is risky to deny "traditional readings" (i.e., the King James Version) in major variants. But why should the KJV have any textual authority? Just because it is the text people are used to does not mean it is right. In fact, the KJV has no authority in textual matters; only ancient manuscripts, versions, and fathers have authority in these matters. It is thus much more risky to go against the preponderance of ancient evidence than it is to deny the reading of the KJV; there is nothing about the KJV text that makes it "safer" to follow.

Laodicea lay in an earthquake-prone region, and a major earthquake devastated the area in A.D. 60, shortly before this epistle was written. However, it is an overstatement to say that Laodicea was "destroyed" by the earthquake, since the city declined aid from Rome, and instead relied on its own resources to recover and rebuild (so Tacitus *Annals* 14.27.1)—unlike Philadelphia and Hierapolis, which did accept Roman aid. This earthquake must have done serious damage in Colossae as well, though Paul makes no mention of it in his epistles. Laodicea, at least, was wealthy enough so as to have no great trouble recovering from the disaster. At any rate, Paul's concerns were spiritual, and life in Laodicea and Colossae appeared to go on with relative normalcy during the rebuilding process.

There is no specific record of the founding of the church at Laodicea. However, Paul indicates in Col 1:6-7 that Epaphras first brought the gospel to Colossae, apparently after being sent by Paul to evangelize the area during the apostle's three-year ministry in Ephesus on his third missionary journey (mid-53 to June 56; see Acts 20:31; 1 Cor 16:6). Colossians 4:12-13 indicates that Epaphras also evangelized nearby Laodicea and Hierapolis, resulting in the close connection between these churches that is evident from Col 2:1 and 4:15-16. Colossians 4:12 may indicate that Epaphras was a native of Colossae. In addition to the ministry of Epaphras, many travelers from the entire region continually passed through Ephesus, and as a result, Luke notes that during Paul's ministry in Ephesus "all those who dwelt in Asia heard the word of the Lord, both Jews and Greeks" (Acts 19:10). Thus, the bulk of the believers at Laodicea probably came to Christ through the work of Epaphras, while others were evangelized by Paul and his ministry team in Ephesus, and still others had come to faith in Christ subsequently through the ministry of other believers.

Although the Laodicean church appeared to be doing reasonably well at the time when Paul wrote, by the end of the first century it had degenerated considerably. Revelation 3:14-21 clearly presents Laodicea as the worst of the seven churches to which the Lord addresses miniature epistles—a complacent and wealthy church which was characterized by spiritual lukewarmness.

Author

The apostle Paul names himself as the writer in 1:1, refers to himself as "I Paul, the prisoner of Christ Jesus in behalf of you Gentiles" in 3:1, and also refers to himself as "the prisoner of the Lord" in 4:1. The connections between this epistle and Colossians, another Pauline Epistle, have already been noted. The themes and language of this book are entirely Pauline, and there simply is no good reason to believe that someone other than Paul wrote it. Pseudonymous letters were composed in the first century (2 Thess 2:2), but were not accepted by the church, since Paul closed every one of his epistles with writing in his own distinctive hand (cf. Gal 6:11; 1 Cor 16:21; 2 Thess 3:17; Phlm 19).

Most liberal scholars deny the authenticity of Ephesians, which is hardly surprising given the fact that the purpose and product of all forms of higher criticism is to deny the truth of Scripture. Hoehner has given a more than adequate rebuttal to the liberal denial of Pauline authorship of Ephesians.[4] Liberal scholars simply emphasize the differences between Ephesians and Paul's other letters, rather than the correspondences, and in the end cannot produce any objective or compelling reason to doubt Pauline authorship.

Date and Occasion of Writing

This epistle was written from Rome to Laodicea early in A.D. 62, near the end of Paul's first Roman imprisonment (cf. 3:1; 4:1; Phlm 22). It was likely not written in the winter, since winter travel was

---

[4] Harold W. Hoehner, *Ephesians: An Exegetical Commentary* (Grand Rapids: Baker, 2002), 2-61.

difficult and dangerous. An alternative date for Ephesians, Colossians, and Philemon is sometime in 61, although Paul indicates in Phlm 22 that he expects to be released soon.

The occasion of writing can be pieced together from the sister epistles of Colossians and Philemon, in conjunction with historical references in the book of Acts: a runaway slave named Onesimus had become a Christian under Paul's ministry as a prisoner in Rome, and had become attached to Paul as one of the apostle's choice servants. This slave was previously known to Paul, for he belonged to Paul's friend Philemon, a wealthy man who hailed from the city of Colossae but had visited Ephesus on business while Paul was teaching in the school of Tyrannus, and had heard the gospel from the apostle there. Paul wished to retain Onesimus' services, but his conscience compelled him to fulfill his legal obligation of sending the runaway back to his master. Thus, Paul decided to write a letter to Philemon (at Colossae) for the release of Onesimus. With Onesimus available as a letter carrier, Paul planned to send another letter at the same time for the instruction of the church at the significant and nearby city of Laodicea, intending for this epistle to be read in the smaller congregation at Colossae as well. Before he wrote the letters, however, Tychicus came and reported the outbreak of heresy in Colossae, prompting Paul to write letters to both churches, applying the themes and theological structure of the letter to Laodicea to the situation of the Colossian church.[5] Paul then sent these letters back with both Tychicus and Onesimus. Apparently Paul wrote Colossians after he wrote Ephesians, since he refers to his letter to the Laodicean church in Col 4:16.

Purpose and Message

The purpose of this epistle is to instruct the spiritually young church at Laodicea regarding the position of the Christian believer in Christ—and therefore in Christ's body, the church—and to explain how the church practically is to function as the body of Christ. The message of this epistle is, Christian believers have freely obtained incredible spiritual benefits in Christ, through whom Jews and Gentiles have been united into one new man—as a result of which Christians are responsible to walk in accordance with their high calling in unity, in newness of mind, in love, in light, and in wisdom, while standing firm against the spiritual forces in the heavenlies.

Outline of Ephesians

I. Salutation 1:1-2
II. The Calling of the Church 1:3–3:21
    A. Praise for God's spiritual blessings 1:3-14
    B. Prayer for wisdom and revelation 1:15-23
    C. Our new position individually 2:1-10
    D. Our new position corporately 2:11-22
    E. Parenthetical expansion of the mystery 3:1-13
    F. Prayer for a greater apprehension of Christ's love 3:14-19
    G. Concluding benediction 3:20-21
III. The Conduct of the Church 4:1–6:20
    A. Walk in unity 4:1-16

---

[5] While both Colossians and Ephesians present the church as a body, and Christ as its Head (Eph 4:15-16; Col 1:18), in Ephesians the focus is on the body, whereas in Colossians it is on the Head. Colossians is more polemical, while Ephesians is more pastoral. Colossians emphasizes the Christian's completeness in Christ, while Ephesians emphasizes the church's unity in Christ. The Spirit is only mentioned one time in Colossians, compared with eleven times in Ephesians.

B. Walk in newness of mind 4:17-32
      1. The new mind of believers 4:17-24
      2. The deeds resulting from the new mind 4:25-32
   C. Walk in love 5:1-2
   D. Walk in light 5:3-14
   E. Walk in wisdom 5:15–6:9
      1. Introduction and relationship between wives and husbands 5:15-33
      2. Relationship between children and parents 6:1-4
      3. Relationship between slaves and masters 6:5-9
   F. Stand in warfare 6:10-20
IV. Closing Remarks 6:21-24

Argument of Ephesians

The body of the book of Ephesians has a clear two-part division: a doctrinal section which describes the believer's position in Christ (1:3–3:21) and an applicational section which describes the believer's practice in Christ (4:1–6:20). The message of chs. 4–6 is, "Be (practically) who you are (positionally)." The body is prefaced by a typical epistolary salutation (1:1-2), and is followed by an epistolary conclusion (6:21-24).

Salutation, 1:1-2

Paul opens the epistle with a typical, brief salutation, of which the most notable element is what is not present, according to the best text—an identification of the addressees (1:1-2).

The Calling of the Church, 1:3–3:21

In 1:3–3:21, Paul sets forth the position of the Christian believer in Christ, and emphasizes the unity of all believers, Jew and Gentile, in Christ's body.

The body of the book of Ephesians opens with a brilliant burst of praise to the triune God for the blessings of salvation (1:3-14). Verses 3-14 comprise a single, well-structured sentence, in which Paul offers praise for blessings from the Father (1:3-6), blessings from the Son (1:7-12), and blessings from the Holy Spirit (1:13-14).[6] Having praised God for the spiritual blessings He has given to believers, Paul then thanks God for the application of these blessings to the Christians at Laodicea, and prays that they would experience their spiritual benefits in Christ in a deeper and fuller way as they grow in the wisdom and knowledge of God (1:15-23). The close of this thanksgiving, which describes how God raised Christ, seated Him far above all the Satanic powers, and made Him head over the church, leads into 2:1-10, in which Paul describes how the Christian believer has been raised and seated with Christ through the power of God—by grace through faith, and not by our own works. Not only has God's power in Christ been manifested through the salvation of the Laodiceans as individuals, it is also manifested through their corporate union, as Gentiles, with Jewish believers into a new race of men, the body of Christ, in which those who once were strangers from God's promises have now been brought near and made fellow-citizens of the household of God (2:11-22).

---

[6] This is the first of at least seven long sentences in this epistle. The others are 1:15-23; 2:1-9; 3:1-13, 14-19; 4:1-6, 11-16.

In ch. 3, Paul offers praise to God for the truths expressed in chs. 1–2, especially the mystery of Jew and Gentile in one body. This chapter is a "bridge" which both concludes the theological division of the epistle and prepares the reader for the exhortations in chs. 4–6. Paul introduces a prayer in 3:1, but he immediately digresses, and does not actually begin the prayer until 3:14. The parenthetical (3:2-13) explains that Paul is not unhappy about his imprisonment, nor is he blaming the Gentiles; therefore his readers need not feel saddened or guilty because of it. Paul's imprisonment actually is connected to the vital role he is playing in revealing the mystery of the church to the Gentiles. Because of the union of Jew and Gentile in one body, Paul praises God, and prays that the Laodiceans would gain a greater apprehension of Christ's unfathomable love (3:14-19). Paul concludes with a doxology which praises God for His incredible power in Christ which brought Jew and Gentile together in the church and reconciled them to Himself through Christ (3:20-21).

The Conduct of the Church, 4:1–6:20

In 1:3–3:21, Paul has laid out the spectacular spiritual blessings of the believer in Christ, and the resulting union of Jew and Gentile in the body of Christ. The high calling of the Christian believer, and the spiritual unity of all Christians in the body of Christ, has obvious practical ramifications for the daily life of Christians, and for their relation to one another in the church. Thus, Paul applies practically in 4:1–6:20 the theological truths developed in 1:3–3:21. The structure of the applicational section is marked by the use of the imperative "walk/live" (περιπατέω) in connection with the inferential conjunction "therefore" (οὖν). Following this structural indicator, believers are to (1) walk in unity (4:1-16); (2) walk in newness of mind (4:17-32); (3) walk in love (5:1-2); (4) walk in light (5:3-14); and (5) walk in wisdom (5:15–6:9). The final section of the second half of the book departs from this pattern in that it begins with the imperative ἐνδυναμοῦσθε (*stand*) in 6:10. This imperative is prefaced by the words Τοῦ λοιποῦ (*finally*), which indicates that it forms the conclusion of the second half of the book.[7]

The first exhortation, which is to walk in unity, is given in 4:1-16.[8] The spiritual unity of all believers in Christ's body forms the basis of the exhortation to live in unity in the church (4:1-6). The means of attaining unity in the faith is by ministering to each other in accordance with the gifts which Christ has given to each member of His body, for the goal of building each other up to spiritual maturity (4:7-16).[9]

The second exhortation, to walk in newness of mind, is given in 4:17-32. Believers have been enlightened from the vanity which once darkened their minds apart from Christ, and therefore ought to live out what they have become positionally (4:17-24). The deeds resulting from the new mind are described in 4:25-32.

Third, Paul briefly exhorts believers to walk in love, just as Christ loved us (5:1-2). This is followed by the fourth exhortation, which is to walk in light—not imitating the dark deeds of the world (5:3-6), but reproving them through our actions as sons of light (5:7-14).

---

[7] Outlines which present 6:10-20 as a third major section of the book do not adequately account for this connection.

[8] The command in 4:1 is actually "to walk worthily of the calling wherewith ye were called." This is apparently a thesis statement for all of 4:1–6:20, with 4:1-16 focusing on the first manner of walking worthily, which is walking in unity.

Note that 4:1 is connected to 3:1 in that both have "I the prisoner of the Lord exhort you." Paul's imprisonment on behalf of the Gentiles gives an additional motivation for the Laodicean Christians to walk worthily of their calling.

[9] Verses 11-16 are a key passage on the purpose of the church, and of ministry within the church: the church exists primarily for its own edification (cf. 1 Cor 12:7; 14:26b).

The fifth and longest exhortation is to walk in wisdom (5:15–6:9). This section is introduced by a general admonition to be filled with the Holy Spirit, resulting in controlled behavior, in contrast to the world's drunkenness with wine, resulting in surrender of control to one's sinful passions (5:15-21). This leads directly into three admonitions regarding how believers are to exercise self-control in their relationships. First, wives are to submit to their husbands as the church submits to Christ, while husbands are to love their wives as Christ loves the church (5:22-33). Second, children are to obey their parents, while parents are to support and encourage their children, rather than pushing them to provocation (6:1-4). Third, slaves are to obey their masters and do their work as unto the Lord, while masters are to treat their slaves as they would want to be treated, remembering their own accountability before the ultimate Master (6:5-9).

Although 6:10-20 is sometimes regarded as a third major section of the book, it is prefaced by the word "finally," which indicates that it forms the conclusion of the applicational section of the book. This section encapsulates the preceding admonitions by explaining how Christians are able to stand firm in their spiritual warfare. Wicked men are only tools and mouthpieces used by Satan and his minions, who are our real enemies—and who have already been put underneath Christ (1:20-21), and underneath the believer in Christ (2:1-6). The Christian lives under constant fire as part of a fierce battle which is being fought in the heavenlies—a war which is not fought, on our part, through direct physical or verbal confrontation, but through truth, righteousness, the gospel, faith, salvation, the Word of God, and prayer.

Closing Remarks, 6:21-24

Ephesians ends with a brief epistolary conclusion in 6:21-24. Paul states his purpose in sending Tychicus to deliver the letter (6:21-22), then writes a brief and impersonal salutation (6:23), and concludes with a short benediction (6:24).

Bibliography for Ephesians

Hoehner's 2002 commentary on Ephesians was his *magnum opus*. While it has justly been recognized as a superb commentary, it is not utterly exhaustive and is not the final word on the book; older commentaries are still worth reading. Weaknesses include: 1) Hoehner frequently wants to accept both of two or more interpretational or syntactical options, when only one can be correct. 2) Hoehner is very weak on text critical issues, including the recipients and title of the epistle. 3) Hoehner is strongly Calvinistic. In sections of the book that deal with deterministic theological issues, Hoehner will jump from an explanation of the text to a discussion of his theology without demonstrating that the latter develops naturally from the former. 4) Hoehner follows Wallace's *Greek Grammar beyond the Basics* unquestioningly most of the time. 5) Hoehner wastes a lot of space responding to various interpretive alternatives and citing secondary literature.

Abbott, T. K. *A Critical and Exegetical Commentary on the Epistles to the Ephesians and to the Colossians*. International Critical Commentary. Edinburgh: T. & T. Clark, 1897.

Barnes, Albert. *Ephesians, Philippians and Colossians*. Notes on the New Testament, ed. Robert Frew. Reprint: Grand Rapids: Baker, 1949.

Barth, Markus. *Introduction, Translation, and Commentary on Chapters 1–3*. Vol. 1 of *Ephesians*. Anchor Bible. Garden City, NY: Doubleday, 1974.

———. *Translation and Commentary on Chapters 4–6*. Vol. 2 of *Ephesians*. Anchor Bible. Garden City, NY: Doubleday, 1974.

Best, Ernest. *A Critical and Exegetical Commentary on Ephesians*. International Critical Commentary. Edinburgh: T&T Clark, 1998.

Bruce, F. F. *The Epistles to the Colossians, to Philemon, and to the Ephesians*. New International Commentary on the New Testament. Grand Rapids: Eerdmans, 1984.

Chafer, Lewis Sperry. *The Ephesian Letter: Doctrinally Considered*. New York: Loizeaux Brothers, 1935.

Constable, Thomas L. *Notes on Ephesians*. 2104 ed. Sonic Light, 2014.

Eadie, John. *Commentary on the Epistle to the Ephesians*. Edinburgh: T. & T. Clark, 1883.

Edwards, Mark J., ed. *Galatians, Ephesians, Philippians*. Ancient Christian Commentary on Scripture, ed. Thomas C. Oden. Downers Grove, IL: InterVarsity Press, 1999.

Ellicott, Charles J. *A Commentary, Critical and Grammatical, on St. Paul's Epistle to the Ephesians, with a Revised Translation*. Andover: Warren F. Draper, 1862.

Foulkes, Francis. *The Letter of Paul to the Ephesians: An Introduction and Commentary*. 2nd ed. Tyndale New Testament Commentaries. Grand Rapids: Eerdmans, 1989.

Hodge, Charles. *A Commentary on the Epistle to the Ephesians*. New York: Robert Carter, 1858.

Hoehner, Harold W. "Ephesians." In *The Bible Knowledge Commentary: New Testament*, ed. John F. Walvoord and Roy B. Zuck, 613-45. Wheaton, IL: SP Publications, 1983.

———. *Ephesians: An Exegetical Commentary*. Grand Rapids: Baker, 2002.

Klein, William W. "Ephesians." In *The Expositor's Bible Commentary: Revised Edition*, ed. Tremper Longman III and David E. Garland, vol. 12, 19-173. Grand Rapids: Zondervan, 2006.

Lenski, R. C. H. *The Interpretation of St. Paul's Epistles to the Galatians and to the Ephesians and to the Philippians*. Columbus, OH: Lutheran Book Concern, 1937.

Lincoln, Andrew T. *Ephesians*. Word Biblical Commentary, vol. 42. Dallas: Word, 1990.

MacArthur, John F., Jr. *Ephesians*. MacArthur New Testament Commentary. Chicago: Moody Press, 1986.

McGee, J. Vernon. *1 Corinthians–Revelation*. Volume 5 of *Thru the Bible with J. Vernon McGee*. Nashville: Thomas Nelson, 1983.

Meyrick, F. "Ephesians." In *The Holy Bible with an Explanatory and Critical Commentary: New Testament*, ed. F. C. Cook, vol. 3, 537-78. New York: Charles Scribner's Sons, 1900.

Moule, H. C. G. *The Epistle to the Ephesians, with Introduction and Notes*. The Cambridge Bible for Schools and Colleges. Cambridge: Cambridge, 1886.

O'Brien, Peter T. *The Letter to the Ephesians*. Pillar New Testament Commentary. Grand Rapids: Eerdmans, 1999.

Robinson, J. Armitage. *St. Paul's Epistle to the Ephesians*. 2nd ed. London: Macmillan, 1904.

Rutherfurd, John. *St. Paul's Epistles to Colossæ and Laodicea*. Edinburgh: T. & T. Clark, 1908.

Schnackenburg, Rudolf. *Ephesians: A Commentary*. Translated by Helen Heron. Edinburgh: T&T Clark, 1991.

Westcott, Brooke Foss. *Saint Paul's Epistle to the Ephesians: The Greek Text with Notes and Addenda*. Reprint: Grand Rapids: Eerdmans, 1952.

Witherington III, Ben. *The Letters to Philemon, the Colossians, and the Ephesians: A Socio-Rhetorical Commentary on the Captivity Epistles*. Grand Rapids: Eerdmans, 2007.

Wood, A. Skevington. "Ephesians." In *Expositor's Bible Commentary*, ed. Frank E. Gaebelein et al., vol. 11, 1-92. Grand Rapids: Zondervan Publishing House, 1978.

Interpretive Guide to Philippians

Philippians is one of the prison epistles, written during Paul's first Roman imprisonment, probably early in A.D. 62. Many expositors say that the theme of Philippians is joy, but its subject is more broad than that. This book is really meant to describe the Christian mind, what the mindset and attitude of Christians should be like. Its positive, encouraging tone has made it a favorite of Christian readers and pastors alike. Philippians is the most warm and personal of the epistles of Paul which were addressed to churches, since it was not written in response to a theological problem, but only as a thank-you letter. However, it is not just a book of warm platitudes; rather, Paul bases his exhortations on historical and theological realities. Philippians contains one of the most important passages in the NT for the doctrine of Christology (2:1-11), and it also supplies key information on the personal background and motivations of the apostle Paul.

Historical Background

The city of Philippi was situated in Macedonia, about ten miles inland from the Aegean Sea and the port city of Neapolis, and about eighty miles northeast of Thessalonica. Philippi was made a Roman colony after the combined armies of Octavian, Anthony, and Lepidus defeated Brutus and Cassius on a plain just west of the city. As a Roman colony, Philippi was granted the same legal privileges as cities in Italy. Roman colonies held a status comparable to that of Alaska and Hawaii in the United States—they and their citizens have all the rights and privileges of other states, even though they are geographically separated from the forty-eight contiguous states. This adds significance to the reference to πολίτευμα (*citizenship*) in 3:20. It should be remembered that Paul could speak to the Philippians as equals in the matter of citizenship, for he too was a Roman citizen.

The church at Philippi was founded by Paul on his second missionary journey (Acts 16:6-40), and in fact was the first church Paul founded in Europe. Paul established a special relationship with this church through the beating that he and Silas willingly suffered there in order to protect the new believers from persecution. When Paul was forced to leave town and travel down the road to Thessalonica, the church at Philippi sent him financial gifts twice during the three weeks he was in that city (Phil 4:16; cf. Acts 17:1-9). Paul briefly revisited Philippi twice at the end of his third missionary journey (Acts 20:1-6). When the Philippians heard that Paul was under house arrest in Rome, they took up a generous collection for Paul, and sent Epaphroditus to Rome to deliver it in person (Phil 2:25; 4:18). This epistle is essentially a thank-you letter for the Philippians' gift.

Author

Paul and Timothy are both named as senders in 1:1, but it is clear that Paul is the sole author of the letter. Paul refers to himself in the first person singular throughout the epistle and includes much material of a personal and autobiographical nature. Timothy is referred to in the third person in 2:19-24. There are no significant liberal challenges to the Pauline authorship of Philippians.

Date and Occasion of Writing

Philippians was written from Rome (1:13; 4:22) to Philippi (1:1) near the end (1:25-26; 2:24) of Paul's first Roman imprisonment (1:12-14), probably early in A.D. 62. The letter was carried to Philippi by Epaphroditus (2:25-30). The occasion of writing was the receipt of a gift from the church at Philippi that was carried to Paul in Rome by Epaphroditus (4:18; cf. 2:25; 4:10-16; 2 Cor 8:1-2; 11:8-9), and was then followed by Epaphroditus' severe illness and recovery (2:26-28). Paul wished to give the Philippians a report on his present condition (1:12-30), to comfort them by the return of Epaphroditus (2:25-30), to express his joy for their gift (4:10-20), and to communicate important theological truths for the edification of the church. Philippians is one of those rare epistles of Paul that is not intended to address a particular problem among the recipients, but rather was written to instruct them and to develop the apostle's friendship with them. There are brief warnings against false teachers (3:2, 15, 18-19) and a short word of admonishment to Euodia and Syntyche (4:2-3), but the space given to these issues indicates that they were not major problems in the church.

Purpose and Message

Paul's didactic purpose in this epistle is to instruct the Philippians concerning the Christian mind. Such themes as joy, unity, humility, selflessness, and contentment are only aspects of the Christian mind, which is the theme that ties the letter together. This is a book about right thinking, and the right living which follows from right thinking. The message of Philippians is that Christians should think in a way that seeks the good of others at any expense and values heavenly things to the exclusion of the things of this world.

Outline of Philippians

I. Introductory Matters 1:1-30
   A. Greeting 1:1-2
   B. Paul's thanksgiving and supplication for the Philippians 1:3-11
   C. Paul's present circumstances and their spiritual implications 1:12-30
II. Exhortation to Have a Sacrificial Mind 2:1-30
   A. Exhortation to have the mind of Christ 2:1-11
   B. Exhortation to live with a sacrificial mind 2:12-18
   C. Exhortation to receive those who demonstrate a sacrificial mind 2:19-30
III. Exhortation to Have a Spiritual Mind 3:1-21
   A. Paul's present example of a spiritual mind contrasted with his past in Judaism 3:1-16
   B. The spiritual mind contrasted with the fleshly mind of the Judaizers 3:17-21
IV. Behavior Which Should Result from Having the Christian Mind 4:1-9
   A. Exhortation to stand fast 4:1
   B. Exhortation to reconcile personal differences 4:2-3
   C. Exhortation to have an attitude of dependence on the Lord 4:4-7
   D. Exhortation to develop the Christian mind 4:8-9
V. Closing Remarks 4:10-23
   A. Concerning the Philippians' gift to Paul 4:10-20
   B. Salutations 4:21-22
   C. Benediction 4:23

Argument of Philippians

The first chapter of Philippians deals with introductory matters which lead into the main argument and introduce its themes. The body of the epistle, in which the main argument is presented, runs from 2:1 to 4:9. The argument is divided into three sections: ch. 2 exhorts the Philippians to have a sacrificial mind, ch. 3 exhorts them to have a spiritual mind, and 4:1-9 applies the theological principles developed in chs. 2–3 to the everyday lives of the believers in Philippi. The remainder of the epistle deals with the personal matter of the gift sent to Paul by the Philippians, followed by standard epistolary salutations and a benediction.

Introductory Matters, 1:1-30

The first major section of the epistle is introductory, dealing with various personal matters regarding Paul's relationship with the Philippians. These include a greeting (1:1-2) a prayer (1:3-11), and a report on Paul's present condition (1:12-30).

Greeting, 1:1-2. Like Paul's other epistles, Philippians begins with a greeting (1:1-2). However, this greeting differs from most of the others in that Paul does not refer to himself as an apostle. He does not need to assert his apostolic authority to the Philippians, because there are no major problems in that church. Instead, he refers to himself and Timothy as "servants." Right from the start, it is clear that this epistle will have a different tone than most of the others.

Paul's thanksgiving and supplication for the Philippians, 1:3-11. As is often his practice in his epistles, Paul follows the greeting with a prayer of thanksgiving and supplication for the Philippians in 1:3-11. This is a personal prayer about Paul's love for the Philippians, but it also introduces such themes of the letter as joy (1:4), the Philippians' gifts to Paul (1:5), and above all the proper way of thinking which leads to righteousness (1:9-11).

Paul's present circumstances and their spiritual implications, 1:12-30. The Philippians knew that Paul was in prison, so after Paul greets the saints and shares his affection for them, he gives them a report on his present condition and its effect on his ministry. He then analyzes his circumstances and challenges the Philippians with spiritual principles from this analysis. Once again, this report lays the groundwork for the main argument in the body of the book by showing how Paul exemplifies a selfless mind in his circumstances. First, in 1:12-20, Paul rejoices that his imprisonment has given him an opportunity to preach the gospel to the whole Roman court, while simultaneously emboldening others to preach the gospel in Paul's absence. Those who held professional jealousy against Paul were preaching the gospel solely to irritate Paul by getting ahead of him in the ministry while he was confined (1:15-17). But Paul had no interest in getting glory for himself, so he simply rejoiced in the proclamation of the gospel (1:18-20).

Next, in 1:21-26, Paul applies a spiritual mentality to his present circumstances. It is better for him to leave this world and to be with Christ in heaven, where his true home is. But he is perfectly willing, and even desirous, to remain in the world for the benefit of the Philippians and other believers. Paul's concern for others thus trumps his concern for himself.

Finally, in 1:27-30, Paul brings the introductory section to a conclusion by challenging the Philippians to live and think as they ought in the midst of Paul's imprisonment and in the light of his example. He exhorts them to remain faithful and united regardless of Paul's condition (1:27), to follow Paul's example in not fearing suffering and persecution (1:28), and to rather graciously accept persecution as God's gift to his saints (1:29), of whom Paul is a prime example (1:30). The gracious acceptance of suffering comes from a mentality that is radically different from the mind of the world, a mind which selflessly sacrifices for the good of others, and which values heavenly things to the exclusion of the things of this world. This nicely introduces the body of the book, in which Paul will describe the Christian mind in more detail and will exhort the Philippians to think and live accordingly.

Exhortation to Have a Sacrificial Mind, 2:1-30

Having introduced the themes of the book in ch. 1, Paul now launches into the main argument to develop these ideas more fully. He begins in ch. 2 by describing the sacrificial mind and exhorting the Philippians to think in this way. The message of ch. 2 is that Christians are to live and think in a way that puts the concerns and needs of others above their own, even at the cost of life itself. This corresponds to the second half of Paul's inner conflict in 1:23-24, which was his desire to remain in this world and suffer in order to minister to the Philippians and to other believers.

Exhortation to have the mind of Christ, 2:1-11. In 2:1-11, Paul exhorts the Philippians to have a mind that seeks to serve and benefit others at one's own expense. The example of Christ is set forth as the ultimate model of such a mind. Verses 1-4 state the thesis of this section by exhorting the Philippians to all have the same mind of love (2:2), which does not seek to promote itself (2:3a), but rather considers other believers and their needs to be more important than one's own (2:3b-4). This mentality is illustrated and modeled in the greatest possible way by the Lord Jesus Christ (2:5-11). First, Christ Jesus, though preexistent (ὑπάρχων) with the external manifestation of the divine essence (ἐν μορφῇ θεοῦ), was even willing to give up the outward appearance of deity, taking on the external manifestation of a servant through the incarnation (2:6-7). In doing so, Christ voluntarily "emptied Himself of the immediate manifestation of His divine essence. . . . [Christ] maintained His [divine] attributes (perfections) and their activity, but in accepting His incarnate state He chose not to externally manifest these attributes (perfections) in the human realm with the manifestation of His humanity, apart from the Father's will and the Spirit's leading."[1] He then willingly humiliated Himself by obeying the Father's command to suffer the cruel death of the cross (2:8). By choosing to humble Himself rather than demanding the glory that was rightly His, Christ was made super-exalted by the Father (2:9-11). The lesson is that the way to become great in the ultimate sense is to follow Christ's example in becoming a servant of all (cf. Mark 10:43-45). The ultimate product and goal of living with a sacrificial mindset is the glory of God (2:11).

Exhortation to live with a sacrificial mind, 2:12-18. In the next paragraph, 2:12-18, Paul exhorts the Philippians to follow Christ's example. Verse 12 begins with the inferential conjunction Ὥστε, "So then." Because the Lord Jesus Christ became obedient unto death, the Philippians are to have the same kind of obedience to God—namely, obedience that will go to any length to serve others and bring glory to God. The sacrificial mindset does not permit dissatisfaction with life circumstances or one's divinely ordained responsibilities (2:14). Living with contentment and obedience to God will result in the sanctification of the Philippians, a strong testimony to the world, and the validation of Paul's ministry (2:15-16). Paul then adds that even as the Philippians present themselves as sacrifices, he himself is poured out as a drink-offering on top of their sacrifice, while the mind of Christ allows both parties to rejoice in their mutual sacrifice.

Exhortation to receive those who demonstrate a sacrificial mind, 2:19-30. After presenting Christ as the example of the sacrificial mind in 2:1-11 and exhorting the Philippians to follow Christ's example in 2:12-18, Paul then commands the church to receive two men who were living demonstrations of the sacrificial mind (2:19-30). In the flow of thought of the chapter, 2:19-30 is connected with 2:12-18 by Paul's desire to know whether the Philippians are pressing on towards sanctification in his absence. However, 2:19-30 also continues the themes of the chapter by presenting Timothy and Epaphroditus as examples of men who model the sacrificial mindset and commanding the church to receive them for this reason. First, Paul says he hopes to send Timothy to Philippi because Timothy is the only one of his available coworkers who genuinely seeks the interests of others, rather than his own interests (2:19-24).

---

[1] James R. Mook, "Class notes for TH702 Christology & Angelology" (Capital Bible Seminary, Spring 2005) 187.

Then, in 2:25-30, Paul states that he deemed it necessary to send Epaphroditus back to Philippi with the letter, because the Philippians had heard that he was gravely ill and were anxious to know what had become of him. Epaphroditus had carried the Philippians' gift to Paul and had voluntarily risked his life in so doing (2:30), thereby demonstrating the mind of Christ which is willing to sacrifice everything for the benefit of others.

Exhortation to Have a Spiritual Mind, 3:1-21

The introductory chapter ended with an admonishment for the Philippians to embrace the same conflict as Paul, graciously accepting suffering and deprivation in this life (1:30). Chapter 2 expanded upon one side of the acceptance of suffering, which is a selfless mentality that is willing to sacrifice anything for the good of others. Chapter 3 expands on the other half of the mentality that allowed Paul to embrace suffering, which was his desire to depart and be with Christ (1:23-24). The message of ch. 3 is that Christians are to live and think in a way that focuses on their advancement in the things of Christ and His heavenly kingdom to the exclusion of advancement in the eyes of men and in the things of this world. Whereas the previous chapter exhorted the Philippians to have the mind of Christ, in this chapter they are exhorted to have the mind of Paul. Paul sets himself forth as an example of one who has repudiated the fleshly mind and now stands in contrast to the legalistic Jews of whose number he once counted himself. Further, while ch. 2 only offered positive examples to emulate, in ch. 3 Paul's positive example is offered by way of contrast with negative examples, including the apostle's own past.

Paul's present example of a spiritual mind contrasted with his past in Judaism, 3:1-16. Chapter 3 opens with the words Τὸ λοιπόν (*Furthermore*; lit., *As for the rest*), which are used to make a transition to the remainder of the instruction that Paul wishes to present. Verse 1 opens with a command to rejoice in the Lord, which is appropriate as an introduction to a chapter that calls believers to a mentality that looks forward to what awaits them in the Lord's presence, regardless of their circumstances in this life. Paul acknowledges that the message of this chapter is only an elaboration on what he has been saying all along, but to repeat the same instruction is good for both him and them (3:1b). This chapter is a warning not to adopt the mindset that Judaizing false teachers were promoting (3:2), since a Christian's glory is in the Lord, not in the flesh (3:3). Paul then sets himself forth as an example of a man who once had, in the flesh, everything that the Judaizers could ever hope to achieve (3:4-6), yet renounced all of his worldly accomplishments and status to serve Christ (3:7-11). What things were of great value to the world were a loss in Paul's mind, because they hindered him from accepting the gospel and were of no worth for eternity. Paul then contrasts his past life in Judaism with his present resolve to leave his past behind, including both failures and successes, and to press on towards the heavenly reward that Christ has promised for those who fulfill their calling in Him (3:12-14). The Philippians are exhorted to follow Paul's example, and not that of the Judaizers who claimed to have already attained the goal in this life (3:15-16).

The spiritual mind contrasted with the fleshly mind of the Judaizers, 3:17-21. Whereas the previous paragraph contrasted Paul's present spiritual mind as a Christian with his past fleshly mind in Judaism, in 3:17-21 the spiritual mind is contrasted with the fleshly mind of the Judaizers. In 3:17, Paul expands the model of a spiritual mind from himself to his coworkers and those who live the way they do. In contrast to Paul's relatively small ministry team, there are many false teachers who have just the opposite mentality, as described in 3:18-19. These are Judaizers who claim to believe in Jesus in some way, but deny the sufficiency of His atonement and therefore the gospel, and are not just sincerely misguided but are in the ministry solely to enhance their status in this life and actually have been hardened beyond any possibility of repentance. But Paul and the Philippians are to have a spiritual perspective which considers heaven to be their true home, while working to gain status and wealth in Christ's kingdom, counting the things the world values as worthless for eternity (3:20-21). The redemption of the body and the subjection of all things to Christ is the ultimate focus of the spiritual mind, and thus the portrayal of this hope in 3:20-21 rounds out the exhortation for the Philippians to have this mind.

Behavior Which Should Result from Having the Christian Mind, 4:1-9

As in most of Paul's other epistles, the doctrinal section of the book is followed by a section which practically applies the theological truths developed to the everyday life of believers. In 4:1-9, Paul uses specific, everyday examples to illustrate how a sacrificial and spiritual mentality will manifest itself in the life of the Christian.

Exhortation to stand fast, 4:1. The transition to the section applying what has been developed in the main argument is indicated by the word Ὥστε (*Wherefore*) in 4:1. In light of the Philippians' hope of future glory in Christ and Paul's example as a man who is still pressing on to that which has not yet been attained (3:1-21), he exhorts the church to vindicate his ministry among them by continuing in the things of the Lord.

Exhortation to reconcile personal differences, 4:2-3. Paul's second application of the Christian mind to the Philippians is much more specific, addressing a personal conflict between two women in the church that had become public knowledge. Here Paul applies the instruction in 2:1-11 to the problem, exhorting the women to be of the same mind, selflessly seeking the good of the other rather than her own interests. In 4:3, he asks a pastor in Philippi to mediate the conflict in another demonstration of concern for others.

Exhortation to have an attitude of dependence on the Lord, 4:4-7. Paul's third application of what has been said is to have an attitude that is dependent on the Lord's provision and promises, not changing circumstances. Believers can rejoice at all times, no matter what the circumstances, if their joy is in the Lord and in view of His promise of future reward (4:4; cf. 3:1). They can have an attitude of obvious selflessness (τὸ ἐπιεικὲς, lit., *considerateness*), not caring about their own advancement in this life, in view of the Lord's soon return (4:5). No circumstance will produce anxiety in the mind of the Christian who commits his cares to God (4:6). God gives believers a peace of mind that transcends circumstances and He protects their minds so that they will attain the goal their heavenly reward (4:7).

Exhortation to develop the Christian mind, 4:8-9. The words Τὸ λοιπόν (*Finally*) in 4:8 indicate that 4:8-9 form the conclusion to the body of the epistle. These verses sum up how the Philippians can practically go about cultivating the Christian mind. First, in 4:8, Paul exhorts the Philippians to let their minds continually be occupied with what is good and right. Second, in 4:9, Paul commands the Philippians to simply follow the example he has presented to them in both word and deed. Verse 9 ends with a short benediction which concludes the body of the letter.

Closing Remarks, 4:10-23

The close of this epistle is structurally similar to several of Paul's other epistles in that he deals with matters concerning his mutual contacts with the recipients and his relationship with them (4:10-20), then moves to a series of salutations (4:21-22) and the benediction (4:23). However, this letter is different in that there are no problems in their relationship, and it is the Philippians' contact with Paul that is the focus.

Concerning the Philippians' gift to Paul, 4:10-20. The word δὲ (*but*) in 4:10 marks a transition from the didactic portion of the epistle to the personal topic of the monetary gift sent to Paul by the Philippians. This paragraph complements the main argument by showing how the Philippians were already demonstrating the Christian mind by thinking selflessly and sacrificially, while Paul was demonstrating the Christian mind by having an internal contentment that depended on the Lord rather than circumstances. Interestingly, Paul does not directly thank the Philippians for their gift, but rejoices in the Lord that they had remembered him in his need (4:10a). He explains that even during the long interval in which they did not have the opportunity to support him, he did not feel any deficiency, since he has learned how to be content in the Lord regardless of his economic circumstances (4:10b-13). Paul then commends them for their faithful giving to him throughout his ministry, uniquely demonstrating the selfless mindset (4:14-16). He reiterates that he is not commending them so they will send more money, but because he, too, is selflessly minded, seeking their own best interests and the heavenly reward that the spiritually minded Christian lives for (4:17). Nevertheless, he has been well supplied by their gift delivered by Epaphroditus as an offering to the Lord (4:18). Since Paul cannot repay the Philippians, he can only promise that God will supply their every need (4:19). Paul concludes the matter with a brief doxology, as the goal of what they are doing and what he is doing is the glory of God (4:20).

Salutations, 4:21-22. According to the typical form of Paul's letters, Paul sends greetings from Rome to Philippi and asks the church to greet the saints on his behalf.

Benediction, 4:23. The epistle ends with a Christian benediction typical of Paul's letters (cf. Gal 6:18; Phlm 25).

Bibliography for Philippians

There is no shortage of available commentaries on Philippians. The challenge is to identify the top two or three most helpful commentaries for one's study. Moule's commentary in the old Cambridge Bible series is one of the best. Other classic commentators include Barnes, Eadie, Ellicott, Gwynn, Lightfoot, and Vaughn. Mook has the best explanation of the *kenosis* of Christ passage. Kent is one of the more conservative modern commentators. O'Brien, Hawthorne, and Fee (NICNT) are the most detailed; among these three, O'Brien is the best and Fee is next. Bockmuehl is one of the best critical commentators. Overall, the two best commentaries on Philippians are probably Moule and O'Brien, while one may take his pick of the others depending upon the goals of his study.

Barnes, Albert. *Ephesians, Philippians and Colossians*. Notes on the New Testament, ed. Robert Frew. Reprint: Grand Rapids: Baker, 1949.

Bockmuehl, Markus N. A. *The Epistle to the Philippians*. Black's New Testament Commentary. Peabody, MA: Hendrickson, 1998.
   Note: Bockmuehl's introduction, and especially "The Purpose and Nature of the Letter" is very helpful in summarizing and critiquing the state of scholarship. He is one of the better critical commentators. He is a professor at Cambridge.

Bruce, F. F. *Philippians*. New International Biblical Commentary, ed. W. Ward Gasque. Peabody, MA: Hendrickson, 1989.
   Note: This is a republication of Bruce's 1983 commentary in the Good News Commentary series.

Constable, Thomas L. *Notes on Philippians*. 2104 ed. Sonic Light, 2014.

Daillé, Jean. *An Exposition of The Epistle of Saint Paul to the Philippians*. Translated by James Sherman. Philadelphia: Presbyterian Board of Publication, 1841.
   Note: This book was originally published in French in the mid-1600s while the author was Minister of the French Reformed Church at Charenton. It is a collection of Daillé's sermons on Philippians.

Eadie, John. *A Commentary on the Greek Text of the Epistle of Paul to the Philippians*. Edinburgh: T. & T. Clark, 1894. Reprint, Minneapolis: James and Klock, 1977.

Eastburn, Manton. *Lectures, Explanatory and Practical, on the Epistle of St. Paul to the Philippians*. New York: G. & C. & H. Carvill, 1833.

Edwards, Mark J., ed. *Galatians, Ephesians, Philippians*. Ancient Christian Commentary on Scripture, ed. Thomas C. Oden. Downers Grove, IL: InterVarsity Press, 1999.

Ellicott, Chas. J. *A Critical and Grammatical Commentary on St. Paul's Epistles to the Philippians, Colossians, and to Philemon*. Andover: Warren F. Draper, 1876.

Fee, Gordon D. *Paul's Letter to the Philippians*. New International Commentary on the New Testament, ed. Gordon D. Fee. Grand Rapids: Eerdmans, 1995.
   Note: Fee's commentary is very detailed, but he is a charismatic.

———. *Philippians*. The IVP New Testament Commentary Series, ed. Grant R. Osborne. Downers Grove, IL: InterVarsity Press, 1999.
   Note: Carson says there is no need to look at this one if you have Fee's NICNT volume.

Garland, David E. "Philippians." In *The Expositor's Bible Commentary: Revised Edition*, vol. 12, 175-261. Grand Rapids: Zondervan, 2006.

Gwynn, J. "Philippians." In *The Holy Bible with an Explanatory and Critical Commentary: New Testament*, ed. F. C. Cook, vol. 3, 579-641. New York: Charles Scribner's Sons, 1900.

Hawthorne, Gerald F., and Ralph P. Martin. *Philippians*. Rev. ed. Word Biblical Commentary, ed. Bruce M. Metzger et al., vol. 43. Nashville: Thomas Nelson, 2004.
   Note: Martin is more critical (i.e., uses higher criticism more) than Hawthorne.

Hawthorne, Gerald F. *Philippians*. Word Biblical Commentary, ed. David A. Hubbard, Glenn W. Barker, and Ralph P. Martin, vol. 43. Waco, TX: Word Books, 1983.

Hendriksen, William. *Exposition of Philippians*. New Testament Commentary. Grand Rapids: Baker, 1962.

Hutchinson, John. *Exposition of Paul's Epistle to the Philippians*. Limited Classical Reprint Library. Edinburgh: T. & T. Clark, 1887. Reprint, Minneapolis: Klock & Klock, 1985.

Kent, Homer A., Jr. "Philippians." In *Expositor's Bible Commentary*, ed. Frank E. Gaebelein et al., vol. 11, 95-159. Grand Rapids: Zondervan Publishing House, 1978.

Lenski, R. C. H. *The Interpretation of St. Paul's Epistles to the Galatians and to the Ephesians and to the Philippians*. Columbus, OH: Lutheran Book Concern, 1937.

Lightfoot, J. B. *Saint Paul's Epistle to the Philippians*. Zondervan Classic Commentary Series. London: Macmillan & Company, 1913. Reprint, Grand Rapids: Zondervan, 1953.

Lightner, Robert P. "Philippians." In *The Bible Knowledge Commentary: New Testament*, ed. John F. Walvoord and Roy B. Zuck, 647-666. Wheaton, IL: SP Publications, 1983.
   Note: Lightner is more of a theologian than an exegete.

Loh, I-Jin, and Eugene A. Nida. *A Translator's Handbook on Paul's Letter to the Philippians*. Helps for Translators. London: United Bible Societies, 1977.

Martin, Ralph P. *The Epistle of Paul to the Philippians: An Introduction and Commentary*. 1st ed. Tyndale New Testament Commentaries, ed. R. V. G. Tasker. Grand Rapids: Eerdmans, 1959.

———. *Philippians*. New Century Bible Commentary, ed. Matthew Black. Grand Rapids: Eerdmans, 1976.

———. *The Epistle of Paul to the Philippians: An Introduction and Commentary*. 2nd ed. Tyndale New Testament Commentaries, ed. Leon Morris. Grand Rapids: Eerdmans, 1987.
   Note: Martin is more sympathetic to critical views than other writers in this series.

McGee, J. Vernon. "Philippians." In *Thru the Bible with J. Vernon McGee*, vol. 5, 286-330. Nashville: Thomas Nelson, 1983.

Melick, Richard R., Jr. *Philippians, Colossians, Philemon*. New American Commentary, ed. David S. Dockery, vol. 32. Nashville: Thomas Nelson, 1991.

Note: This is a good series, but Melick is not as strong as some of the other writers.

Mook, James R. Class notes for TH702 Christology & Angelology. Capital Bible Seminary, Spring 2005.
Note: Mook has the best analysis of the kenosis of Christ, which is found on pp. 177-99.

Moule, H. C. G. *The Epistle of Paul the Apostle to the Philippians*. Cambridge Greek Testament for Schools and Colleges, ed. J. Armitage Robinson. Cambridge: Cambridge, 1897.

———. *The Epistle to the Philippians*. The Cambridge Bible for Schools and Colleges, ed. J. J. S. Perowne. Cambridge: Cambridge, 1895.
Note: Moule writes out the argument of Philippians, which is very helpful. This is an excellent commentary.

Müller, Jac. J. *The Epistles of Paul to the Philippians and to Philemon: The English Text with Introduction, Exposition and Notes*. New International Commentary on the New Testament, ed. F. F. Bruce. Grand Rapids: Eerdmans, 1955.

O'Brien, Peter T. *The Epistle to the Philippians: A Commentary on the Greek Text*. New International Greek Testament Commentary, ed. I. Howard Marshall and W. Ward Gasque. Grand Rapids: Eerdmans, 1991.

Silva, Moisés. *Philippians*. Wycliffe Exegetical Commentary, ed. Kenneth Barker. Chicago: Moody Press, 1988.

———. *Philippians*. 1st ed. Baker Exegetical Commentary on the New Testament, ed. Moisés Silva. Grand Rapids: Baker Book House, 1992.

———. *Philippians*. 2nd ed. Baker Exegetical Commentary on the New Testament, ed. Robert Yarbrough and Robert H. Stein. Grand Rapids: Baker, 2005.

Vaughn, Charles John. *Epistle to the Philippians*. Limited Classical Reprint Library. London: Macmillan and Co., 1872. Reprint, Minneapolis: Klock & Klock, 1985.

Vincent, Marvin R. *A Critical and Exegetical Commentary on the Epistles to the Philippians and to Philemon*. International Critical Commentary, ed. Samuel Rolles Driver, Alfred Plummer, and Charles Augustus Briggs. Edinburgh: T. & T. Clark, 1897.

Walvoord, John F. *Philippians: Triumph in Christ*. Chicago: Moody Press, 1971.

Interpretive Guide to Colossians

Colossians is a very didactic, content-oriented book which is aimed at refuting a theological heresy—yet it is intensely practical at the same time, since this heresy was threatening the very foundation of the Colossian church. The Person of Christ is the central theme of the book, which makes it an ideal book to study to refocus one's attention from the things of this world to the things of Christ. This book also reveals the futility of seeking spiritual growth through fleshly methods and philosophies—certainly a temptation in every generation.

Historical Background

The town of Colossae was situated in the Lycus River valley in the Roman province of Asia, not far from Laodicea and Hierapolis, and about a hundred miles east of Ephesus. The native population of the area was Phrygian, with a large number of Greek settlers. There was also a significant population of Jews in the area (cf. Josephus *Ant.* 12.147-53), who had become Hellenized by the first century B.C.[1] From an economic and political standpoint, Colossae was a relatively insignificant city, being overshadowed by its much larger neighbor Laodicea. Nevertheless, this city became a strategic battleground for the faith near the end of Paul's first Roman imprisonment, which is why he addressed an epistle to its church.

The city of Colossae was evangelized by one of Paul's associates, Epaphras (1:7), probably during Paul's three-year ministry in Ephesus (cf. Acts 19:10). Epaphras, a native Colossian who was likely converted in Ephesus and thereafter became one of Paul's companions, apparently planted the churches at nearby Laodicea and Hierapolis as well (4:12-13). Paul had not personally visited these churches (2:1), though he had met some believers from these cities elsewhere—notably, Epaphras, Philemon, and Onesimus, among others. At the time of writing, Epaphras was in prison with Paul for his Christian ministry (Col 4:12-13; Phlm 23). Various statements in the book indicate that the majority of the Colossian Christians were Gentiles who were saved out of a pagan background (1:21, 27; 2:13; 3:5-7).

The Colossian Heresy

It is evident from the contents of Colossians that the epistle was written to counteract heretical teaching in the church at Colossae. The nature of this heresy can be pieced together from Paul's warnings in 2:8-23 and the emphases of the epistle. The heresy is described as "philosophy," "vain deceit," "the tradition of men," and "the rudiments of the world" (2:8). It involved circumcision (2:11), the observance of Jewish rituals (2:16-17, 20-22), the worship of angels (2:18; cf. 2:15), self-abasement (2:18, 23), visions (2:18), and secret knowledge (2:18, 23; cf. 2:1-4). In certain Jewish sects, angels "were regarded as controlling the communication between God and man, and so needed to be placated by keeping strict legal observances."[2] Such a view of angels is commonly espoused in Pseudepigraphal literature and in the literature of the Qumran sect. However, the Colossian heresy cannot be regarded as strictly Jewish, since it was being practiced (or was in danger of being practiced) by a Christian church that was composed mainly of Gentiles who were saved out of a pagan background. On the other hand, it was not uncommon for Hellenistic Jews to adopt aspects of Greek thought in their religious practices, and there was a large Jewish community in Colossae. It therefore seems that this heresy applied Hellenistic Jewish mysticism to

---

[1] P. T. O'Brien, "Colossians, Letter to the" (in *Dictionary of Paul and His Letters*; Downers Grove: IVP, 1993), 147.

[2] O'Brien, "Colossians," 149.

Christianity. It contained some elements in common with later Gnosticism, but was more Jewish. It was ascetic, mystical, and legalistic. But one must be careful about reading the teachings of later Gnostics, such as Valentinus' series of divine eons, into Colossians.

Paul says in 2:4 that the things he wrote about Christ in 1:9–2:3 are intended to counteract the Colossian heresy, which has led some to suggest that the Colossian heresy, like later Gnosticism, attacked the Person of Christ. However, it is more likely that this heresy only implicitly denied the sufficiency and supremacy of Christ by seeking spiritual fulfillment through rituals, asceticism, and communication with angels (cf. 2:18-19). In refuting this heresy, Paul transfers to Christ all the roles attributed by the Colossian heresy to angels, legal observances, and Jewish rituals. For example, the angels who were worshipped by the mystical sect (2:18) were created by and for Christ (1:15-17), who is the Head over all principality and power (2:10), and despoiled them at the cross (2:15); all the treasures of wisdom and knowledge are hidden in Christ (2:3), not in mystical experiences (2:18); and Christ alone supplies everything that the Christian needs for life (2:19).

Thus, the Colossian heresy does not seem to have directly attacked justification by faith or the divinity of Christ, but it had implications for both. It was probably presented as a means of sanctification and spiritual growth, but implied that Christ's work was insufficient. Note that Paul's prayer in 1:9-12 assumes the justification of the Colossian Christians, but prays for their growth. The Colossian heresy was basically a mix of ascetic, mystic, and Jewish legalistic practices which were held to make the person who practiced them more spiritual.

Paul was led by the Holy Spirit to write an epistle to the church in the small town of Colossae, not just to help that individual church, but to help the church at large in subsequent generations. The Colossian heresy became very prominent in the early centuries of church history, in more developed forms, because it was the natural outgrowth of Greek or Hellenistic Jewish thought applied to Christianity. Paul's letter to the Colossian church gave a clear rebuttal to the later heresy of Gnosticism, as well as to alternative forms of the heresy at Colossae. His letter remains an antidote to heretical teaching today, for many modern false teachers have adopted aspects of Gnosticism, denigrating the Person of Christ, and laying great stress upon mystical experiences as the pathway to sanctification.

Author

As in many of Paul's other epistles, Paul and Timothy are both named as senders in the first verse, but it is clear from the personal references throughout rest of the letter that Paul is the sole author. In addition to the heading in 1:1, Paul names himself as the author in 1:23, and again in the last verse (4:18).

Though all agree that these references show that the letter claims to be Pauline, some critics have disputed the authenticity of Colossians since the mid-nineteenth century on the basis of its writing style and supposed theological differences between Colossians and the epistles accepted as genuinely Pauline by the critics. For a response to these claims, see P. T. O'Brien, "Colossians, Letter to the" (in *Dictionary of Paul and His Letters*; Downers Grove: IVP, 1993), 150-52. In brief, the vocabulary of Colossians is not significantly different from the other Pauline epistles. The style of Colossians is closer to 2 Corinthians than to Ephesians or Romans because Colossians is more emotionally charged. For example, whereas Ephesians has several very long sentences, in Colossians Paul often seems to break off in mid-sentence and begin a new thought. The claim that Paul could not have written a letter in this way is greatly exaggerated. As for the supposed theological differences, it should be noted that there are no theological *contradictions* between Colossians and other Pauline letters, only different theological *emphases* as a response to the Colossian heresy. Finally, the claim that Colossians has to be post-Pauline, because the Gnostic heresy it opposes did not develop until the second century, falters on two false assumptions: (1) it is not clear that Paul is in fact opposing a Gnostic heresy in Colossians; and (2) if the description of the Colossian heresy does in fact fit Gnosticism, this would not prove that Colossians is late, but rather that Gnosticism is early.

Positive evidence in favor of Pauline authorship is the statement in 4:18 that Paul signed the book in his own distinctive hand, which he says in 2 Thess 3:17 is the mark of authenticity in every one of his epistles. The early church would never have accepted as genuinely Pauline a letter which did not have Paul's signature on it.

Date and Occasion of Writing

Colossians was written while Paul was in prison (1:24; 4:3)—a condition that only fits his first Roman imprisonment, since he anticipates a soon release in Phlm 22, and since Rome was a common destination for runaway slaves. There are close linkages between Ephesians (Laodiceans), Colossians, and Philemon, which indicate that all three epistles were written at the same time. Tychicus delivered the letters to Laodicea and Colossae, while Onesimus delivered the intensely personal letter to Philemon. Colossians was written from Rome to Colossae early in A.D. 62, near the end of Paul's first Roman imprisonment.

The occasion of writing can be summarized as follows: as Paul was preparing to write a letter to Philemon (at Colossae) for the release of Onesimus, sending at the same time a letter to the nearby church at the large city of Laodicea, Tychicus (or perhaps someone else) came and reported the heresy in Colossae, prompting Paul to write a letter to the Colossian church as well.

Purpose and Message

Colossians was written to counteract a Hellenistic Jewish heresy in Colossae that sought to achieve sanctification through mysticism, legalism, and asceticism (cf. 2:4). The message of the book is that Jesus Christ is the Creator, Sustainer, and Lord of all, the Head of the church, the Fulfillment of the Law, the Victor over principalities and powers, the Embodiment of God's fulness, and the Source of all the treasures of wisdom and knowledge—therefore do not seek spiritual growth in the flesh; rather, live as new men in Christ.

Outline of Colossians

I. Salutation 1:1-2
II. Doctrinal: Instruction regarding the Person of Christ 1:3–2:7
    A. Paul's thanksgiving for the Colossians' faith in Christ 1:3-8
    B. Paul's desire for the Colossians' fuller knowledge of Christ 1:9-23
    C. Paul's joy in suffering for Christ on behalf of the Colossians 1:24-29
    D. Paul's struggle for the Colossians' growth in Christ 2:1-5
    E. Conclusion: Exhortation to live in Christ as you began in Christ 2:6-7
III. Polemical: Defense of the Sufficiency of Christ 2:8-23
    A. Warning against captivation by philosophy in disregard of Christ's fullness 2:8-15
    B. Warning against ensnarement by symbols in disregard of Christ's reality 2:16-17
    C. Warning against seeking to connect with angels in disconnect to Christ 2:18-19
    D. Warning against seeking sanctification through the Law in disregard of the Christian's death to the Law 2:20-23
IV. Applicational: Exhortation to Life in Christ 3:1–4:6
    A. Exhortation to set your mind on things above 3:1-4
    B. Exhortation to put away the deeds of the old man 3:5-11
    C. Exhortation to put on the deeds of the new man 3:12-17

D. Exhortation to relate to men as unto the Lord 3:18–4:1
  E. Exhortation to be witnesses of the Lord 4:2-6
V. Closing Remarks 4:7-18
  A. Commendation of Tychicus and Onesimus 4:7-9
  B. Salutations from those with Paul 4:10-14
  C. Salutations from Paul 4:15-18

Argument of Colossians

The body of the book of Colossians has a clear three-part structure, consisting of a section of doctrinal instruction concerning the Person of Christ (1:3–2:7), a polemical section defending the sufficiency of Christ (2:8-23), and an applicational section exhorting the Colossian Christians to the proper manner of life in Christ (3:1–4:6). The body is prefaced by an epistolary salutation (1:1-2), and is followed by an epistolary conclusion (4:7-18).

Salutation, 1:1-2

The letter to the church at Colossae begins with a typical, brief epistolary salutation (1:1-2).

Doctrinal: Instruction regarding the Person of Christ, 1:3–2:7

Paul opens the body of the book by thanking God for his readers' faith in Christ, and the resulting love of the brethren which they had demonstrated (1:3-8). Paul is setting them up for the argument that their faith in Christ is essentially incompatible with fleshly means of sanctification. After thanking God for the Colossians' salvation, Paul informs them how he desires their spiritual progress through growth in spiritual wisdom and understanding, especially in the knowledge of Christ (1:9-23). This paragraph contains rich doctrinal truths which include some of the strongest affirmations of the supremacy of Christ in all of Scripture. Paul then alludes to his present condition as a prisoner, and speaks of his joy in suffering for Christ on behalf of the Colossians, with the aim of making them perfect in Christ (1:24-29). Paul reveals his great struggle—through prayer and otherwise—for the Colossian and Laodicean Christians, that they would grow in knowledge of Christ, rather than being deceived through crafty speech (2:1-5). Paul concludes the section by stating the point of what he is saying, which is that the Colossians are to live the Christian life the same way they began it, namely, through Christ Jesus the Lord (2:6-7).

Polemical: Defense of the Sufficiency of Christ, 2:8-23

In 2:8-23, Paul uses the reality of Christ's supremacy to challenge the Colossians to renounce the effort to achieve sanctification through fleshly means. The Colossians should not be captivated by vain philosophy and human traditions, since all of God's fullness dwells in Christ, who removed the curse of the Law from us and despoiled the principalities and powers (2:8-15). Jewish observances are merely a shadow of Christ's reality (2:16-17). Worshipping angels and glorying in visions are fleshly endeavors, which, far from connecting the believer with spiritual power, actually result in a disconnect from Christ, who is the only source of the Christian's spiritual nourishment (2:18-19). Since the Colossians died with Christ from the ordinances of the Law, it makes no sense that they would go back to them, for they only contain an outward show of wisdom, and do not produce true righteousness (2:20-23).

Applicational: Exhortation to Life in Christ, 3:1–4:6

Having given the negative exhortation, Paul now turns to the positive in 3:1–4:6. Since the Colossians have been raised and seated with Christ, they ought to set their minds on heavenly things, not on the ordinances of men (3:1-4). As new men in Christ, they ought to put to death the deeds of the flesh, and not to put any stock in the supposed spiritual superiority of one race over another (3:5-11). Having put away the deeds of the old man, they are to put on the works of the new man in Christ (3:12-17). All human relationships are to be governed by one's relationship to the Lord, for whom we are really working, and to whom we are ultimately accountable (3:18–4:1). These principles are also to govern our relationship with the world, to whom we are be witnesses for the Lord (4:2-6).

Closing Remarks, 4:7-18

As Paul brings the letter to a close, he commends the messengers he has sent with the letter, Tychicus and Onesimus (4:7-9). He then sends greetings from those who were with him (4:10-14). He concludes the letter by greeting the church personally, and giving closing personal instructions (4:15-18).

Bibliography for Colossians

Abbott, T. K. *A Critical and Exegetical Commentary on the Epistles to the Ephesians and to the Colossians*. International Critical Commentary. Edinburgh: T. & T. Clark, 1897.

Alexander, W. "Colossians." In *The Holy Bible with an Explanatory and Critical Commentary: New Testament*, ed. F. C. Cook, vol. 3, 643-85. New York: Charles Scribner's Sons, 1900.

Barnes, Albert. *Ephesians, Philippians and Colossians*. Notes on the New Testament, ed. Robert Frew. Reprint: Grand Rapids: Baker, 1949.

Barth, Markus and Helmut Blanke. *Colossians: A New Translation with Introduction and Commentary*. Translated by Astrid B. Beck. Anchor Bible, vol. 34B. New York: Doubleday, 1994.

Bruce, F. F. *The Epistles to the Colossians, to Philemon, and to the Ephesians*. New International Commentary on the New Testament. Grand Rapids: Eerdmans, 1984.

Carson, Herbert M. *The Epistles of Paul to the Colossians and Philemon: An Introduction and Commentary*. Tyndale New Testament Commentaries. Grand Rapids: Eerdmans, 1960.

Constable, Thomas L. *Notes on Colossians*. 2104 ed. Sonic Light, 2014.

Dunn, James D. G. *The Epistles to the Colossians and to Philemon: A Commentary on the Greek Text*. New International Greek Testament Commentary. Grand Rapids: Eerdmans, 1996.

Eadie, John. *A Commentary on the Greek Text of the Epistle of Paul to the Colossians*. New York: Robert Carter, 1856.

Ellicott, Chas. J. *A Critical and Grammatical Commentary on St. Paul's Epistles to the Philippians, Colossians, and to Philemon*. Andover: Warren F. Draper, 1876.

Geisler, Norman L. "Colossians." In *The Bible Knowledge Commentary: New Testament*, ed. John F. Walvoord and Roy B. Zuck, 667-86. Wheaton, IL: SP Publications, 1983.

Harris, Murray J. *Colossians & Philemon*. Exegetical Guide to the Greek New Testament. Grand Rapids: Eerdmans, 1991.

Lightfoot, J. B. *Saint Paul's Epistles to the Colossians and to Philemon: A Revised Text with Introductions, Notes, and Dissertations*. 9th ed. London: Macmillan, 1890.
   Note: I think this is really only the third revised edition, and the ninth printing. The third edition would be dated to 1879.

MacArthur, John, Jr. *Colossians & Philemon*. The MacArthur New Testament Commentary. Chicago: Moody Press, 1992.

MacLaren, Alexander. *The Epistles of St. Paul to the Colossians and Philemon*. 2nd ed. The Expositor's Bible, ed. W. Robertson Nicoll. London: Hodder and Stoughton, 1888.

McGee, J. Vernon. *1 Corinthians–Revelation*. Volume 5 of *Thru the Bible with J. Vernon McGee*. Nashville: Thomas Nelson, 1983.

Melick, Richard R., Jr. *Philippians, Colossians, Philemon*. New American Commentary, ed. David S. Dockery, vol. 32. Nashville: Thomas Nelson, 1991.

Moo, Douglas J. *The Letters to the Colossians and to Philemon*. Pillar New Testament Commentary. Grand Rapids: Eerdmans, 2008.

Moule, H. C. G. *The Epistles to the Colossians and to Philemon: with Introduction and Notes*. The Cambridge Bible for Schools and Colleges. Cambridge: Cambridge, 1893.

O'Brien, Peter T. *Colossians, Philemon*. Word Biblical Commentary 44. Waco, TX: Word Books, 1982.

Rutherfurd, John. *St. Paul's Epistles to Colossæ and Laodicea*. Edinburgh: T. & T. Clark, 1908.

Still, Todd D. "Colossians." In *The Expositor's Bible Commentary: Revised Edition*, ed. Tremper Longman III and David E. Garland, vol. 12, 263-360. Grand Rapids: Zondervan, 2006.

Vaughan, Curtis. "Colossians." In *Expositor's Bible Commentary*, ed. Frank E. Gaebelein et al., vol. 11, 161-226. Grand Rapids: Zondervan Publishing House, 1978.

———. *Colossians and Philemon*. Bible Study Commentary. Grand Rapids: Zondervan, 1980.

Wilson, R. McL. *A Critical and Exegetical Commentary on Colossians and Philemon*. International Critical Commentary. London: T & T Clark, 2005.

Witherington III, Ben. *The Letters to Philemon, the Colossians, and the Ephesians: A Socio-Rhetorical Commentary on the Captivity Epistles*. Grand Rapids: Eerdmans, 2007.

Wright, N. T. *The Epistles of Paul to the Colossians and to Philemon: An Introduction and Commentary*. Tyndale New Testament Commentaries. Grand Rapids: Eerdmans, 1986.

Interpretive Guide to 1 Thessalonians

First Thessalonians is a very warm, personal, and tender letter which gives basic instruction for new believers. It provides unique insight into the heart of the apostle Paul for a young church, and reveals his manner of dealing with baby Christians. Both of the Thessalonian epistles are rich in eschatological teaching—teaching which is considered by many today as best avoided by immature believers, but which Paul considered essential to their grounding in the faith (cf. 2 Thess 2:5). When Paul preached at Thessalonica, the Jews there accused him of proclaiming the reign of a new King, Jesus (Acts 17:7), and there is a reference to Christ's coming in every chapter of 1 Thessalonians (1:10; 2:19; 3:13; 4:13-18; 5:23).

Historical Background

Thessalonica was a populous city enjoying good fortune throughout most of the Hellenistic and Roman period. It was founded (at or near the site of Therma ["hot springs"]) at the head of the Thermaic Gulf (now called the Gulf of Salonika) about 315 B.C. by Cassander, formerly a general of Alexander the Great and, when the city was founded, king of Macedonia. As an important military and commercial port, it became the principal city of Macedonia. It was designated the capital of one of the four administrative districts into which Rome divided Macedonia in 168 B.C. In 146 B.C. it became the capital of the now-unified province of Macedonia. In the same year the Egnatian Way, connecting Asia Minor with the Adriatic Sea (and Rome beyond the Adriatic), was put through. It was on this road that Paul and his coworkers traveled from Philippi to Thessalonica. . . . In return for its support of Antony and Octavian, Thessalonica became a free city in 42 B.C. It remained the most important and populous city of Macedonia into the third or fourth century A.D. As Salonika it is the second largest city of modern Greece and still an important seaport.[1]

Paul and Silas planted the church at Thessalonica on Paul's second missionary journey, as recorded in Acts 17:1-9 (cf. 1 Thess 2:1-12). Paul and Silas travelled to Thessalonica after they were beaten and cast into prison in Philippi, then released. In only three weeks of teaching and preaching, "some" of the Jews were persuaded, "a great multitude" of the devout Greeks, and "not a few" leading women (Acts 17:4). Paul's ministry in Thessalonica ended abruptly when the Jews instigated a riot, forcing him to leave with Silas and Timothy under cover of darkness and travel to Berea. In Phil 4:15-16, Paul states that the Philippian church sent him monetary support twice while he was in Thessalonica, while in 1 Thess 2:9 and 2 Thess 3:7-9, Paul states that he and his ministry team also worked to support themselves while they ministered.

Author

Paul, Silvanus (Silas), and Timothy are all named as senders in 1:1, but it is clear that Paul took the lead role in the composition of 1 Thessalonians. Paul refers to himself in the first person singular three times (2:18; 3:5; 5:27) and refers to Timothy in the third person twice (3:2, 6). The reason that Silas and Timothy are named as co-senders is that they were Paul's ministry partners on his second missionary journey, and had helped plant the church in Thessalonica. Although they were not directly the authors of the epistle, they were with Paul when he wrote, and were in agreement with what he was writing.

---

[1] J. W. Simpson Jr., "Thessalonians, Letters to the" (in *Dictionary of Paul and His Letters*; Downers Grove: IVP, 1993), 933.

Even within the world of liberal scholarship, few question the authenticity of 1 Thessalonians. There are abundant personal details in the book which correspond perfectly with Paul's travels in the book of Acts, and the language and structure of the book are thoroughly Pauline.

Date and Occasion of Writing

Paul states in 2:17 that he wrote this epistle within a short time after he had planted the church at Thessalonica. Since Paul had only been able to minister in Thessalonica for three weeks (Acts 17:2), he sought to revisit the city quickly in order to give further instruction to these baby Christians, but Satan had hindered him twice (2:18). Thus, after Paul had been driven out of Berea and had fled to Athens (Acts 17:10-34), he sent Timothy back to Thessalonica in order to reassure the church concerning Paul's afflictions, and to find out whether the new believers were remaining strong in their faith (3:1-5). Timothy returned to Paul with a good report (3:6-8), but Paul still longed to see the Thessalonians in order to supply that which was lacking in their faith (3:9-10). Since he was temporarily unable to return to Thessalonica in person to instruct this young church, he wrote an epistle to them in order to give them the communication he wished he could deliver in person.

The occasion for the writing of 1 Thessalonians was the report Timothy brought back to Paul on the state of the church (3:6). Paul indicates in 1:7-8 that he had already conducted evangelistic work in the region of Achaia, where Corinth and Athens were located, by the time of writing. According to Acts 18:5, Timothy came to Paul from Macedonia early in Paul's one and a half year ministry in Corinth (cf. Acts 18:11), which terminated around the time of Gallio's brief stint as proconsul (July 1–Sept. ?, 51). First Thessalonians must therefore have been written in the spring of A.D. 50.

Purpose and Message

Paul's purpose in writing 1 Thessalonians was to shore up the faith of young Christians in a church he had recently planted. It is apparent from Acts 17:5-9, 13 and 1 Thess 2:14 that the Thessalonian believers faced intense opposition because of their Christian faith. In addition, many in the church had been saved out of a pagan background (1:9), and needed a better grounding in Christian doctrine. The message of 1 Thessalonians is, I am encouraged by your example of faith, and I have great affection for you and joy because of you, though I am unable to visit you immediately; thus, I exhort you to continue to grow in your Christian faith by walking in a manner that pleases the Lord, and by comforting one another with the hope of resurrection life with Christ. I know that God will direct our way to you, and that He will sanctify you and complete your salvation.

Outline of 1 Thessalonians

I. Salutation 1:1
II. Personal: Paul's Desire for the Thessalonians' Growth 1:2–3:13
    A. Thanksgiving for the Thessalonians' example of faith 1:2-10
    B. Paul's example of faith 2:1-12
    C. Thanksgiving for the Thessalonians' steadfastness 2:13-16
    D. Paul's longing for the Thessalonians 2:17-20
    E. Timothy's visit and report 3:1-10
    F. Concluding doxology 3:11-13
III. Hortatory: Paul's Directions for the Thessalonians' Growth 4:1–5:24
    A. Exhortation to moral purity 4:1-8
    B. Encouragement to love of the brethren 4:9-12

C. Comfort concerning the resurrection 4:13-18
   D. Reminder concerning the second advent 5:1-11
   E. Directions regarding conduct in the church 5:12-24
IV. Closing Remarks 5:25-28

Argument of 1 Thessalonians

First Thessalonians opens with a standard epistolary salutation (1:1), and closes with a typical epistolary conclusion (5:25-28). Two major divisions are easily recognized in the body of the book: 1:2–3:13, which is a personal section that concerns Paul's relationship to the Thessalonians, and 4:1–5:24, which is doctrinal and hortatory. Both major divisions are concluded by a doxology.

Salutation, 1:1

First Thessalonians begins with a typical salutation that names Paul and his two primary coworkers on his second missionary journey (1:1).

Personal: Paul's Desire for the Thessalonians' Growth, 1:2–3:13

The personal section of the epistle, in which Paul expresses his joy for the Thessalonians' faith and his desire for their continued growth, follows a general chronological order, from Paul's thanksgiving for the Thessalonians' faith (1:2-10), to a recollection of his ministry among them (2:1-12), to a thanksgiving for their continued steadfastness (2:13-16), to Paul's frustration in not having been able to revisit the church (2:17-20), to a summary of Timothy's visit to Thessalonica and return (3:1-10). This section is long by necessity, so Paul can explain how much he cares about the Thessalonian church, and what has transpired since his brief time among them.

Paul opens the body of the epistle by thanking God for the example of the Thessalonians' faith (1:2-10). He then encourages these baby Christians by reminding them of the faithfulness of himself and his ministry partners, who are examples to be emulated (2:1-12). After recalling his ministry among the Thessalonians, Paul thanks God that they remained steadfast in their faith even in the face of persecution (2:13-16). He then relates how he earnestly longs to be with them again, but that Satan hindered him twice (2:17-20). Because of his tender concern for the Thessalonian church, Paul sent Timothy back to Thessalonica in his place, both to reassure the church concerning Paul's afflictions, and to find out whether the new believers were remaining strong in their faith (3:1-5). Timothy returned to Paul with an encouraging report (3:6-8), but Paul still longed to see the Thessalonians in person in order to perfect that which was lacking in their faith (3:9-10). Paul closes the personal section of the book with a doxology in which he prays for his return to Thessalonica and for the continued growth of the Thessalonian believers (3:11-13).

Hortatory: Paul's Directions for the Thessalonians' Growth, 4:1–5:24

The hortatory section of the book opens with a thesis statement in which Paul urges the believers to continue to progress in the Christian life as they had begun it (4:1). He first exhorts the Thessalonians to take care to be morally pure (4:2-8)—probably not because sexual sin was a greater problem in the Thessalonian church than elsewhere, but because this is the sort of general exhortation that Paul would give to any group of young Christians. Paul follows this exhortation with an encouragement to love of the brethren—a quality which the Thessalonians had already demonstrated, but in which Paul wished for them to abound more and more (4:9-12). Paul then comforts the church, and instructs them to comfort each other, by instructing them concerning our hope of resurrection at the rapture of the church (4:13-18).² Paul then reminds the Thessalonians about the second advent, of which he had already given them instruction, and calls the Thessalonians to walk in accordance with their calling as those destined for salvation in the day when the Lord judges the world (5:1-11). This is followed by a series of short admonitions exhorting the Thessalonians to proper conduct in the church (5:12-22). The hortatory section of the book is concluded by a short doxology (5:23-24).

Closing Remarks, 5:25-28

Paul concludes 1 Thessalonians with closing personal exhortations (5:25-27) and a short benediction (5:28).

---

² Paul says the Thessalonians were "ignorant" of the rapture (4:13), which indicates that they, like the Corinthians (1 Cor 15:12, 18), did not know that dead believers would be raised. This is interesting in light of 1:10 and 5:1-2, which state that the Thessalonians were fully aware of apostolic teaching concerning the second coming of Christ, and that they were in fact waiting for His coming. Thus, they correctly understood that living believers would be saved alive at the second coming, but they did not know what would happen to those who died beforehand. Paul teaches them about the rapture because that is when all Church Age believers will be raised. Paul specifies that it is only those who are "in Jesus" (4:14) who will be raised at the rapture, since OT saints are raised at the end of the tribulation (so Dan 12:1-3). This is an event in which both living and dead believers will be raised (4:15), which means it cannot be identical with the second advent—a posttribulational rapture would leave no one in mortal bodies to walk into the kingdom. In the coming which Paul describes, believers meet the Lord in the air (4:16-17), in contrast to the second coming, in which the saints emerge from heaven to return to the earth with Christ (Rom 8:19; Col 3:4; 1 Thess 3:13; Jude 14-15; Rev 19:14).

Bibliography for the Thessalonian Epistles

Hiebert is the most helpful of the modern commentators, and probably the best commentator overall.

Alexander, W. "1 Thessalonians." In *The Holy Bible with an Explanatory and Critical Commentary: New Testament*, ed. F. C. Cook, vol. 3, 687-731. New York: Charles Scribner's Sons, 1900.

———. "2 Thessalonians." In *The Holy Bible with an Explanatory and Critical Commentary: New Testament*, ed. F. C. Cook, vol. 3, 704, 732-48. New York: Charles Scribner's Sons, 1900.

Barnes, Albert. *Thessalonians, Timothy, Titus, and Philemon*. Notes on the New Testament, ed. Robert Frew. Reprint: Grand Rapids: Baker, 1949.

Beale, G. K. *1-2 Thessalonians*. IVP New Testament Commentary Series. Downers Grove, IL: InterVarsity Press, 2003.

Best, Ernest. *A Commentary on the First and Second Epistles to the Thessalonians*. Harper's New Testament Commentaries. Peabody, MA: Hendrickson, 1986.

Bruce, F. F. *1 & 2 Thessalonians*. Word Biblical Commentary, vol. 45. Waco: Word, 1982.

Constable, Thomas L. "1 Thessalonians." In *The Bible Knowledge Commentary: New Testament*, ed. John F. Walvoord and Roy B. Zuck, 687-711. Wheaton, IL: SP Publications, 1983.

———. "2 Thessalonians." In *The Bible Knowledge Commentary: New Testament*, ed. John F. Walvoord and Roy B. Zuck, 713-25. Wheaton, IL: SP Publications, 1983.

Constable, Thomas L. *Notes on 1 Thessalonians*. 2104 ed. Sonic Light, 2014.

Constable, Thomas L. *Notes on 2 Thessalonians*. 2104 ed. Sonic Light, 2014.

Couch, Mal. *The Hope of Christ's Return: Premillennial Commentary on 1 & 2 Thessalonians*. Chattanooga, TN: AMG Publishers, 2001.

Demarest, Gary W. *1, 2 Thessalonians, 1, 2 Timothy, Titus*. The Communicator's Commentary, vol. 9. Word: Waco, 1984.

Eadie, John. *A Commentary on the Greek Text of the Epistle of Paul to the Thessalonians*. Edited by William Young. London: MacMillan, 1877.

Ellicott, C. J. *A Critical and Grammatical Commentary on St Paul's Epistles to the Thessalonians, with a Revised Translation*. London: Parker, Son, and Bourn: 1862.

Findlay, George G. *The Epistles to the Thessalonians: With Introduction, Notes and Map*. Cambridge Bible for Schools and Colleges. Cambridge: Cambridge, 1891.

Frame, James Everett. *A Critical and Exegetical Commentary on the Epistles of St. Paul to the Thessalonians*. International Critical Commentary. Edinburgh: T. & T. Clark, 1912.

Furnish, Victor Paul. *1 Thessalonians, 2 Thessalonians*. Abingdon New Testament Commentaries. Nashville: Abingdon, 2007.

Gaebelein, A. C. *The First and Second Epistles to the Thessalonians: A Complete Analysis of First and Second Thessalonians with Annotations*. New York: Our Hope, n. d.

Green, Gene L. *The Letters to the Thessalonians*. Pillar New Testament Commentary. Grand Rapids: Eerdmans, 2002.

Hiebert, D. Edmond. *The Thessalonian Epistles: A Call to Readiness*. Chicago: Moody Press, 1971.

Lillie, John. *Lectures on the Epistles of Paul to the Thessalonians*. Edinburgh: Oliphant, Anderson, & Ferrier, 1881.

MacArthur, John, Jr. *1 & 2 Thessalonians*. MacArthur New Testament Commentary. Chicago: Moody Press, 2002.

Marshall, I. Howard. *1 and 2 Thessalonians*. New Century Bible Commentary. Grand Rapids: Eerdmans, 1983.

Martin, D. Michael. *1, 2 Thessalonians*. New American Commentary, vol. 33. Nashville: Broadman & Holman, 1995.

McGee, J. Vernon. *1 Corinthians–Revelation*. Volume 5 of *Thru the Bible with J. Vernon McGee*. Nashville: Thomas Nelson, 1983.

Milligan, George. *St Paul's Epistles to the Thessalonians: The Greek Text with Introduction and Notes*. New York: MacMillan, 1908.

Morris, Leon. *The Epistles of Paul to the Thessalonians: An Introduction and Commentary*. 2nd ed. Tyndale New Testament Commentaries. Grand Rapids: Eerdmans, 1984.

———. *The First and Second Epistles to the Thessalonians*. Rev. ed. New International Commentary on the New Testament. Grand Rapids: Eerdmans, 1991.

Plummer, Alfred. *A Commentary on St. Paul's First Epistle to the Thessalonians*. London: Robert Scott, 1918.

———. *A Commentary on St. Paul's Second Epistle to the Thessalonians*. London: Robert Scott, 1918.

Richard, Earl J. *First and Second Thessalonians*. Sacra Pagina Series, vol. 11, ed. Daniel J. Harrington. Collegeville, MN : Liturgical Press, 1995.

Thomas, Robert L. "1 Thessalonians." In *Expositor's Bible Commentary*, ed. Frank E. Gaebelein et al., vol. 11, 227-98. Grand Rapids: Zondervan Publishing House, 1978.

———. "1 Thessalonians." In *The Expositor's Bible Commentary: Revised Edition*, ed. Tremper Longman III and David E. Garland, vol. 12, 361-439. Grand Rapids: Zondervan, 2006.

———. "2 Thessalonians." In *Expositor's Bible Commentary*, ed. Frank E. Gaebelein et al., vol. 11, 299-337. Grand Rapids: Zondervan Publishing House, 1978.

———. "2 Thessalonians." In *The Expositor's Bible Commentary: Revised Edition*, ed. Tremper Longman III and David E. Garland, vol. 12, 441-85. Grand Rapids: Zondervan, 2006.

Vine, W. E. with C. F. Hogg. *Vine's Expository Commentary on 1 & 2 Thessalonians*. Nashville: Thomas Nelson, 1997.

Walvoord, John F. *The Thessalonian Epistles*. Findlay, OH: Dunham, 1955.

Wanamaker, Charles A. *The Epistles to the Thessalonians: A Commentary on the Greek Text*. New International Greek Testament Commentary. Grand Rapids: Eerdmans, 1990.

Witherington, Ben III. *1 and 2 Thessalonians: A Socio-Rhetorical Commentary*. Grand Rapids: Eerdmans, 2006.
> **Note:** Witherington has done a huge amount of research in the primary sources and secondary literature, but also has a tendency to overstate his case, and to force everything into his categories. Witherington is Wesleyan, and argues that believers can lose their salvation. Posttribulational. Interprets the text by backgrounds.

Interpretive Guide to 2 Thessalonians

Second Thessalonians is a warm and encouraging letter from the apostle Paul to a church he had recently planted on his second missionary journey. Paul's purpose is not just to encourage the young Christians of Thessalonica, but also to gently correct problems that had developed in their church, and to strengthen and comfort the church through these corrections. This short epistle is tightly packed with great doctrinal truths, especially concerning end time events and church discipline procedures.

Author

Paul, Silvanus (Silas), and Timothy, the ministry team on Paul's second missionary journey, are all named as senders in 1:1, but it is clear that Paul took the lead role in the composition of 2 Thessalonians. Paul refers to himself in the first person singular in 2:5, and he personally signs the letter in 3:17-18.

Some critical scholars deny the authenticity of 2 Thessalonians, but their arguments are generally recognized as far from compelling. Some say that 2 Thessalonians is too similar to 1 Thessalonians to be authentic, because Paul supposedly would not write two similar epistles close in time to each other. Others highlight differences between the two epistles, claiming that 2 Thessalonians is cold and 1 Thessalonians warm, and that 2 Thessalonians contains different teaching on the second coming than 1 Thessalonians. However, these differences are not contradictions, but are merely different emphases in response to different situations. The difference in Paul's tone between the two epistles is greatly exaggerated by some; in fact he is warm in 2 Thessalonians as well. With regard to the similarities, these would seem to be evidence of the authenticity of 2 Thessalonians, since it is entirely plausible that Paul would have to write a follow-up letter to the Thessalonian church, just as he later wrote two letters to the Corinthian church. Finally, it is hard to see how 2 Thessalonians could be a successful forgery when Paul specifically says he wrote the last two verses with his own distinctive hand in order to authenticate the letter to the recipients (2 Thess 3:17-18). With so many other Pauline epistles available for comparison, the early church certainly would have known Paul's handwriting, and would have rejected this epistle if the handwriting was not Paul's. Pauline authorship of 2 Thessalonians was never questioned by the early church, and is directly affirmed in the writings of many early fathers.

Date and Occasion of Writing

Various internal features of 2 Thessalonians indicate that it is a sequel to 1 Thessalonians: (1) The senders of the both epistles are the same—Paul, Silvanus, and Timothy—and it is known that these three men formed Paul's ministry team on his second missionary journey. (2) The problems addressed in 2 Thessalonians are a natural development from the situations spoken of in 1 Thessalonians. Paul's admonition in 1 Thess 4:11 to "be quiet, and to do your own business, and to work with your hands" apparently reflected an opposite tendency at Thessalonica, and, according to 2 Thess 3:11, Paul subsequently heard that some Thessalonian believers were refusing to work. Also, Paul's instruction regarding the rapture and the second coming in 1 Thess 4:13–5:11 was apparently exploited by false teachers, who, according to 2 Thess 2:1-2, wrote false epistles in Paul's name claiming that the Lord was just about to return. (3) The entire first half of 1 Thessalonians (1:2–3:13) rehearses the history of Paul's relationship to the Thessalonian church, whereas 2 Thessalonians says nothing about this history, and therefore seems to assume the background of this personal communication given in 1 Thessalonians.

Since 2 Thessalonians was evidently written shortly after 1 Thessalonians, it must have been composed late in A.D. 50. The place of writing was Corinth, during Paul's second missionary journey. The occasion of writing, as has already been indicated, was a report Paul heard of problems in the

Thessalonian church concerning false teaching on the Lord's return, and concerning believers who were refusing to work. This false teaching was promulgated, in part, by a spurious epistle or epistles claiming Pauline authority.

Purpose and Message

The purpose of 2 Thessalonians was to encourage the Thessalonian believers to remain steadfast in their faith by correcting misinformation they had received regarding the day of the Lord, and by lovingly disciplining brothers who refused to work. The message of 2 Thessalonians is, remain steadfast in your faith by being encouraged in the midst of persecution, by not believing claims that the day of the Lord is imminent, and by working to meet your own needs.

Outline of 2 Thessalonians

I. Salutation 1:1-2
II. Encouragement in the Midst of Persecution 1:3-12
III. Response to False Teaching concerning the Day of the Lord 2:1-17
    A. Refutation of the imminence of the second advent 2:1-12
    B. Exhortation to doctrinal steadfastness 2:13-15
    C. Prayer for comfort and establishment 2:16-17
IV. Exhortation to Obedience 3:1-16
    A. Expression of mutual confidence in the Lord's establishment 3:1-5
    B. Exhortation to withdraw from disorderly brothers 3:6-15
    C. Prayer for God's peace and presence 3:16
V. Closing Remarks 3:17-18

Argument of 2 Thessalonians

The body of 2 Thessalonians is easily divided into three parts, following the chapter divisions. The second and third divisions are marked by a concluding doxology.

Salutation, 1:1-2

Second Thessalonians opens with a typical epistolary salutation which names Paul and his two primary ministry partners on his second missionary journey (1:1-2).

Encouragement in the Midst of Persecution, 1:3-12

Paul begins the body of the epistle, as is typical, with a thanksgiving to God for his readers (1:3-12). However, Paul relates this thanksgiving to the problems in Thessalonica regarding false teachers, and false teaching on eschatology. Paul states that the opposition the believers are experiencing is merely part of God's plan to increase the judgment of the wicked and the reward of the righteous (1:3-6). Paul then describes how both believers and unbelievers will be recompensed in the day when the Lord returns to judge the world (1:7-10), and prays for the Thessalonians' growth in the Christian faith (1:11-12).

Response to False Teaching concerning the Day of the Lord, 2:1-17

The thanksgiving leads directly into a refutation of false teaching concerning the day of the Lord (2:1-17). The Thessalonians had been disturbed by false teachers claiming apostolic authority, who were teaching that the second advent (= the day of the Lord) was imminent (2:1-2).[1] Paul affirms that the second coming cannot be imminent, since it will be preceded by an unprecedented worldwide rebellion against God, leading up to the ultimate expression of evil at the end of the age through the revelation of the man of sin (= the antichrist) and the termination of the Holy Spirit's special ministry of convicting the world of sin, righteousness, and judgment (2:3-10; cf. John 16:7-11; Acts 14:16; 17:30). Since all unbelievers will have heard the gospel by the midpoint of the tribulation (cf. Rev 14:1-8), all who still refuse to repent by the midpoint will be judicially hardened, accepting the antichrist's mark and sealing their eternal fate (cf. Rev 14:9-12). God's purpose in allowing the antichrist to come to power, and his purpose in removing the Holy Spirit's restraining influence, is to ensure the judgment of those who refused to believe, and also to lead the world to the fullest possible expression of wickedness so as to force Him to judge and leave no question as to the justice of the judgment (2:11-12). After explaining why the second advent is not imminent, Paul then encourages and exhorts the Thessalonian believers to doctrinal steadfastness (2:13-15). Paul closes the section regarding the day of the Lord by praying for the comfort and establishment of the Thessalonian believers (2:16-17).

Exhortation to Obedience, 3:1-16

In 3:1-5, Paul transitions to the final topic of the epistle by requesting prayer for himself and his coworkers (3:1-2), then by expressing confidence that the Lord will establish and protect the Thessalonian believers as well, as they follow apostolic teaching (3:3-5). Paul proceeds to command the Thessalonian believers to withdraw from disorderly brothers, referring primarily to people he had heard about who were able to work but refused to do so, though he might also have had in mind those who were promulgating false teaching regarding the Lord's return (3:6-15). Paul closes the exhortation to obedience with a prayer for God's peace and presence with the Thessalonian believers (3:16).

Closing Remarks, 3:17-18

Second Thessalonians closes in typical epistolary fashion, with the added note that Paul signs every one of his epistles to verify their authenticity, given the circulation of spurious letters in his name (3:17-18; cf. 2:2).

Bibliography

For a bibliography of the Thessalonian epistles, see the Interpretive Guide to 1 Thessalonians.

---

[1] Probably these false teachers were teaching a posttribulational rapture—they were probably denying the tribulation period outright—since that is the only way the second coming could be imminent without the rapture having occurred.

Interpretive Guide to 1 Timothy

First and Second Timothy and Titus are collectively known as the Pastoral Epistles, since they are epistles written to pastors, rather than to churches. These letters were composed in the final years of Paul's life, and they represent the apostle's instructions to the next generation of church leaders. First Timothy and Titus are official letters, stating church policy, while 2 Timothy is intensely personal. Together, the three Pastoral Epistles contain the most specific NT instruction regarding the operation of the local church and the calling of the pastor.

Historical Background to the Pastoral Epistles

The events and travels in Paul's ministry which he notes in the Pastoral Epistles (1 & 2 Timothy, Titus) do not fit into the historical narratives of Acts, and therefore must have occurred later. Since the book of Acts ends when Paul was released from his first Roman imprisonment in the spring of A.D. 62, Paul's subsequent activities must be pieced together from various statements made in the Pastoral Epistles. The difficulty of doing so shows how blessed we are to have the historical background in Acts in order to make sense of historical references in Paul's other epistles. The relevant biblical data is presented below, followed by an attempted solution.

Historical or geographical references in Titus:
- 1:5: *For this cause left I thee in Crete, that thou shouldest set in order the things that were wanting, and appoint elders in every city, as I gave thee charge . . . .*
- 3:12: *When I shall send Artemas unto thee, or Tychicus, give diligence to come unto me to Nicopolis: for there I have determined to winter.*

Historical or geographical references in 1 Timothy:
- 1:3: *As I exhorted thee to tarry at Ephesus, when I was going into Macedonia, that thou mightest charge certain men not to teach a different doctrine . . . .*
- 3:14-15: *These things write I unto thee, hoping to come unto thee shortly; but if I tarry long, that thou mayest know how men ought to behave themselves in the house of God, which is the church of the living God, the pillar and ground of the truth.*
- 4:13: *Till I come, give heed to reading, to exhortation, to teaching.*

Historical or geographical references in 2 Timothy:
- 1:15: *This thou knowest, that all that are in Asia turned away from me; of whom are Phygelus and Hermogenes.*
- 1:16-18: *The Lord grant mercy unto the house of Onesiphorus: for he oft refreshed me, and was not ashamed of my chain; but, when he was in Rome, he sought me diligently, and found me (the Lord grant unto him to find mercy of the Lord in that day); and in how many things he ministered at Ephesus, thou knowest very well.*
- 4:9-10: *Give diligence to come shortly unto me: for Demas forsook me, having loved this present world, and went to Thessalonica; Crescens to Galatia, Titus to Dalmatia.*
- 4:11: *Only Luke is with me. Take Mark, and bring him with thee; for he is useful to me for ministering.*
- 4:12: *But Tychicus I sent to Ephesus.*
- 4:13: *The cloak that I left at Troas with Carpus, bring when thou comest, and the books, especially the parchments.*

- 4:14-15: *Alexander the coppersmith did me much harm: the Lord will render to him according to his works: of whom do thou also beware; for he greatly withstood our words.*
- 4:20: *Erastus remained at Corinth: but Trophimus I left at Miletus sick.*
- 4:21: *Give diligence to come before winter.*

References to Paul's intent to visit Spain:
- Rom 15:24: *. . . whensoever I go unto Spain (for I hope to see you in my journey, and to be brought on my way thitherward by you, if first in some measure I shall have been satisfied with your company) . . . .*
- Rom 15:28: *When therefore I have accomplished this, and have sealed to them this fruit, I will go on by you unto Spain.*

References to Paul's release (or anticipated release) after his first imprisonment:
- Acts 28:30-31: *And he remained two whole years in his own rented quarters, and welcomed all that went in unto him, preaching the kingdom of God, and teaching the things concerning the Lord Jesus Christ with all boldness, unhindered.*
- Phil 1:25-26: *And having this confidence, I know that I shall abide, yea, and abide with you all, for your progress and joy in the faith; that your glorying may abound in Christ Jesus in me through my presence with you again.*
- Phil 2:24: *. . . but I trust in the Lord that I myself also shall come shortly.*
- Phlm 22: *But withal prepare me also a lodging: for I hope that through your prayers I shall be granted unto you.*

Luke states in Acts 28:30-31 that Paul was released from prison after "two full years"; various other chronological indicators fix the date of Paul's release as the spring of A.D. 62. In Romans 15:24-29 (written late A.D. 56), Paul states that he originally planned to travel on to Spain after his visit with the Roman church. However, Paul made these plans on the assumption that he would just be passing through Rome, and pausing to minister there before proceeding on to Spain. Since, in fact, he was subsequently imprisoned for nearly five years, the last two of which were spent at Rome (Acts 24:27), the apostle changed his plans. He states in the Prison Epistles (written early A.D. 62) that his intention was to visit the churches at Philippi (Phil 1:25-26; 2:24) and Colossae (Phlm 22; cf. Col 4:9) upon his release in prison, where he felt that a visit was owed. Thus, in the summer and fall of 62, Paul likely traveled through Macedonia and Asia Minor, probably returning to Rome for the winter of 62/63 in order to prepare for his long-anticipated trip to Spain. Because of the confidence with which Paul writes in Rom 15:24-29, one would expect that he did in fact preach the gospel in Spain as he had planned (cf. Acts 1:8; 13:47). This is also indicated by Paul's statement in 2 Tim 4:7 that he had "finished the course," and there is excellent evidence from the writings of the early church that Paul traveled to Spain.[1]

After ministering in Spain in A.D. 63, Paul returned to the region around the Aegean Sea in 64, or in the winter of 63/64. From here one can attempt to correlate the events in Titus and/or 1 Timothy with those in 2 Timothy, or one can postulate that they occurred in different years. The least problematic scenario is to view the epistles of Titus and 1 Timothy as having been written in 64, and the events in these books as not connected to the events in 2 Timothy. According to this reconstruction, Paul had traveled to Spain with such usual ministry partners as Luke, Timothy, and Titus. When he returned east, he ministered briefly in Crete—either spending the winter of 63/64 there, or else merely stopping at a Cretan port on his return voyage—and left Titus in Crete to establish the churches there (Tit 1:5), while he sailed on to Ephesus with Timothy (1 Tim 1:3). While in Ephesus (most likely), Paul wrote his letter to Titus. Paul then left Timothy in Ephesus to minister there, while he traveled on to Macedonia (1 Tim 1:3), where he wrote 1 Timothy. Paul was rejoined by Timothy and Titus in Nicopolis, in central Greece,

---

[1] See *1 Clement* 5.7; *Acts of Peter* 1-3, 40; *Muratorian Fragment*.

during the winter of 64/65 (Tit 3:12). When spring arrived, Paul evidently sent Timothy to Bithynia, where he was to join the now-martyred apostle Peter's former ministry partner, Mark.[2] Paul himself traveled south to Corinth, where Erastus, a native Corinthian, remained (2 Tim 4:20; cf. Rom 16:23). It was probably from Corinth that Paul sent two coworkers to two areas of the Roman Empire that were still relatively unreached with the gospel: Titus was sent to Dalmatia, in what is now Croatia (2 Tim 4:10), while Crescens was sent to faraway Gaul (2 Tim 4:10).[3] (Some suggest that these two were dispatched from Rome after Paul was imprisoned.) Paul then sailed to Miletus on the SW coast of Asia Minor, where he left Trophimus sick (2 Tim 4:20). He proceeded to sail north to Ephesus, where Onesiphorus ministered to him (2 Tim 1:16-18). Paul then sailed north to Troas, where Carpus ministered to him (2 Tim 4:13), apparently with the intent of rejoining Timothy in Bithynia. However, Paul was suddenly arrested in Troas at the instigation of an anti-Christian idol-maker, Alexander the coppersmith (2 Tim 4:14), who would also pose a danger to Timothy when he passed through the town on his way to visit Paul in Rome (2 Tim 4:15). Because Nero's persecution of Christians in Rome had now reached a fevered pitch, Paul was treated differently after his arrest in Troas than after previous arrests: as a leading Christian he was considered an enemy of the state and probably would have been executed in Troas if he had not immediately appealed for a trial before the emperor in Rome. (Some suggest that Paul was rushed to Rome before he could ask Luke to bring his books and cloak from Carpus' house [2 Tim 4:13].) When Paul was arrested, Demas left him for fear of his life and traveled to Thessalonica (2 Tim 4:9-10). The leaders of the churches in Asia Minor, including Phygelus and Hermogenes, also renounced their affiliation with Paul for fear of their lives (2 Tim 1:15), although Onesiphorus did not, and actually visited Paul in Rome (2 Tim 1:16-18). Luke, too, stuck with Paul, traveling with him on the prison ship to Rome once again (2 Tim 4:11; cf. Acts 27). It was probably after his arrest in Troas when Paul sent Tychicus back to Ephesus to minister there in his place (2 Tim 4:12).

If all of the events in the Pastoral Epistles are thought to have occurred during the same year, the following possible scenario results: after unknown events in A.D. 64, Paul spent the winter of 64/65 in Crete with Timothy and Titus. When normal travel resumed after the winter, Paul and Timothy sailed to Ephesus, while Paul left Titus in Crete to establish the churches there (Tit 1:5). Paul likely wrote his epistle to Titus while in Ephesus. Paul then left Timothy in Ephesus to minister there, while he traveled north to the port of Troas (2 Tim 4:13), and then from Troas into Macedonia (1 Tim 1:3), where he apparently wrote 1 Timothy (1 Tim 1:3). Paul then traveled through Macedonia to Corinth, where Erastus, a native Corinthian, remained (2 Tim 4:20; cf. Rom 16:23). At some point, Paul sent Titus to Dalmatia, probably intending to rejoin him in Nicopolis (Tit 3:12),[4] and sent Crescens to Galatia or Gaul (2 Tim

---

[2] Second Timothy 1:15 implies that Timothy was near Asia, but not in Asia (since he had not turned away from Paul). Second Timothy 4:13 implies that Timothy would have to pass through Troas in order to travel to Rome, which implies that he was in a region to the east of Troas. The area just to the north of the province of Asia and to the east of Troas is Bithynia, where Paul had once wished to minister but was providentially redirected (Acts 16:7). Peter had subsequently planted churches in Bithynia (1 Pet 1:1), and Paul may have wanted Timothy to help Mark in his ministry to these churches. That Timothy was ministering with or near Mark is shown by 2 Tim 4:11.

[3] Alternatively, Paul may have sent Crescens to Galatia from Miletus; the word Γαλατίαν can be understood as a reference to either Gaul or Galatia. While it is possible that Paul decided that a member of his team should make a return visit to Galatia, it seems that Paul's focus late in his life was on evangelizing unreached regions of the world, and on instructing newly reached Gentiles in the central area of the Roman Empire (cf. Rom 15:20-21). Various references in the church fathers support the interpretation of 2 Tim 4:10 as a reference to Gaul, as does the tradition of the churches of Vienne and Mayence in France, which name Crescens as their founder.

[4] It is difficult to fit the activities of Titus, as recorded in the Pastoral Epistles, into one year. It would seem that Titus should have spent the bulk of one year in Crete in order to establish the churches there, before traveling to Nicopolis to spend the winter with Paul. A trip to Dalmatia would take considerable time, not just for travel but also for the work of planting churches in a newly evangelized area.

4:9-10). Paul sailed from Corinth to Miletus in Asia Minor, where he left Trophimus sick (2 Tim 4:20). Paul apparently intended to rejoin Timothy in Ephesus (1 Tim 3:14-15; 4:13), and then travel with him to Nicopolis, where they would spend the winter with Titus (Tit 3:12). However, Paul was suddenly arrested, apparently at the instigation of Alexander the coppersmith (2 Tim 4:14-15), and was taken to Rome for trial and eventual execution.

While trying to work out Paul's activities between his first and second Roman imprisonments is a difficult problem, the most probable solution sees him returning to Macedonia and Asia in 62, wintering in Rome in 62/63, ministering in Spain in 63, returning east early in 64, writing 1 Timothy and Titus sometime in 64, spending the winter of 64/65 in Nicopolis, and finally being arrested in Troas in the late spring or early summer of 65. Second Timothy was written in the late summer or early fall of 65, and Paul was executed by Nero in the winter of 65/66.[5]

Addressee

Timothy is the best known pastor of the generation which succeeded the apostles as leaders of the early church and continued the traditions begun by the apostles. Timothy was a man of spiritual sincerity (Phil 2:19-21; 2 Tim 1:5), faithfulness in ministry (Phil 2:22-23), and doctrinal understanding (1 Cor 4:17; 2 Tim 2:7). But by some modern standards he would not have made an ideal church leader, since he evidently was naturally timid and did not have a forceful personality (1 Cor 16:10; 1 Tim 4:12; 2 Tim 1:6-7). He also had a tendency to discouragement (1 Tim 4:14), and he was often weak and sickly (1 Tim 5:23). However, God actually prefers to use weak people (1 Cor 1:26-31), so Timothy's résumé seemed ideal to the Lord, who chose him for the pastoral ministry (1 Tim 1:18).

Acts 16:1-2 indicates that Timothy's original home was Lystra, or possibly nearby Derbe (Acts 20:4), in southern Galatia, in what is now south-central Turkey. His mother and grandmother were devout Jews who passed their faith on to young Timothy, but Timothy's father was an unbelieving Greek who forbade him to be circumcised (Acts 16:1-3; 2 Tim 1:5).[6] Paul evidently met Timothy as a young man on his first missionary journey (A.D. 47–48) and led him to faith in Jesus as the promised Messiah (1 Tim 1:2, 18). It was probably at his baptism when Timothy made a confession of his Christian faith "in the presence of many witnesses" (1 Tim 6:12). Paul also knew Timothy's believing mother, Eunice, and his believing grandmother, Lois (2 Tim 1:5). Paul determined early in his second missionary journey (A.D. 49) to mentor Timothy as a ministry partner, but he had to circumcise him first, since Jews would have no respect for an uncircumcised man with a Jewish mother (Acts 16:3). Paul also communicated some ministry gift to Timothy at an ordination ceremony, laying his hands on him and (presumably) praying to impart this gift to him (1 Tim 1:6). Other elders also laid their hands on Timothy (1 Tim 4:14), and miraculous prophetic utterances were given concerning the young man (1 Tim 1:18; 4:14).

After this commissioning, Paul, Silas, and Timothy visited the other Galatian churches that Paul and Barnabas had planted previously (Acts 16:4-5). They then passed quickly through western Turkey (Asia Minor), and crossed the Aegean Sea to the Macedonian city of Thessalonica, where Paul and Silas were beaten and briefly imprisoned (Acts 16:6-40). After Paul and Silas were released, they went with Timothy to Thessalonica, and then to Berea (Acts 17:1-13). When threats were made against Paul's life, he

---

[5] According to Eusebius' *Chronicle*, Paul was martyred in Nero's fourteenth year, A.D. 67. However, the reference in Eusebius is problematic, since Eusebius says that Peter was martyred at the same time, whereas Paul was evidently arrested after Peter's execution, since Peter speaks of Paul as still active in ministry in 2 Pet 3:15-16. If Hebrews was written after Paul's execution and Timothy's imprisonment for standing by Paul (cf. Heb 13:23), 2 Timothy would have been written early in the fall of 65, about a year after Nero began his pogrom.

[6] Timothy's mother presumably did not want to marry an unbeliever, but most marriages were arranged by the bride's father (cf. 1 Cor 7:36-38).

traveled further south by himself while Silas and Timothy remained in Berea to minister to the newborn Christians there (Acts 17:14-15). While Paul was in Athens, he sent Timothy back to Thessalonica to check on the believers there (1 Thess 3:1-2), and Timothy brought Paul a good report back from Thessalonica after Paul had traveled on to Corinth (Acts 18:5; 1 Thess 3:6). Timothy's report prompted the writing of 1 Thessalonians, and Timothy is named in 1 Thess 1:1 as a cosender of that epistle, along with Paul and Silas. Timothy is again named as a cosender of 2 Thessalonians (2 Thess 1:1), which was written soon after 1 Thessalonians (late A.D. 50). During the eighteen months in which Paul ministered in Corinth (Acts 18:11), Timothy and Silas ministered alongside him, preaching "the Son of God, Jesus Christ" (2 Cor 1:19).

There is no direct mention of Timothy's activities during the next five years, until the latter part of Paul's third missionary journey (A.D. 56). At that time Timothy was found ministering with Paul in Ephesus, until he was sent into Macedonia as part of an "advance team" to prepare for Paul's travels through Greece (Acts 19:22). Paul states in 1 Cor 4:17 and 16:10 that he intended to send Timothy to the church at Corinth (1 Cor 4:17; 16:10). Timothy is also named as a cosender of 2 Corinthians (2 Cor 1:1). Timothy is again named in Paul's letter to the Romans, which was written from Corinth within three months of the writing of 2 Corinthians (Rom 16:21). Timothy accompanied Paul at least as far as Asia Minor on Paul's journey to Jerusalem, early in A.D. 57 (Acts 20:4).

The biblical record is silent concerning Timothy's activities for another five years, until early in A.D. 62. At that time, it is clear that Timothy is by Paul's side during the apostle's first Roman imprisonment. Timothy is named as a cosender of the letter to Philemon (Phlm 1), the letter to the church at Philippi (Phil 1:1), and the letter to the church at Colossae (Col 1:1). Paul states in Phil 2:19-24 his intention to send Timothy to Philippi shortly, and he commends Timothy's selfless character in the highest possible terms.

It is evident from 1 & 2 Timothy that Timothy continued to minister alongside Paul after Paul's release from prison in early A.D. 62. Probably Timothy traveled to Spain with Paul and Titus, and then back to the east, where Paul left him in Ephesus on a temporary ministry assignment (1 Tim 1:3). Timothy rejoined Paul later in the same year (A.D. 64), but Timothy was sent away on another ministry assignment again the next year (A.D. 65). Paul was arrested and taken to Rome while Timothy was away, and in 2 Timothy Paul urges Timothy to come to him before winter (2 Tim 4:21). Hebrews 13:23 indicates that Timothy not only was successful in reaching Rome before Paul's execution, but that he was also imprisoned briefly for his unabashed association with Paul. In Heb 13:23, Barnabas (whom, I argue, wrote Hebrews) states his intention to travel to Jerusalem soon with Timothy, just prior to the open revolt of the Jews in June, A.D. 66. Timothy was thus deprived of his mentor about seventeen years after Paul had first taken him under his wing.

Hebrews 13:23 is the last direct mention of Timothy in the Bible. The fourth century church historian Eusebius (*H. E.* 3.4.6) states that Timothy was the leading pastor of the church at Ephesus. If this is true (as seems likely), then Timothy ministered side by side with the apostle John in his later years, though John, like the other apostles, had an itinerant ministry and was not permanently tied to one local church. The church at Ephesus is presented in Rev 2:1-7 as the prototypical church of the apostolic era, where it is described as faithfully maintaining moral and doctrinal soundness, but flagging in its zeal for the Lord. This was not just Timothy's fault, but it is evident that the energy of the church did wane late in the first century A.D., after the initial wave of apostolic preaching, miracle-working, and missionary journeys. Rather than continuing to undertake bold missionary journeys to far-flung, unevangelized parts of the world in fulfillment of the Great Commission, the second generation became essentially introverted and focused on its own concerns within the Roman Empire. According to one source, Timothy suffered a martyr's death under Diocletian (Sept. 14, 81–Sept. 18, 96) or Nerva (Sept. 18, 96–Jan. 27/28, 98), and January 24 or 26 is traditionally celebrated as the date of his martyrdom.

Authorship of the Pastoral Epistles

The Pastoral Epistles were unanimously accepted by the early church as authentically Pauline.[7] Although heretics such as Marcion, Tatian, and Basilides rejected the authority of some or all of the Pastorals due to Paul's contradiction of their heresies, their judgment was never accepted by the Christian church. There were no further challenges to the Pauline authorship of the Pastorals until F. C. Baur's denial of their authenticity in 1835 through the use of higher criticism. Today, nearly all critical scholars reject Pauline authorship of the Pastoral Epistles. One would think that with such unanimity and dogmatism, there must be major problems with the view that Paul was the author of these epistles. However, liberal arguments against accepting Pauline authorship of the Pastoral Epistles are surprisingly weak. Probably the strongest argument is that the language of the Pastorals is more classical than the language of Paul's other epistles. Second Timothy 4:11 gives a reasonable explanation for this stylistic difference, however: Luke had to have been Paul's amanuensis for 2 Timothy, since Paul says, "Only Luke is with me." It is reasonable to suppose that Luke may have been Paul's amanuensis for other letters as well—1 Timothy, Titus, and possibly Ephesians and Colossians. That the language of the Pastorals includes many "Lucanisms" is therefore not surprising. It should be noted that these stylistic differences are limited to "warp and woof" words, i.e., conjunctions, prepositions, and adverbs, and are not related to content. Most scholars who accept the authenticity of the Pastoral Epistles assume that Luke Atticized Paul's Greek.

All of the other differences in terminology and content between the Pastorals and Paul's other epistles can be attributed to differences in audience and purpose. There are in fact differences in content and terminology between every one of Paul's epistles due to the different situations they address. In fact, probably the primary reason why critical scholars today reject Pauline authorship of the Pastorals is simply that they do not want to question the dominant paradigm. The weight of scholarly opinion is considered to be sufficient evidence in itself to discredit the Pastorals. The critics make no serious attempt to harmonize the message of the Pastorals with the message of Paul's other epistles, and instead simply seek to find as many contrasts and differences as possible, and to focus on these differences to support their denial of Pauline authorship. Critics are also troubled by the quotation of Luke 10:7 in 1 Tim 5:18, which contradicts their denial of the fact that NT books were viewed as Scripture from the day they were written, and which also precludes a late date for the composition of Luke's Gospel.[8]

Because the Pastoral Epistles themselves claim to have been written by Paul (1 Tim 1:1; 2 Tim 1:1; Tit 1:1), and they were unanimously accepted as Pauline by the early church, the burden of proof is on those who seek to deny Pauline authorship. Specifically, they need to prove that it was impossible for Paul to have written these letters, which they cannot do. Paul personally signed all of his letters in his own distinctive hand, which was recognized by the early church, and which distinguished his authentic letters from forgeries (2 Thess 3:17-18). To the Christian believer, the Holy Spirit bears witness to the truth and power of the Pastoral Epistles as the living and active Word of God in a way that makes them qualitatively different from any other work of literature.

---

[7] E. E. Ellis, "Pastoral Letters" (in *Dictionary of Paul and His Letters*; Downers Grove: IVP, 1993), 659.

[8] Other arguments made by the critics are: (1) the historical data in the Pastorals do not fit into Acts; (2) the description of church organization in the Pastorals is too advanced for the mid-60s; and (3) the Pastorals are written against the Gnostic heresy, which did not develop until the early second century. In reply, (1) the book of Acts ends with Paul's release from prison, implying that he engaged in further ministry; (2) there is no proof that church organization developed as gradually as the critics imagine (cf. Acts 6:1-6; 14:23; 15:2-6; 20:17-28; 1 Cor 11–14; Phil 1:1; 1 Pet 5:1-4); and (3) Gnosticism developed earlier than the critics claim, although the heresies Paul attacks in the Pastorals are still more Jewish than later Gnosticism.

Date and Occasion of Writing

In the aftermath of Paul's first missionary journey, Paul and the churches he founded were opposed by Jewish false teachers who claimed to believe that Jesus was the Messiah, but who also demanded submission to the Law as an additional condition for salvation. However, as the center of the church shifted to the Hellenistic world, the heresies which Paul fought incorporated increasingly more Hellenized forms of Judaism. These heresies would develop into full-blown Gnosticism by the late first century. Thus, while Paul's earlier letters focused on arguing against salvation through the works of the Law, his later letters are directed against variegated Jewish-pagan philosophies. Gnosticism is directly named and attacked in 1 Tim 6:20, and is implied in numerous other passages.

The occasion of writing 1 Timothy was that Paul had left Timothy alone in Ephesus (1:3), and wanted to give him instruction on how to oversee the churches in his absence (3:14-15). Although Paul had surely left Timothy to minister alone many times previously, this time was different because it was late in Paul's life, and the apostles were quickly moving off the scene. Paul wanted to leave a repository of instruction for the next generation of leaders in the church, and ultimately for all subsequent generations.

As noted above, 1 Timothy was written between A.D. 62 and 65, most likely in 64.

Purpose and Message

Paul's purpose in writing 1 Timothy was to instruct Timothy on how to oversee the church in the apostle's absence, and to exhort him to remain faithful to his calling (cf. 3:14-15). The message of 1 Timothy is, be faithful to your calling as a minister of the Word by turning away from vain philosophy, by maintaining the proper roles of men and women, by appointing qualified elders and deacons, by protecting the doctrinal purity of the church, and by properly treating various groups of people in the church.

Outline of 1 Timothy

I. Salutation 1:1-2
II. Exhortation to Faithfulness to the Word 1:3-20
    A. Warning against getting sidetracked 1:3-11
    B. Paul's example of faithfulness 1:12-17
    C. Exhortation to follow Paul's example 1:18-20
III. Directions for Maintaining Proper Roles in the Church 2:1–3:13
    A. Exhortation to intercessory prayer 2:1-7
    B. Exhortation to the proper roles of men and women 2:8-15
    C. Exhortation to the appointment of qualified elders and deacons 3:1-13
IV. Directions for Guarding the Purity of the Church 3:14–4:16
    A. The purpose of Paul's directions 3:14-16
    B. Warning against doctrines of demons 4:1-5
    C. Exhortation to faithful ministry 4:6-16
V. Directions for Proper Treatment of Groups in the Church 5:1–6:2
    A. Directions for treatment of the old and young 5:1-2
    B. Directions for treatment of widows 5:3-16
    C. Directions for the treatment of elders 5:17-25
    D. Directions for the treatment of slaveowners 6:1-2
VI. Conclusion 6:3-21

A. Warning against the allure of philosophy and money 6:3-10
B. Charge to faithfulness 6:11-16
C. Warning to the wealthy 6:17-19
D. Final charge to Timothy 6:20-21a
E. Closing benediction 6:21b

Argument of 1 Timothy

The body of 1 Timothy begins with an exhortation for Timothy to be faithful to his calling as a minister of the Word and an overseer of the church (1:3-20), then proceeds to explain how he is to do this by giving directions on how to maintain proper roles in the church (2:1–3:13), to guard the purity of the church (3:14–4:16), and to properly treat various groups of people in the church (5:1–6:2). Paul concludes the letter with final warnings and admonitions (6:3-21).

Salutation, 1:1-2

Paul's first letter to Timothy begins with a warm personal greeting (1:1-2).

Exhortation to Faithfulness to the Word, 1:3-20

Paul begins the body of the letter with an exhortation for Timothy to be faithful to his calling as a minister of the Word (1:3-20). He first warns Timothy—and those whom he oversees—against getting sidetracked, since there were an increasing number of teachers in the church who had become preoccupied with extrabiblical Jewish legends (like those in the Pseudepigrapha) and philosophy, and this had led some into grand philosophical discussions of the Law which had the appearance of profundity (1:3-11). Paul warns Timothy that such discussions are superfluous and contrary to his calling; he should just stick to the Word. Paul then encourages Timothy by setting forth his own example of faithfulness (1:12-17). He closes the exhortation by commanding Timothy to follow Paul's example of faithfulness to his calling, in contrast to those who have been caught up in philosophy and shipwrecked their faith as a result (1:18-20).

Directions for Maintaining Proper Roles in the Church, 2:1–3:13

Having given this charge to Timothy, Paul now turns to instruction concerning behavior in the church, of which Timothy was an overseer. In 2:1-7, Paul commands that intercessory prayer be offered in behalf of the governing authorities in order to create a peaceable environment for the spread of the gospel. It is specifically men who are to lead in prayer (2:8); women are to be modest, quiet, and in subjection to the men who are in authority over them (2:9-14), while demonstrating good works in their proper God-ordained role (2:15).[9] Paul then lays out the qualifications of elders and deacons, since Timothy (not the congregation) was to appoint and oversee them (3:1-13; cf. Tit 1:5).[10]

---

[9] Verses 11-12 give a blanket prohibition against women teaching men and exercising authority over men, and make no exception for where this teaching or authority is exercised. The issue is not *where* the teaching occurs, but *who* is there.

Directions for Guarding the Purity of the Church, 3:14–4:16

In 3:14-15, Paul gives his reason for writing to Timothy: he wants Timothy, as an overseer of the church, to know how to administer the local church, in case Timothy is left to minister on his own for an extended period of time. This is an important matter, since the church is the repository and guardian of God's truth in the world, which Paul summarizes in 3:16. After describing the mystery of godliness, Paul warns against those who will fall away from it in the latter days by giving heed to the doctrines of demons—possibly a reference to mystic ascetic practices, or perhaps a reference to modern vegetarianism based on a Darwinian worldview, and to the denigration of a monogamous life in secular thought (4:1-5). Paul then instructs Timothy on how he, as a minister of Christ, is to function in such a way as to guard against error and to promote truth (4:6-16).

Directions for Proper Treatment of Groups in the Church, 5:1–6:2

In 5:1–6:2, Paul instructs Timothy concerning how various groups of people are to be treated in the church. First, in 5:1-2, he gives directions for Timothy's relation to old and young men and women in the church, as their overseer. Second, in 5:3-16, he gives detailed guidelines for the relief of widows, which are intended to ensure that the church only supports those who genuinely need support, and who are worthy of support. Widows who were placed on the church payroll were to serve the church through prayer and good works, rather than doing whatever they wanted to do with their time. Third, Paul gives directions for the oversight of elders (pastors) in 5:17-25, including procedures for remuneration (5:17-18), for discipline (5:19-21), for ordination (5:22), and for wise conduct (5:23), with a concluding reminder that the Lord is the ultimate judge and will reveal the true worth of a man's work (5:24-25). Finally, Paul exhorts Timothy to instruct believing slaves to honor their masters and serve them faithfully in order to protect the church's reputation (6:1-2).

Conclusion, 6:3-21

As Paul brings the letter to a conclusion, he warns Timothy against the allure of philosophy and false intellectualism, which will result in the rejection of sound doctrine, and against the love of money, which leads men away from the faith and brings grief, not happiness (6:3-10). He then commands Timothy to flee from these things, and to be faithful to his calling to serve the King of kings (6:11-16). Paul instructs Timothy to warn the wealthy against putting their trust in money or thinking of themselves as superior to poor people, and instead to use their temporal riches for eternal gain (6:17-19). Paul then gives one final charge to Timothy, which is once again a warning against being sucked into sophisticated philosophical discussions, maintaining a pure and simple faith instead (6:20-21a). Paul closes the epistle with a short benediction (6:21b).

---

[10] Both elders (3:2) and deacons (3:12) are to be "husbands of one wife," implying that they are male. The expression "husband of one wife" is illuminated by the parallel expression "wife of one husband" in 5:9. This expression is meant to exclude from the pastorate a man who has been divorced and remarried to a different wife.

Note that the "women" described in 3:11 are deacons' wives. (Greek uses the same word [γυνή] for both "woman" and "wife"; there is no special term for "wife.") Paul gives separate qualifications for the wives of deacons because deacons' wives would be more involved in their ministry than elders' wives would be in theirs. The deacon's wife may have been expected to serve with him, and especially to minister to the women in the congregation.

Bibliography for the Pastoral Epistles

Barcley, William Bayless. *A Study Commentary on 1 and 2 Timothy*. Webster, NY: Evangelical Press, 2005.

Barnes, Albert. *Thessalonians, Timothy, Titus, and Philemon*. Notes on the New Testament, ed. Robert Frew. Reprint: Grand Rapids: Baker, 1949.

Blaiklock, E. M. *The Pastoral Epistles*. Bible Study Commentary. Grand Rapids: Zondervan, 1972.

Collins, Raymond F. *1 & 2 Timothy and Titus: A Commentary*. New Testament Library. Louisville: Westminster John Knox Press, 2002.

Constable, Thomas L. *Notes on 1 Timothy*. 2104 ed. Sonic Light, 2014.

Constable, Thomas L. *Notes on 2 Timothy*. 2104 ed. Sonic Light, 2014.

Constable, Thomas L. *Notes on Titus*. 2104 ed. Sonic Light, 2014.

Demarest, Gary W. *1, 2 Thessalonians, 1, 2 Timothy, Titus*. The Communicator's Commentary, vol. 9. Word: Waco, 1984.

Earle, Ralph. "1 Timothy." In *Expositor's Bible Commentary*, ed. Frank E. Gaebelein et al., vol. 11, 339-90. Grand Rapids: Zondervan Publishing House, 1978.

———. "2 Timothy." In *Expositor's Bible Commentary*, ed. Frank E. Gaebelein et al., vol. 11, 391-418. Grand Rapids: Zondervan Publishing House, 1978.

Fee, Gordon D. *1 and 2 Timothy, Titus*. New International Biblical Commentary. Peabody, MA: Hendrickson, 1988.

Fiore, Benjamin. *The Pastoral Epistles: First Timothy, Second Timothy, Titus*. Sacra Pagina Series, vol. 12, ed. Daniel J. Harrington. Collegeville, MN: Liturgical Press, 2007.

Greene, Oliver B. *The Epistles of Paul the Apostle to Timothy and Titus*. Greenville, SC: Gospel Hour, 1964.

Guthrie, Donald. *The Pastoral Epistles: An Introduction and Commentary*. Rev. ed. Tyndale New Testament Commentaries Grand Rapids: Eerdmans, 1988.

Harvey, H. *Commentary on the Pastoral Epistles, First and Second Timothy and Titus; and the Epistle to Philemon*. An American Commentary on the New Testament, ed. Alvah Hovey. Philadelphia: American Baptist Publication Society, 1890.

Hiebert, D. Edmond. *First Timothy*. Chicago: Moody Press, 1957.

———. *Second Timothy*. Chicago: Moody Press, 1958.

———. "Titus." In *Expositor's Bible Commentary*, ed. Frank E. Gaebelein et al., vol. 11, 419-49. Grand Rapids: Zondervan Publishing House, 1978.

———. *Titus and Philemon*. Chicago: Moody Press, 1957.

Humphreys, A. E. *Timothy and Titus: With Introduction and Notes*. Cambridge Bible for Schools and Colleges. Cambridge: Cambridge, 1895.

Jensen, Irving L. *1 & 2 Timothy and Titus: A Self-Study Guide*. Chicago: Moody, 1973.

Johnson, Luke Timothy. *The First and Second Letters to Timothy: A New Translation with Introduction and Commentary*. Anchor Bible, vol. 35A. New York: Doubleday, 2001.

Kelly, J. N. D. *A Commentary on the Pastoral Epistles*. Grand Rapids: Baker, 1963.

Kent, Homer A., Jr. *The Pastoral Epistles: Studies in 1 and 2 Timothy and Titus*. Rev. ed. Salem, WI: Sheffield Publishing Company, 1986.

Knight, George W., III. *The Pastoral Epistles: A Commentary on the Greek Text*. New International Greek Testament Commentary. Grand Rapids: Eerdmans, 1992.

Köstenberger, Andreas. "1 Timothy." In *The Expositor's Bible Commentary: Revised Edition*, ed. Tremper Longman III and David E. Garland, vol. 12, 487-561. Grand Rapids: Zondervan, 2006.

———. "2 Timothy." In *The Expositor's Bible Commentary: Revised Edition*, ed. Tremper Longman III and David E. Garland, vol. 12, 563-600. Grand Rapids: Zondervan, 2006.

———. "Titus." In *The Expositor's Bible Commentary: Revised Edition*, ed. Tremper Longman III and David E. Garland, vol. 12, 601-25. Grand Rapids: Zondervan, 2006.

Lea, Thomas D., and Hayne P. Griffin, Jr. *1, 2 Timothy, Titus*. New American Commentary, ed. David S. Dockery, vol. 34. Nashville: Broadman Press, 1992.

Liftin, A. Duane. "1 Timothy." In *The Bible Knowledge Commentary: New Testament*, ed. John F. Walvoord and Roy B. Zuck, 727-48. Wheaton, IL: SP Publications, 1983.

———. "2 Timothy." In *The Bible Knowledge Commentary: New Testament*, ed. John F. Walvoord and Roy B. Zuck, 749-60. Wheaton, IL: SP Publications, 1983.

———. "Titus." In *The Bible Knowledge Commentary: New Testament*, ed. John F. Walvoord and Roy B. Zuck, 761-67. Wheaton, IL: SP Publications, 1983.

MacArthur, John, Jr. *1 Timothy*. The MacArthur New Testament Commentary. Chicago: Moody Press, 1995.

———. *2 Timothy*. The MacArthur New Testament Commentary. Chicago: Moody Press, 1995.

———. *Titus*. The MacArthur New Testament Commentary. Chicago: Moody Press, 1996.

Marshall, I. Howard, with Philip H. Towner. *A Critical and Exegetical Commentary on the Pastoral Epistles*. International Critical Commentary, ed. J. A. Emerton, C. E. B. Cranfield, and G. N. Stanton. Edinburgh: T&T Clark, 1999.

McGee, J. Vernon. *1 Corinthians–Revelation*. Volume 5 of *Thru the Bible with J. Vernon McGee*. Nashville: Thomas Nelson, 1983.

Mounce, William D. *Pastoral Epistles*. Word Biblical Commentary, vol. 46. Nashville: Thomas Nelson, 2000.

Quinn, Jerome D. and William C. Wacker. *The First and Second Letters to Timothy: A New Translation with Notes and Commentary*. Eerdmans Critical Commentary. Grand Rapids: Eerdmans, 2000.

Quinn, Jerome D. *The Letter to Titus: A New Translation with Notes and Commentary and An Introduction to Titus, I and II Timothy, The Pastoral Epistles*. Anchor Bible, vol. 35. New York: Doubleday, 1990.

Towner, Philip H. *1-2 Timothy & Titus*. IVP New Testament Commentary Series. Downers Grove, IL: InterVarsity Press, 1994.

———. *The Letters to Timothy and Titus*. New International Commentary on the New Testament. Grand Rapids: Eerdmans, 2006.

Wace, H. "Timothy and Titus, The Pastoral Epistles." In *The Holy Bible with an Explanatory and Critical Commentary: New Testament*, ed. F. C. Cook, vol. 3, 760-818. New York: Charles Scribner's Sons, 1900.

Witherington, Ben III. *A Socio-Rhetorical Commentary on Titus, 1-2 Timothy and 1-3 John*. Volume 1 of *Letters and Homilies for Hellenized Christians*. Downers Grove, IL: InterVarsity Press, 2006.

Interpretive Guide to 2 Timothy

The epistle of 2 Timothy is unique in content in the New Testament; it is a solemn charge to a young man whom Paul had discipled as a pastor, and it represents Paul's final charge to Timothy before his death. The aim of Paul's charge is to both warn and exhort Timothy to be faithful in the ministry to which he was called. Paul wrote this letter as he sat on death row in Rome, awaiting execution by the evil emperor Nero. Part of Paul's aim in writing was to urge Timothy to come and see him one last time; but Paul could not be sure that he would in fact see Timothy again, and so the bulk of the letter reads like a dying general's heroic speech to his colonel, exhorting him to fight the war with courage and determination after he has taken over command of the troops.

Second Timothy is often preached during the ordination service for a new pastor, and no book of the Bible is more fitting for such an occasion. Paul addresses the problems that make some pastors quit the ministry, such as fear, discouragement, and weariness. He also addresses problems that make some pastors have an unfruitful ministry, like a lack of focus on the Word, and getting sidetracked by disputes and philosophical arguments. But 2 Timothy is not just a book for pastors; there is a sense in which all Christians are ministers of God. In fact, 2 Timothy contains the key verse for the well-known AWANA (Approved Workmen Are Not Ashamed) children's ministry—*Give diligence to present thyself approved unto God, a workman that needeth not to be ashamed, handling aright the word of truth* (2:15). The book also contains an extended warning concerning apostasy in the last days (3:1–4:5) that is often, and justly, applied to our contemporary context.

Second Timothy is a very somber book, and it stands as a stern warning against both apostasy and unfaithfulness in ministry. It should be remembered, however, that Paul was convinced of the genuineness of Timothy's faith (1:5), and that this letter was meant to encourage Timothy to keep going in ministry in the face of difficulties. Every indication from church history is that Timothy did in fact persevere in ministry until the end of his life, in accordance with Paul's charge. This book should, however, scare pastors and theologians who are not actually saved (2:23-26), as well as pastors who are saved but who have forsaken the ministry or the Word of God (2:5; 4:3-5). While some of this book's exhortations can make us uncomfortable, those who respond properly to these exhortations should be encouraged and uplifted, rather than discouraged or worried.

Author

Paul names himself as the author of this epistle in the very first verse (1:1), and the intensely personal nature of the letter is such that only Paul could have written it. There would be no reason for a forger to create a letter like this one. Regarding the liberal challenge to Pauline authorship of the Pastorals, see the introduction to 1 Timothy.

Date and Occasion of Writing

For the historical background to the Pastorals, see the introduction to 1 Timothy. The occasion of writing 2 Timothy was Paul's sudden arrest and imprisonment in Rome in the summer of A.D. 65. Paul wrote 2 Timothy as a farewell letter, but also to give Timothy an update on his condition. Timothy had heard that Paul had been arrested, but did not know what had transpired since; events must have moved very quickly in the turmoil that gripped Rome near the end of Nero's reign. Paul wanted to give Timothy a final word of exhortation, and also wanted to urge him to come visit him, and to bring his cloak before the onset of winter.

Purpose and Message

Paul's primary purpose in writing 2 Timothy was to give his protégé Timothy a final charge to be faithful in ministry, and by so doing to leave a charge to future pastors throughout the age of the church. The message of 2 Timothy is, be faithful to your calling as a minister of the Word, not entangling yourself in philosophy or being carried away with the world's errors; stick to the Bible alone, and study and teach it in simple faith.

Outline of 2 Timothy

I. Salutation 1:1-2
II. Introduction: the imperative for faithfulness in ministry 1:3-18
   A. Thanksgiving for Timothy's faith 1:3-14
   B. Examples of unfaithfulness and faithfulness 1:15-18
III. Charge to Timothy 2:1–4:8
   A. Charge to perseverance in ministry 2:1-13
   B. Warning against entanglement in philosophy 2:14-26
   C. Warning against corruption at the end of the age 3:1-13
   D. Charge to faithfulness to the Word as the counter to false intellectualism 3:14-17
   E. Final charge to Timothy 4:1-8
IV. Closing remarks 4:9-22
   A. Personal remarks 4:9-18
   B. Final directions and salutations 4:19-21
   C. Closing benediction 4:22

Argument of 2 Timothy

Second Timothy is essentially Paul's final charge to his protégé, Timothy, in which he challenges Timothy to be faithful to his calling. The epistle is introduced by a greeting (1:1-2) and a statement of the imperative to remain faithful in ministry (1:3-18). The main body of the epistle consists of a charge to Timothy (2:1–4:8). The letter ends with a lengthy section of closing remarks (4:9-22).

Salutation, 1:1-2

This short epistle opens with a typical salutation which emphasizes Paul's hope of resurrection life in Christ Jesus even as he faces death (1:1-2).

Introduction: The Imperative for Faithfulness in Ministry, 1:3-18

The salutation is followed by a thanksgiving, in which Paul thanks God for Timothy's faith, and challenges him to continue in the same (1:3-14). He follows this in 1:15-18 with examples of unfaithfulness (Phygelus and Hermogenes) and faithfulness (Onesiphorus).

Charge to Timothy, 2:1–4:8

Paul then calls Timothy to perseverance in ministry, and to have a life that is focused completely on serving the Lord (2:1-13). Paul then warns Timothy against getting sidetracked by becoming involved in philosophical argumentation, which results in confusion, not clarity, and leads men to depart from the simple truths of the Christian faith (2:14-26). In the last days, the deceptions of intellectual sophistication will grow (or, we may say now, is growing) exponentially worse, as will the moral state of professing Christians who pursue this false intellectualism (3:1-13).[1] The way to prevent deception is not to study false doctrine and to argue with false teachers, but is rather to study the Bible with the aim of understanding and obeying it by faith (3:14-17). Paul gives his final charge to Timothy in 4:1-8, setting forth his own life as an example to emulate.

Closing Remarks, 4:9-22

Paul closes the epistle with personal remarks in 4:9-18, final salutations and directions in 4:19-21, and a benediction in 4:22.

Bibliography

For a bibliography of the Pastoral Epistles, see the Interpretive Guide to 1 Timothy.

---

[1] It is important to note that the verb ἐνστήσονται in 3:1 is in the future tense, meaning that these grievous times were yet to come when Paul wrote. The preceding and following context shows that Paul is really describing grievous times for the church, more than for secular society. The world has always been the world, but the church in the last days is said to become exceptionally bad. Especially notable is the reference to the "silly women" who are "ever learning, and never able to come to the knowledge of the truth" in 3:6-7, which appears to be a prophecy of female involvement in academia, particularly in the fields of biblical studies and theology. For all of world history before the last half of the twentieth century, nearly all academic study was done by men, whereas today women are coming to dominate academia, and are increasingly writing and teaching in evangelical seminaries and pastoring evangelical churches.

Interpretive Guide to Titus

As the apostle Paul saw his own life and ministry drawing to a close, he saw fit to write letters to two of his longtime ministry partners in order to leave them written instructions on how to oversee churches. The closer of these two ministry partners to Paul was Timothy, who was half-Jewish, and whose mother and grandmother had raised him with knowledge of the Jewish Scriptures. The other recipient of the apostle's final words of instruction to the next generation of church leaders was an uncircumcised Greek Christian named Titus who had been saved out of a pagan background early in Paul's ministry. Paul evidently began discipling Titus first, but he felt a greater affinity for Timothy due to their shared background in Judaism and Timothy's more advanced knowledge of the Hebrew Scriptures. Pastor Titus, appropriately, was assigned to oversee the churches in Crete, which was as thoroughly Gentile a place as there was in the Roman Empire. If Timothy stood for the Christian who had received a godly heritage and who ministered in a culture with some biblical influence, Titus stood for the man who was saved out of raw paganism, and who ministered in areas that had no historic biblical influence.

The subjects Paul addresses in his letter to Titus are closely related to the problems which Titus faced in the Cretan churches. Cretan culture was morally "low" even by pagan standards, and Cretan converts to Christianity had to be trained to live differently than the way they were raised, and differently than the people around them. The Cretan Christians had to lead a separated lifestyle. In this letter, Paul addresses several specific cultural problems within the Cretan churches, and emphasizes the connection between doctrine and lifestyle. Whereas 1 Timothy focuses on doctrinal issues, Titus has more of a practical emphasis.

As Paul's number two protégé, both the man Titus and the letter written to him are often overshadowed by Timothy and the two epistles which he received from Paul. However, people who were saved in young adulthood from an entirely non-Christian background are more likely to identify with Titus, as are pastors who minister among peoples who need to be culturally reoriented in order to put Christian values into practice.

Author

Paul names himself as the author of this epistle in the very first verse (1:1), and there is no good reason to doubt the church's acceptance of this letter as authentically Pauline. On the liberal denial of the Pauline authorship of the Pastorals, see the introduction to 1 Timothy. The liberal denial is just that—it is a pure denial for anti-Christian theological reasons, without any legitimate reasons to question Pauline authorship, and in the face of very strong evidence in support of Pauline authorship.

Addressee

Paul calls Titus "my true child according to a common faith" (Tit 1:4), which indicates that Titus was saved through Paul's ministry,[1] but which also shows Paul's affection for him. Titus was apparently saved as a young man through Paul's early ministry in Damascus, Tarsus, or Antioch—presumably Antioch, since Titus accompanied Paul and Barnabas from Antioch to the Jerusalem Council in A.D. 49 (Gal 2:1-3).[2] Paul's ministry in Antioch began in A.D. 42, one year before the famine (Acts 11:25-30).

---

[1] Some suggest that the parent-child metaphor merely refers to a teacher-student mentoring relationship; but see 1 Cor 4:14-15; 2 Cor 12:14-15; Gal 4:19; Phlm 10.

Since Acts 11:19-30 describes a great spiritual revival in Antioch in that year, it is likely that Titus was saved in A.D. 42. Titus was probably born around A.D. 22, which would have made him an ideal age to be a protégé of Paul and Barnabas in A.D. 49. In A.D. 64, when this epistle was written, Titus was likely in his early forties.

The fact that Titus was uncircumcised (Gal 2:3) indicates that his parents were not Jewish and were not proselytes to Judaism—this man was saved out of raw paganism. If, as seems likely, Titus was raised in Antioch, he would have been accustomed to life in a large metropolis, surrounded by diverse peoples, cultures, languages, and customs. He would have spoken both Syriac and Greek, though he would also have heard many other languages spoken in the marketplace, especially Latin and Jewish Palestinian Aramaic. If he was of the native stock of the region, he would have had a somewhat darker complexion than Greeks or Romans, though he would not have seemed out of place anywhere in the Mediterranean world. As an uncircumcised Gentile, he would find more natural acceptance among Gentiles than a Jew such as Paul would have had—Paul's evident success in ministry among Gentiles notwithstanding.

Titus evidently showed spiritual sincerity, zeal, and pastoral giftedness, for Paul took him under his wing, and brought him to Jerusalem as a representative of Gentile Christianity, when the great question of whether circumcision was necessary for salvation was posed to the apostles and elders in Jerusalem (Acts 15:1-3; Gal 2:1-3). Titus returned to Antioch with Paul and Barnabas after the Jerusalem Council, and he evidently continued to minister in Antioch while Paul departed on his second missionary journey. Although Titus is not mentioned by name in the book of Acts, references to him in 2 Corinthians show that he was in fact ministering with Paul at least during his third missionary journey (A.D. 53–57). Most likely, when Paul revisited Antioch in the winter of A.D. 52/53, after his second missionary journey, he selected Titus to be a primary ministry partner on his subsequent journey. Titus evidently ministered with Paul in Ephesus during the bulk of his three years of ministry there (Acts 19; 20:31). Toward the end of this ministry period Paul was informed of problems in the church at Corinth, and he sent Titus to deliver the letter of 1 Corinthians and to report on the state of the Corinthian church. Paul could not wait to hear Titus' report, so he journeyed into Macedonia where he met Titus as he was returning. Titus reported that Paul's letter was generally well received (2 Cor 7:6-16), but he also revealed continuing problems in the Corinthian church. Thus, Paul wrote 2 Corinthians and sent Titus back to Corinth with an unnamed brother, possibly Luke, to deliver the letter (2 Cor 8:16-24). Paul told the Corinthians that he and Titus walked "in the same spirit" and "in the same steps" (2 Cor 12:18). Second Corinthians 8 indicates that Titus was also the leader of the group of men designated to carry to Jerusalem the collection taken up in the Greek churches for the impoverished saints in Judea (cf. Rom 15:25-28; 1 Cor 16:1-4). Titus successfully fulfilled the difficult and sensitive task of mediation at Corinth, as Paul enjoyed a good three month visit there immediately afterward (Acts 20:3), during which he wrote the epistle to the Romans. These interactions show that Titus was a man of great spiritual concern, tact, and administrative ability.

There is no direct mention of Titus' activities during the eight years between the writing of 2 Corinthians (A.D. 56) and the writing of Paul's letter to him (A.D. 64). However, this letter shows that Titus had remained a regular ministry partner of Paul during this period. Whether Titus ministered in Antioch during Paul's four and a half year imprisonment, or whether he ministered elsewhere, is mere speculation. But it is certain that Titus resumed ministry alongside Paul after the apostle's release from prison in A.D. 62. Early in A.D. 64, it is clear that Paul wanted Titus by his side, but felt it necessary to leave him in the island of Crete temporarily in order to establish its troubled, shallow churches. Paul intended for Titus to rejoin him in Nicopolis that winter, while replacing him on Crete with Artemas or Tychicus (Tit 3:12).

---

[2] An alternate hypothesis is that Titus was saved during Paul's first missionary journey, and that he became an attendant of Paul and Barnabas after John Mark had gone home. Support for this hypothesis is that Galatians 2:1-3 can be read to indicate that Titus was known to the churches in Galatia. Against this hypothesis, Paul also names in Galatians 2 several other persons who had never visited Galatia (Peter, James, and John). Also, there is no indication in the epistle to the Galatians, or anywhere else in the NT, that Titus was closely associated with the Galatian churches.

The final mention of Titus in the New Testament is in 2 Tim 4:10, where Paul states that Titus had left him (evidently with permission) in order to minister in Dalmatia, in what is now Croatia. Titus was a natural choice to organize churches in areas such as Crete and Dalmatia which had very little Jewish influence.

Although the last mention of Titus in the Bible places him in Dalmatia, church tradition located Titus in Crete during the later years of his ministry.[3] If this tradition is correct, then Titus returned to Crete and entered into a settled pastoral ministry there after the death of Paul, similar to the way that Timothy appears to have done in Ephesus. From an early period the church of Gortyna on Crete housed a coffin with what it held to be Titus' body. After that city was destroyed by Muslim invaders in 823, Titus' skull was moved to the city of Heraklion (a.k.a. Iráklion, Candia), the rest of his bones evidently having been lost. Sometime later, after another invasion, Titus' skull was transported to St. Mark's Basilica in Venice. In 1966, Titus' skull was returned to Crete in an ornate reliquary, which today is situated near the entrance to the Church of Saint Titus in Heraklion. The reliquary is carried through the city in a procession every year on August 25, which is Titus' feast day in the Orthodox churches. If the reliquary does indeed contain Titus' skull—or, for that matter, the skull of some other Christian—it will be found to have been robbed of its contents following the rapture of the church of God from the earth, which Titus played a vital role in establishing nearly two thousand years ago.

Date and Occasion of Writing

On the historical background to the Pastorals, see the introduction to 1 Timothy. The most likely scenario is that Paul's letter to Titus was written in A.D. 64, between Paul's first and second Roman imprisonments. After Paul had ministered in Spain in A.D. 63, likely with Titus and Timothy, he sailed back to the east early in A.D. 64, landing at Crete. Paul then left Titus in Crete to give direction to the churches there (Tit 1:5), which had many problems, while he sailed on to Ephesus with Timothy (1 Tim 1:3). It seems that Paul wrote this letter to Titus shortly after arriving in Ephesus, sending it with Zenas the lawyer and Apollos (Tit 3:13). The occasion of writing the epistle to Titus was Paul's desire to give Titus written instructions on how to exercise his oversight of the churches in Crete.

Purpose and Message

Paul's primary purpose in writing this letter to Titus was to instruct him on how to oversee the churches in Crete in Paul's absence. This letter could also be read in the churches of Crete for their own instruction, as well as in other Christian churches throughout the world. Paul's message to Titus was, appoint qualified elders in Crete, teach the Cretan Christians the sort of godly behavior that results from faith, and enforce your authority over the church. This message to Christian leaders and churches today is, make sure your elders are qualified, and exhort all Christians to live a righteous and holy life, since God has saved us in order to make us a holy people.

Writing Style

On the writing style of the Pastoral Epistles, see the introduction to 1 Timothy (under "Authorship"). It is interesting that the letter to Titus contains fewer uses of the terms "Jesus" (4x) and "Christ" (4x) than any other book in the NT except James and the short epistles of 2 & 3 John. Titus and the Johannine epistles are the only NT books in which the word κύριος (*Lord*) never appears. Every book of the NT

---

[3] See, among other sources, Eusebius *Church History* 3.4.6.

does use the word "God," and this is Paul's preferred term in his epistle to Titus, since it would have been the word best understood by those with a background in Greek paganism. The word "Lord" would have been used more frequently when addressing Jews, due to the frequent use of this term in the reading of the OT Scriptures.

Textual Base

The letter to Titus contains no especially noteworthy or unusual textual variants. Titus and 3 John are the only books of the New Testament which contain no textual notes in the 1901 American Standard Version (ASV). The UBS[4] Greek text notes only four variants (in 1:4, 10; 3:1, 15). Two of these are minor variations in the salutation and benediction, which follow the pattern of variants in the salutation and benediction of most other NT epistles. The variants in 1:10 and 3:1 involve merely the presence or absence of the conjunction καί (*and/even*). Six additional variants are noted in the second edition of Metzger's *Textual Commentary*. Two of these (on 1:9, 11) are merely of historical interest, since they are read only by one manuscript from the thirteenth century. Another variant, the various subscriptions after 3:15, is also mainly of historical interest. The variant in 2:5 involves two synonyms (οἰκουργούς and οἰκουρούς). The variant in 2:7 is typical for words in a list of character qualities, and the original reading is readily apparent. Finally, the variant reading in 3:9 is merely the difference between a singular (ἔριν) and a plural (ἔρεις).

Outline of Titus

I. Salutation 1:1-4
II. Directives regarding the oversight of the church 1:5–3:11
    A. Instructions for the appointment of elders 1:5-16
        1. Qualifications of elders 1:5-9
        2. Warning against unqualified elders 1:10-16
    B. Instructions for proper Christian behavior 2:1-15
    C. Instruction on the doctrinal basis for Christian conduct 3:1-7
    D. Exhortation to faithful teaching 3:8-11
III. Closing remarks 3:12-15
    A. Personal remarks 3:12-14
    B. Closing salutation 3:15a
    C. Benediction 3:15b

Argument of Titus

As Paul's letter to Titus was written to instruct him on how to direct the churches in Crete, the main body of the epistle consists of directives regarding the oversight of the church (1:5–3:11). In accordance with typical epistolary style, the letter is introduced by a greeting (1:1-4) and ends with a section of brief closing remarks (3:12-15).

Salutation, 1:1-4

The short epistle to Titus begins with a lengthy salutation, in which Paul emphasizes the connection between knowledge of the truth and a godly lifestyle (1:1-4).

Directives regarding the Oversight of the Church, 1:5–3:11

The body of the epistle to Titus (1:5–3:11) consists of Paul's specific instructions to Titus regarding how he is to direct the churches in Crete.

Instructions for the appointment of elders, 1:5-16. The first and most basic matter to be addressed is the appointment of an elder (pastor) in each of the Cretan churches (1:5-16).[4] Paul began by presenting a list of requisite qualifications that each elder must meet—which included administrative abilities (1:6), a righteous character (1:7-8), and doctrinal understanding and soundness (1:9). Paul then explained the reason why enforcement of this standard was necessary—there were many unqualified elders who were wreaking havoc in the church (1:10-16).

Instructions for proper Christian behavior, 2:1-15. In ch. 2, Paul expands the demand for righteousness and blamelessness to encompass all groups of people in the church, not just the pastors. He directs specific instruction to older men (2:2), older women (2:3), younger women (2:4-5), younger men (2:6), Titus himself (2:7-8), and slaves (2:9-10). Because of the problem in Crete with a culture that minimized the importance of good works, Paul emphasizes the basis for his instruction: God saved us in order to make us a holy people (2:11-14). Chapter 2 concludes with an exhortation to Titus to communicate this teaching authoritatively—once again, because of the cultural resistance to it (2:15).

Instruction on the doctrinal basis for Christian conduct, 3:1-7. In 3:1-7, Paul expands further on the doctrinal basis for the practical directives which Titus was to deliver to the Cretan church.[5] Christians are to do good works (3:1-2) because, whereas we were characterized by evil works before we were saved (3:3), God saved us through His mercy and grace (3:4-6), in order to make us fit to receive eternal life (3:7).

Exhortation to faithful teaching, 3:8-11. The body of the epistle to Titus closes with a final exhortation for Titus himself to be faithful in teaching and exhorting the church in accordance with Paul's straightforward instruction, while refusing to be drawn into fruitless theological arguments (3:8-11).

Closing Remarks, 3:12-15

The closing remarks in Paul's letter to Titus are found in 3:12-15. Paul states his intentions for Titus' dealings with Paul's other coworkers, and for Titus' return to Paul (3:12-13). After a final exhortation in accordance with the theme of the epistle (3:14), Paul concludes with a brief closing salutation (3:15a) and a benediction (3:15b).

---

[4] The reason why Titus had to appoint pastors was probably not that the Cretan churches did not have pastors. It is because the Cretan churches were spiritually immature, and they had unqualified pastors—or, at a minimum, they were taught by unqualified itinerant preachers (1:10-11). Aside from the mention of Cretans in Jerusalem on the day of Pentecost (Acts 2:11) and the mention of Paul's brief layover in Crete on his way to Rome (Acts 27), there is no direct mention of any apostolic missionary activity on the island in order to establish its churches prior to Paul's work with Titus there.

[5] The typical pattern in Pauline epistles is a doctrinal section followed by a practical section which applies Christian doctrine to Christian practice. Thus, it is somewhat unusual that Paul saves the doctrinal basis for his practical exhortations until the final chapter of Titus. This is because the major problem in Crete was not doctrinal *per se*, but practical.

Bibliography

For a bibliography of the Pastoral Epistles, see the Interpretive Guide to 1 Timothy.

Interpretive Guide to Philemon

There is something about the book of Philemon that always seems to give a special joy to the reader. Philemon is unique among New Testament books, and perhaps among Old Testament books also, in that it is entirely positive. There are no rebukes, only encouragements and exhortations. There is no complaining and no mention of conflict. There is no mention of heresy or problems in the church. There are no warnings against disobedience or false teachers. There is no mention of spiritual problems in the life of Philemon or of anyone else. Paul does mention that he is in prison, but he looks forward to his soon release (v. 22). Because the book of Philemon is so positive, it can be a very refreshing book to read and study—and, in fact, Paul says that Philemon has refreshed his heart and will do so again (vv. 7, 20-21). The reason why this book is so positive is that it presents a model for how godly, mature believers ought to relate to one another, and it just so happens that, ideally, our relationships with our fellow believers will be mutually refreshing and uplifting. The way Paul used his ecclesiastical authority is also instructive—rather than commanding Philemon to do the right thing, he appealed to him to do it voluntarily, with no threat of retaliation if he refused.

This is a very warm and personal letter. It shows the depth of emotion that Paul felt—his inner passion, his zeal, his true character. Not only is it addressed specifically to one of Paul's close friends, it concerns a personal issue between them and another of Paul's closest personal friends, who had previously wronged the other. Since most ordinary letters in the NT period were quite short and concerned with personal matters, Philemon, 2 John, and 3 John are the closest to typical first century letters of all the NT epistles. This is, however, no ordinary letter—it is a special message from God to the church of Jesus Christ.

Historical Background

Colossians 4:9 indicates that Philemon was a resident of the town of Colossae, and there are several indications in the letter to Philemon that he was a wealthy man. His house was large enough to serve as a meeting place for a church (v. 2), he owned slaves, and he had room to lodge Paul (v. 22). Paul indicates in v. 19 that Philemon was saved under his ministry. Most likely, Philemon visited Ephesus on business while Paul was teaching in the school of Tyrannus, and heard the gospel from the apostle there. Philemon's wife is named as Apphia (v. 2), and the pastor of the church that met in his house is named as Archippus (v. 3; cf. Col 4:17).

Onesimus was a slave belonging to Philemon who had run away—not, apparently, because he had been mistreated by Philemon, but more likely because he was able to steal money from Philemon (v. 18), which would potentially allow him to live comfortably elsewhere. Onesimus made his way to Rome, a common destination for escaped slaves, who could easily blend in with the masses of people in the city. Onesimus must have known Paul from Paul's previous contacts with Philemon. It is unlikely that Onesimus would have showed himself to Paul if he were trying to remain hidden. Apparently while Onesimus was in Rome, he realized his need for a Savior, and sought out Paul as the man whom he knew could tell him how to be saved. Paul, who was under house arrest, was likely surprised by the unexpected visitor, but quickly bonded with him and took him under his wing. Onesimus proved himself to be a faithful companion and valuable servant to Paul. Paul realized, however, that since Onesimus legally was still the property of Philemon, the right thing to do was to send him back to his master, even though he would have liked to have kept him for himself. Thus, Paul wrote the letter to Philemon and had Onesimus carry it in order to request that the runaway be forgiven and manumitted.[1]

---

[1] A certain Onesimus who was bishop of Ephesus sometime during the reign of Trajan (98–117) is mentioned in Ignatius *Ephesians* 1.3; 2.1; 6.2, but it is not likely that he was the same Onesimus who had been Philemon's slave.

Author

Paul and Timothy are named as senders in 1:1, but the intensely personal nature of the letter shows that Paul is the only author. Timothy is named because he was with Paul at the time of writing. All but the most extreme critics accept Pauline authorship of Philemon.

It is possible that Paul had an amanuensis for this epistle, as for his other letters, and that in v. 19 he took the pen from the amanuensis. It is also possible that Paul wrote this entire letter in his own hand, as argued by Longenecker.[2]

Date and Occasion of Writing

The epistle to Philemon was delivered at the same time as Laodiceans (Ephesians) and Colossians, near the end of Paul's first Roman imprisonment, probably early in A.D. 62. This is indicated by Paul's reference to himself as a prisoner (vv. 9-10) and to his anticipation of soon release (v. 22). It is also indicated by the parallel personages named in each letter, and by the correspondence between Eph 1:15, Col 1:4, and Phlm 5. The occasion of writing was the conversion of Philemon's runaway slave Onesimus in Rome while Paul was in prison, and Onesimus' subsequent ministry to Paul. Roman law required runaway slaves to be returned to their masters. Paul wished to retain Onesimus for his service to him, but did not want to break the law by harboring a runaway—particularly, a runaway who belonged to a good Christian friend who had not mistreated him and would not mistreat him. Thus, he sent Onesimus back to Philemon with a request for him to be freed and forgiven all debts so he could return to Rome as Paul's servant. According to Col 4:7, Onesimus was from Colossae and traveled to Colossae with Tychicus. Most likely, Tychicus delivered the letters to the churches at Laodicea and Colossae, while Onesimus personally presented himself to Philemon with the letter from Paul.[3] It is also possible that Tychicus presented Onesimus to Philemon with Paul's letter.

Philemon's response is not specifically recorded, but when Paul says under the inspiration of the Holy Spirit that he has confidence in Philemon's obedience and knows that he will do even beyond what was requested (v. 21), it is safe to assume that this is what happened. It is not likely that this letter would have been preserved if Philemon's response did not meet Paul's expectations.

Purpose and Message

The purpose of the epistle to Philemon was to move Philemon to free his runaway slave Onesimus and forgive his debts so he could return to Rome as Paul's servant. The message of the book corresponds to its purpose: I plead with you to forgive and free Onesimus, and I offer to repay whatever he owes you. I rejoice in confidence that you will do the right thing.

Probably one reason why Paul did not send Onesimus back to Philemon immediately is that there was little travel between Rome and Asia during the winter due to treacherous weather.

[2] Richard N. Longenecker, "Ancient Amanuenses and the Pauline Epistles" (in *New Dimensions in New Testament Study*, Grand Rapids: Zondervan, 1974), 291.

[3] Philemon could have no doubt that the letter from Paul was authentic, since Tychicus would attest to it, and Paul wrote at least part of it in his own hand.

Although this purpose and message relate to a specific personal situation, Paul was an apostle who wrote under inspiration, and he knew that he was writing Scripture. Thus, there is another purpose for writing this epistle which looks beyond the immediate situation with Onesimus and Philemon and seeks to provide a model for the way in which Christians ought to interact with one another in love.

This letter was preserved by the church as Scripture because the church preserved all the writings of the apostles, but also because the letter was addressed to the whole church, and not just to Philemon. It contributes to the Bible's overall message in that it teaches by way of example principles regarding how believers ought to relate to each other and use ecclesiastical power.

Outline of Philemon

I. Salutation vv. 1-3
II. Commendation vv. 4-7
III. Appeal vv. 8-20
IV. Closing matters vv. 21-25
    A. Anticipation of the outcome vv. 21-22
    B. Greetings vv. 23-24
    C. Benediction v. 25

Argument of Philemon

The book of Philemon follows a neat four-part epistolary structure: salutation (vv. 1-3), commendation (vv. 4-7), appeal (vv. 8-20), and epilogue (vv. 21-25).

The salutation (vv. 1-3) is typical of Paul's letters, but more personal. Although it says that Paul and Timothy are addressing Philemon, Apphia, Archippus, and their house church, the focus immediately narrows, and Paul addresses Philemon personally in a heart to heart appeal. But Paul did not want to begin his appeal immediately, without first preparing Philemon and greeting him appropriately. He wanted Philemon to know that he cared about him, considered him a dear friend, and was not merely writing to get something from him. Thus, he thanks God for him and commends him in vv. 4-7.

The appeal itself is contained in vv. 8-20. Paul has the authority to command Philemon to release Onesimus, but he will not use that authority because he wants to give Philemon an opportunity to show his heart of love. Paul offers Philemon a way to refuse the request (vv. 15-16) to make clear there is no compulsion. The bond between Paul and Onesimus was so strong that Paul, who had little income, offered to repay Onesimus' debts (vv. 18-19).

After the appeal, closing matters are addressed in vv. 21-25. First, Paul anticipates a positive outcome, both in Philemon's response to his request and in his own release from prison (vv. 21-22). The letter is concluded by standard epistolary greetings (vv. 23-24) and a short benediction (v. 25).

Bibliography for Philemon

There are many good commentaries on Philemon, especially conservative ones. Alexander's commentary is outstanding. Hiebert's volume is a must read. Lightfoot and Moule are classics. Jensen is surprisingly helpful. Many evangelical commentaries on Philemon, particularly older ones, contain extensive discussions of the issue of slavery.

Alexander, W. "Philemon." In *The Holy Bible with an Explanatory and Critical Commentary: New Testament*, ed. F. C. Cook, vol. 3, 819-44. New York: Charles Scribner's Sons, 1900.

Barnes, Albert. *Thessalonians, Timothy, Titus, and Philemon*. Notes on the New Testament, ed. Robert Frew. Reprint: Grand Rapids: Baker, 1949.

Barth, Markus and Helmut Blanke. *The Letter to Philemon: A New Translation with Notes and Commentary*. Eerdmans Critical Commentary. Grand Rapids: Eerdmans, 2000.
Note: This is a critical (liberal) commentary. It is thorough, but seems way too long for such a short epistle.

Bruce, F. F. *The Epistles to the Colossians, to Philemon, and to the Ephesians*. New International Commentary on the New Testament. Grand Rapids: Eerdmans, 1984.

Carson, Herbert M. *The Epistles of Paul to the Colossians and Philemon: An Introduction and Commentary*. Tyndale New Testament Commentaries. Grand Rapids: Eerdmans, 1960.

Constable, Thomas L. *Notes on Philemon*. 2104 ed. Sonic Light, 2014.

Cox, Samuel. *The Epistle to Philemon*. Reprint: Klock & Klock, 1982.

Deibler, Edwin C. "Philemon." In *The Bible Knowledge Commentary: New Testament*, ed. John F. Walvoord and Roy B. Zuck, 769-75. Wheaton, IL: SP Publications, 1983.

Dunn, James D. G. *The Epistles to the Colossians and to Philemon: A Commentary on the Greek Text*. New International Greek Testament Commentary. Grand Rapids: Eerdmans, 1996.

Ellicott, Chas. J. *A Critical and Grammatical Commentary on St. Paul's Epistles to the Philippians, Colossians, and to Philemon*. Andover: Warren F. Draper, 1876.

Fitzmyer, Joseph A. *The Letter to Philemon: A New Translation with Introduction and Commentary*. Anchor Bible, vol. 34C. New York: Doubleday, 2000.

Harris, Murray J. *Colossians & Philemon*. Exegetical Guide to the Greek New Testament. Grand Rapids: Eerdmans, 1991.

Harvey, H. *Commentary on the Pastoral Epistles, First and Second Timothy and Titus; and the Epistle to Philemon*. An American Commentary on the New Testament, ed. Alvah Hovey. Philadelphia: American Baptist Publication Society, 1890.

Hiebert, D. Edmond. *Titus and Philemon*. Chicago: Moody Press, 1957.

Jensen, Irving L. *Colossians and Philemon: A Self-Study Guide*. Chicago: Moody, 1973.

Lightfoot, J. B. *Saint Paul's Epistles to the Colossians and to Philemon: A Revised Text with Introductions, Notes, and Dissertations*. 9th ed. London: Macmillan, 1890.
   Note: I think this is really only the third new edition, and the ninth printing. The third edition would be dated to 1879.

MacArthur, John, Jr. *Colossians & Philemon*. The MacArthur New Testament Commentary. Chicago: Moody Press, 1992.

MacLaren, Alexander. *The Epistles of St. Paul to the Colossians and Philemon*. 2nd ed. The Expositor's Bible, ed. W. Robertson Nicoll. London: Hodder and Stoughton, 1888.

McGee, J. Vernon. *1 Corinthians–Revelation*. Volume 5 of *Thru the Bible with J. Vernon McGee*. Nashville: Thomas Nelson, 1983.

Melick, Richard R., Jr. *Philippians, Colossians, Philemon*. New American Commentary, ed. David S. Dockery, vol. 32. Nashville: Thomas Nelson, 1991.

Moo, Douglas J. *The Letters to the Colossians and to Philemon*. Pillar New Testament Commentary. Grand Rapids: Eerdmans, 2008.

Moule, H. C. G. *The Epistles to the Colossians and to Philemon: with Introduction and Notes*. The Cambridge Bible for Schools and Colleges. Cambridge: Cambridge, 1893.

Müller, Jac. J. *The Epistles of Paul to the Philippians and to Philemon: The English Text with Introduction, Exposition and Notes*. New International Commentary on the New Testament, ed. F. F. Bruce. Grand Rapids: Eerdmans, 1955.

Nordling, John G. *Philemon*. Concordia Commentary. Saint Louis: Concordia, 2004.
   Note: This is a conservative Lutheran commentary. It is thorough, but seems way too long for such a short epistle. Nordling has an extensive discussion of slavery in the Roman world and in the NT.

O'Brien, Peter T. *Colossians, Philemon*. Word Biblical Commentary 44. Waco, TX: Word Books, 1982.

Rupprecht, Arthur A. "Philemon." In *Expositor's Bible Commentary*, ed. Frank E. Gaebelein et al., vol. 11, 451-64. Grand Rapids: Zondervan Publishing House, 1978.

———. "Philemon." In *The Expositor's Bible Commentary: Revised Edition*, vol. 12, 627-43. Grand Rapids: Zondervan, 2006.

Vaughan, Curtis. *Colossians and Philemon*. Bible Study Commentary. Grand Rapids: Zondervan, 1980.

Vincent, Marvin R. *A Critical and Exegetical Commentary on the Epistles to the Philippians and to Philemon*. International Critical Commentary, ed. Samuel Rolles Driver, Alfred Plummer, and Charles Augustus Briggs. Edinburgh: T. & T. Clark, 1897.

Wilson, R. McL. *A Critical and Exegetical Commentary on Colossians and Philemon*. International Critical Commentary. London: T & T Clark, 2005.

Witherington III, Ben. *The Letters to Philemon, the Colossians, and the Ephesians: A Socio-Rhetorical Commentary on the Captivity Epistles*. Grand Rapids: Eerdmans, 2007.

Wright, N. T. *The Epistles of Paul to the Colossians and to Philemon: An Introduction and Commentary.* Tyndale New Testament Commentaries. Grand Rapids: Eerdmans, 1986.